The Holy Wells of
Bath and Bristol Region

Monuments in the Landscape

Volume VI

The Holy Wells of
Bath and Bristol Region

by
Phil Quinn

Logaston Press

LOGASTON PRESS
Little Logaston Woonton Almeley
Herefordshire HR3 6QH

First published by Logaston Press 1999
Copyright © Phil Quinn 1999

ISBN 1 873827 90 3

Set in Times by Logaston Press
and printed in Great Britain by
The Cromwell Press, Wiltshire

Contents

Please Note

Many of the wells mentioned in this book are situated on private land and permission from the owner must, therefore, be obtained before visiting them. Those where the map refernce is marked with an * indicate that the well and/or associated building is accessible or visible to the general public without permission being required.

The following points should also be observed:

1. When visiting sites in the countryside, always follow the Countryside Code.

2. On all sites, extreme care should be taken.

3. Any artefacts found on sites should be reported to the nearest museum.

4. Under no circumstances should visitors dig on or around any site. Any damage could result in prosecution.

5. It is an offence under the 1979 Ancient Monuments and Archaeological Areas Act to use metal detectors on or near scheduled ancient monuments. In addition, simple 'treasure hunting' near ancient monuments can well damage evidence to such an extent that archaeologists are unable to interpret it fully in the future.

Acknowledgements

Documentary source material for the information contained within this book appears in the Bibliography. Much of this material came from the record offices and libraries of Bristol, Gloucestershire and Somerset and I would like to thank the staff of the following establishments for their considerable help in searching for often obscure material and also for offering useful advice: Bath Public Library; Bristol Central Reference Library; Bristol Record Office; Gloucestershire Record Office Gloucestershire Local Studies Library; Somerset Record Office; Somerset Local Studies Library; Weston-super-Mare Public Library.

I am also very grateful to Dr Michael Costen of Bristol University for his encouragement and great help in this project especially in regard to place-names and Anglo-Saxon boundaries; Mr Chris Richards of North Somerset Museum Service for sharing his encyclopaedic knowledge of North Somerset; and Miss Jennifer Scherr of Bristol University for sending me copies of her papers. A great deal of information was provided by local people who responded to my requests for holy well lore; parish councils and local history societies fielded my requests and I owe a great debt of thanks here too. Furthermore, much material came from chance encounters with local people when I was engaged on field work. Other information was kindly supplied by members of the audiences to whom I gave illustrated talks on local holy wells. For the latter two sources I frequently do not have the names of those involved but the following are known to me and I warmly acknowledge the valuable information which they have given, information that would otherwise not have appeared in this book:

North Somerset
Banwell Bridewell: Mr Chris Richards; *Backwell* Willings Well: Dr Michael Costen; *Barrow Gurney* Fairy Well: Mr Frank Patch; Barrow Fountain: Mr Tony Parsons of Felton & Mr R.L. Woolley

of Wraxall; *Blagdon* Timsell Well: Mr John Chamberlain; *Butcombe* Cleeve's Well: Mrs Mary Bendall; *Charlcombe* St Alphage's Well—soot & baptisms: Mr Roger Parry; *Churchill* Hylisbrook Spring—Romans: Mr Chris Richards; *East Harptree* Kings Castle Well—wishing well: Mrs Margaret Hale; *Easton-in-Gordano* canopied well: Mr Gerald Hart; Pill Spout: Mr R.L. Woolley of Wraxall; *Flax Bourton* Puxpit—haunting: Mrs Mary Carnell of Barrow Gurney; *Hinton Charterhouse* (Ela's Well—blind woman: Mr Len Lambert; Ladywell: Mr Robin Robertson-Glasgow; *Hutton* Ludwell—Romans: Mr Chris Richards; *Keynsham* Hawkeswell—eyes: Mrs Merle Wade of Whitchurch; *Long Ashton* Drop Spring—bottles: Mr Ron Kingston; *Marksbury* Rattlespring: Mr Arthur Moon of Timsbury; *Nailsea* Nailsea Spa: Mrs Phyllis Horman; *Nempnett Thrubwell* Thrubwell: Mr Summers; *Stowey-Sutton* Petrifying spring wayside shrine: Mr Mike Chapman of Bath; *Tickenham* Sunnyside spring: Miss Doris Fisher; *Timsbury* Mermaid Well: Mr Arthur Moon; *Wellow* St Julian's Well—pool: Mr Eric Turner; wishing well: Mrs Small of Trowbridge; *Weston-super-Mare* Ernall's Spring: Mr Chris Richards; *Wrington* Abspit Pond: Mr Chris Richards; *Compton Bishop* Mrs Margaret Jordan.

Bath

Haswell—Nemlett name: Dr Michael Costen; Rosamund's Well—healing stream: Mr Mike Chapman; Holloway spring—chapel: Mr Nigel Locke; Sham Castle Holy Well-location: Mrs M Zalipka; Bath Abbey estate: Dr Michael Costen.

Bristol

Cotham Bewell—uneasiness: Mrs Anne Freeman; *Shirehampton* Bucklewell—eyes: Mr Little; *Bedminster* Flowerwell—floor name: Dr Michael Costen; *Knowle* Hollybrook Well—name: Dr Michael Costen; *Hanham* Stone Hill spring & Hanham Court ghost: Mr David Elliott; Brislington St Anne's Well—ghost: Mr Clive Porter.

South Gloucestershire

Cold Ashton Hammeswelle: Dr Richard Wharton & Mr Peter Williamson; *Cromhall* Tortworth Park lake: Mr Roger Howell of

Tytherington; *Dodington* Dodington Hall wishing well: Sir Simon Codrington; *Dyrham & Hinton* Hinton Chapel well: Mrs Jennifer Hutchinson; *Marshfield* Cadwell Hill—hauntings: Mr Richard Knight; *Olveston* Miles Well: Mr Eric Garrett; Tithing boundary: Mrs Judy Pullin; Rams Well—derivation: Dr Michael Costen; *Pilning & Severn Beach* haunted pool: Mr Jeffrey Rawlinson; *Pucklechurch* St Aldam's Well: healing a boy: Mrs Anne Freeman of Bristol; *Rockhampton* Pennywell: E.J. Ford; Stone—haunted pool: Mrs Anne Riddiford of Thornbury; *Tytherington* pools: Mr Roger Howell; *Siston* St Anne's Well—pins & loss of flow: Mrs Diane Webb; *Thornbury* St Arild's Well: Mrs Jane Bradshaw of Oldbury-on-Severn; *Tortworth* Virgin's Well: Mrs C. Robertson; *Wick & Abson* haunted well: Mrs Joan Hall.

Special thanks go to Anne Freeman and all members of the Source, past and present, especially Marilyn Morris and Christine Bowles for support and encouragement.

The following organisations are involved in the research and conservation of holy wells and spas, and welcome any interest in their work:

The Source (Bristol & Avon holy wells group), c/o 29 Rozel Road, Horfield, Bristol BS7 8SQ

The Wellsprings Fellowship (reserach, restoration and maintenance of holy and historic wells in Wales), The Lodge, Penpont, Brecon, Powys LD3 8EU

Clifton Spa Pump Room & Clifton Rocks railway Group (Clifton Spa restoration), Bruce Tyldesley, Flat 5, 8 Marloes Road, London W8 5LJ, or Kathy Crossthwaite, 22 Cornwallis Crescent, Clifton, Brostol, BS8 4PJ

Source (National holy wells journal), Swn y Môr, 96 Terrace Road, Mount Pleasant, Swansea SA1 6HU

British Spas Federation, c/o Bath Spa Project, Abbey Chambers, Abbey Churchyard, Bath, BA1 1LY Tel: 01225 477710

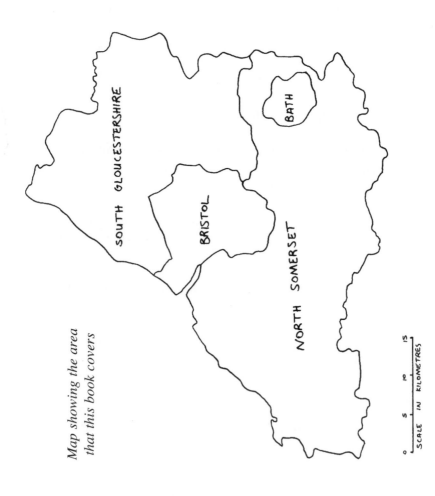

*Map showing the area
that this book covers*

SOUTH GLOUCESTERSHIRE

BATH

BRISTOL

NORTH SOMERSET

0   5   10   15

SCALE IN KILOMETRES

CHAPTER I
What is a Holy Well?

Many of us will have our own ideas on what holy wells are all about. Perhaps the most common idea is that they are places which once held religious significance to past generations, when people were perhaps more superstitious and credulous. We might also think that holy wells in the modern landscape are of little more than curiosity value. Equally we might see them from within the context of folklore where the wells are repositories of an bizarre range of customs and beliefs which may hint at arcane rituals and secret knowledge. Modern open-minded Christians and modern pagans will have their own set of values by which to judge the nature of a holy well, the very age of the holy well tradition offering another strand of legitimacy for their faiths.

Whatever our starting point, the study and appreciation of holy wells is a study in holism, of sacred sites within a sacred landscape peopled with semi-mythological figures and spirits. It is a world of primitive folk medicine linked with elements of religious ritual, of ghosts and the needs of the living, a need to acknowledge places of power within the land and the changing nature of human societies and how we relate to the land.

Definition

A truly acceptable definition of a holy well has long eluded researchers and devotees alike but for the sake of argument we could say that *a holy well is essentially a natural source of water where people went to improve the condition of their lives, in terms of health, wealth or spirituality.*

Many people are interested to find that most holy wells are not in fact wells as we conventionally imagine them to be—excavated

1

shafts within the earth allowing water to be drawn up from deep below. Many are surface springs, often dammed to form small pools or troughs surrounded by other protective masonry ensuring the water is not polluted. The 'well' part of their name derives from the Old English (Anglo-Saxon) word for spring—*wella*.

A universal phenomenon

It might also be surprising to learn that holy wells are found not only in Britain, on mainland Europe and the Bible lands, but throughout the world. There is no major culture or religion which does not hold within it a living tradition of sacred and venerated springs, this assertion could be taken back through time and shown to hold true in many of the extinct cultures and nations for which we have historical or archaeological record. For example, the history and mythology of ancient Greece provides many instances of sacred waters being venerated or incorporated within religious establishments. Holy wells are known from the civilisations of Asia, Africa and the Americas as well as within the surviving 'primitive' cultures of people such as the Australian Aborigines and the Kalahari Bushmen.

With such a vast historical and geographical range it can safely be assumed that veneration of sacred springs is an ancient, and probably innate, human experience which pre-dates the establishment of organised religion.

Central themes

A number of themes appear to be common to holy wells no matter what the time period or the culture. Chief of these is a desire to venerate a chosen spring and imbue it with supernatural qualities: claiming it is the home of spirits or deities, or associating it with holy figures who have passed on some of their sanctity to the waters. In Britain, especially in the western lands, a great number of ancient saints have bequeathed their names to holy wells, some of whom can be confirmed as historically genuine people but many more are at best semi-historical, and some barely hide traits that were once held by pagan deities.

Holy wells are frequently believed to possess healing water, the cures effected by either drinking, bathing or a mix of both. The cure of infertility is a universal trait, while many cultures also acknowledge the power of the well in curing eye complaints, (perhaps the most common cure to be found at the British holy well). Offerings were made to the wells, either as a direct gesture to the resident spirit or as part of a general belief that doing so was part of the established regime by which wishes would be granted. Important ritual centres could develop around the springs and play a central role in the cosmology of many religions. Many wells were 'dressed', that is decorated, with flowers or paintings, strips of cloth or bedecked with statuettes. The so-called 'rag wells' where strips of cloth were tied to neighbouring trees, are a well-known feature of British holy well lore, but are also common in Central America, Africa and throughout Eurasia.

What drew people to see a natural spring as particularly important and cause them to treat it with respect and veneration? Most holy wells are renowned for the never-failing quality of their waters, which flow even in times of drought when most other sources of water have dried up. When people were more dependant on a reliable local source of water for their very survival such constant springs would have meant the difference between life and death. It is thus not hard to visualise pagan peoples investing these sites with magical powers, seeing them as inhabited by some living spirit or deity who was the guardian of the water and who allowed it to flow for the benefit of the people.

Some springs are the headwaters of major rivers and, in times when rivers were believed to be sacred, people would see their headwater springs as the source of such holiness. In folklore from around the world, there are tales of goddesses living in these headwater springs, sometimes a young goddess drowns in them and becomes the river which then bears her name. In the Bristol region there are some noted headwater springs: the Seven Wells at Doddington is the source of the Bristol Frome and was held in high regard by local people. The River Avon flows from two Gloucestershire headwaters: its western branch from Joyce's Pool, Didmarton where there is a legend of a young girl drowning, whilst its eastern branch rises at St Mary Magdalen's Spring, alias the Wor Well, at Tetbury which was renowned for its petrifying properties and also its healing powers—especially in the cure of sore eyes.

Occasionally, it was the peculiar behaviour of a spring which drew comment and veneration. Those springs that were either erratic in their flow or made unusual noises became notable features in the landscape. So too were the 'petrifying wells'—those springs which deposited a thick limy crust on objects which fell into them, seemingly turning items to stone.

The Seven Wells at Doddington is one of many springs where a number appears as part of the name. 'Seven' is by far the most frequent number to appear and in this region there is also the case of the *westran seofen wyllas* or 'western seven wells' which are mentioned in an Anglo-Saxon boundary charter at South Stoke. At many of these 'number wells' the visitor will be hard pressed to find the number of springs described, and it seems likely that where several springs rose close together the word 'seven' was applied no matter how many springs were actually present, as seven is a number long held to have magical associations and was probably thought fitting as a description for multiple springs, especially when they rose on a boundary or some other important site.

Important and holy wells are frequently found on boundaries, usually of manors, parishes or counties. When early boundaries were established the use of permanent and remarkable natural features to demarcate them made perfect sense as they would be easy to find in cases of boundary dispute, and the more important the well in local minds the more value in incorporating it within a boundary. Equally it was the case that ordinary springs could become of greater local importance when employed in marking a boundary. Thus it is now often hard to say whether wells on boundaries are notable because they were incorporated into a boundary or whether they rose to prominence first and were later incorporated into a boundary.

A singular feature of holy wells is that throughout great changes in religion and politics they survive relatively intact from one age to the next. Individual wells may not survive periods of social upheaval but the *idea* of holy wells does—a testament to their deep seated appeal to the human mind.

CHAPTER II
Holy Wells Through Time

With holy wells being arguably such an ancient and cross-cultural phenomenon their changing role throughout human society can be plotted much more easily than other features in the landscape. Our knowledge of very early human interaction with sacred waters in this region is poor due to the lack of archaeological and documentary data, however by inference from living cultures which display a similar technology and structure to our hunter-gatherer ancestors it can be suggested that during prehistory certain springs and pools may well have been thought to have unique powers.

Mesolithic and Neolithic
Excavations at three spring sites in north Somerset have shown that the semi-nomadic hunter-gatherer peoples of the Mesolithic period (10,000 - 3500BC), who were starting to domesticate livestock and thus engage in very primitive agriculture, camped by springs which today have a reputation for the constancy of their flow. At Charlcombe Bay, Weston-in-Gordano, and the Whirleypool at Wraxall, excavation of flint debris has shown that these people had spent time nearby, but we have no indication of how they viewed these springs beyond their utilitarian value. However, a certain licence can be allowed at the third site—the Sacred Spring at Bath—as its unique and dramatic thermal qualities have influenced all visitors for the past two thousand years, bringing forth great religious and medicinal beliefs in the natural powers resident here. The flint blades found in the hot spring may well have simply been camp debris, but it is likely that such a dramatic site would also have engendered a spiritual or religious feeling.

Evidence of Neolithic involvement with local holy wells is less convincing. The only suggestion of activity in this period (3500 - 2000BC) is a ceremonial stone macehead of the late Neolithic or early Bronze Age period, discovered near three spring-fed pools at Stidcote Farm, Tytherington.

Bronze Age and Iron Age

The Bronze Age (2000 - 600BC) is a period for which, throughout Europe, there is extensive archaeological evidence of water cults. So-called 'water hoards' — collections of high status metal work such as swords, cauldrons and shields along with pottery, wooden implements and occasionally human remains — have been found in rivers, pools and adjacent to springs, all in contexts which suggest a ritual deposition. Various suggestions have been made as to why a water cult came into existence or reached such a level of development. The most popular explanation is that such activity was a direct response to the deteriorating climatic conditions experienced during this time, ritual offerings to a water deity perhaps seen as pleas for clemency from a harsh climate.

Despite the discovery of Bronze Age water hoards across the country there have been few local discoveries of such material. However, this may simply represent a lack of archaeological investigation. The only well site where there is unequivocal evidence of Bronze Age ritual deposition is in the hamlet of Cross just over the county boundary in the Somerset Mendips. Here a gold bracelet, dated to the Bronze Age, was found in 1898 when workmen were refashioning the spring which rises in the middle of the settlement.

It was during the Bronze Age that most of our standing stones and round barrows were erected and elsewhere in Britain it has been proven that there are strong associations between holy wells and both standing stones and burial mounds. Nowhere are these associations very common, but they exist in sufficient numbers to prove some connection. In this region a standing stone — the Bethel Stone — once stood near Abspit Pond, Wrington and a stone at Portbury once accompanied a small pool next to the parish church, whilst 6km to the south-east of the Bethel Stone a stone circle once stood less than 200m north of St Anthony's Well at Chew Stoke. The only other possible stone-and-well connection is on the upper slopes of Burrington Combe in the parish of Priddy where the field name 'Hawskwell Quoit' is recorded in the 1838 Burrington Tithe Awards. 'Quoit' is an unusual place name element and in this region almost invariably refers to a standing stone with a folklore of being thrown by giants or the devil.

There is more evidence of barrows associated with holy wells. Two important sites in north Bristol, the Bewell in Cotham and the supposed St Anne's Well at Horfield were both near round barrows, whilst at Weston-super-Mare, Ernall's Spring rose at the foot of an enigmatic mound known as 'Ernall's Tump'. At Pucklechurch the Bridewell (*aka* St Bridget's Well) has a tumulus to keep it company and at Compton Martin the name of the haunted Barrow Well also suggests a tumulus nearby.

However, with the Iron Age (600BC - 43AD) comes more substantive evidence for local prehistoric activity around sacred waters.

The city of Bath provides two of the most important local sites for Iron Age holy well activity. As might be expected the Sacred Spring, the main hot spring rising in the heart of the city, provides some key evidence. Here, silver coins of the Dobunni tribe, an Iron Age people resident throughout much of Gloucestershire and the Cotswolds, were found when extensive excavations were undertaken in 1979 - 80. These coins demonstrate ritual activity here in the years just preceding the Roman conquest. Two kilometres to the west, a pair of Celtic spoons were uncovered, in the middle of the 19th century, on the banks of Locksbrook stream within the field known as Haswell, a site which has now been transformed into Locksbrook cemetery. Immediately to the west of Haswell field there was once a field called Nemlet, a name which may stem from a Celtic root-word *nemeto-* which means 'sacred grove', a theory given added weight by the discovery of a minor Roman cemetery here. The Bath area can therefore prove to have been a focus of Iron Age ritual activity.

Elsewhere in the region such direct evidence of Iron Age activity is lacking. One of the few possible exceptions is a curious structure on the northern slopes of Worlebury Hill at Kewstoke which was believed to have been a votive pit that may or may not once have held water. When excavated this pit produced artefacts ranging in date from the Iron Age to the medieval period and appears to have been associated with a small stone structure that has traditionally been ascribed as the chapel of St Kew, an enigmatic, probably semi-mythical Dark Age figure.

Another coastal sacred water site which may have Iron Age associations is the Monks Well on Steep Holm island, for in the scrub woodland immediately above the well a small, carved stone head was discovered in the 1980s which Celtic expert Dr Anne Ross declared to be a Celtic 'shouting head'—a symbol of life which may once have adorned a shrine near to the well.

The Roman period
An alternative dating of the Steep Holm 'shouting head' places it within the Romano-British period (43 - 410AD). If this is indeed the case, then it is part of a comparatively rich array of material from this period, the richest so far in terms of artefacts and proven ritual associations.

It is certain that when the Romans invaded Britain they would have encountered a water cult (or cults) where offerings were made to springs and pools. Following the pattern of previous territorial conquests a process of assimilation would follow whereby local deities were incorporated within the local Romanised pantheon and, by their attributes, equated to the main Roman deities. Thus at Bath the presiding deity over the hot springs was Sulis-Minerva; from this, and the local uniqueness of the first name, it can be assumed that the pre-Roman Celtic water spirit here was indeed called Sulis.

It is very hard to prove just how assimilated Celtic holy well belief became in the Roman period. It can be certain, however that new practices and emphases were brought in by the Romans and a good case in point is the use of votive shaft wells. These specially constructed sites are known throughout Britain and the material excavated from within them strongly suggests a ritual usage— indeed, skulls, both human and animal, are commonly found. Locally there is the shaft well at the appropriately named Pagan's Hill in the parish of Chew Stoke, excavated in 1951 by Philip Rahtz and Leslie G. Harris. Rahtz and Harris had discovered the remains of a hexagonal Roman temple and further excavation led to the discovery of a shaft well just to the north-east of the temple. Within the well were found a number of artefacts, the most interesting of which was the small statue of a dog, probably associated with the cult based in the temple. Representations of dogs are found at other Roman temple sites in the west such as Lydney in Gloucestershire and Nettleton Shrub in Wiltshire. Another possible Roman shrine site is at the Monks Well on Steep Holm island where the carved stone head, described above in the section on the Iron Age, could just as easily date from the Roman period and be part of a small shrine which may have once stood above the spring, the only regular source of water on this otherwise waterless island.

Other possible Roman sites with watery associations include the Hylisbrook Spring at Churchill, where a Romano-British building has been tentatively identified and contemporary artefacts discovered. The Stidcote Pools in Tytherington, mentioned earlier in connection with the discovery of a stone macehead, may also have been the focus of Roman religious activity, for the remains of a tessellated pavement, perhaps from a shrine, have been found close by. Another Roman pavement may have stood near Bedminster's Flowerwell as the first element of this name is from the Old English word *flor* meaning 'floor', a word normally reserved for descriptions of Roman tessellated pavements. Further Roman buildings were discovered near the spring at Stonehill, Hanham, in association with a coin hoard. However, popular folk belief in Roman involvement at other sites is harder to prove. Wraxall's Whirleypool is commonly said to have been a Roman swimming pool, though this is a groundless belief only given weight in the popular mind by the presence of a Roman villa close by. When the derivation of Olveston's 'Rams Well' is examined, it doesn't originate from a contraction of 'Roman's Well' as is popularly believed, instead it is more likely to derive from the Old English *hramsawelle* — 'wild garlic spring'.

Roman involvement is also suggested at St Pancras' Well, Marshfield, as this Roman saint is rarely used in dedications, and where the name does occur there are often strong Roman connections. Thus it is not perhaps surprising to find that a small Romano-British settlement once existed adjacent to the spring at the hamlet of West End. It would admittedly be pure speculation to suggest that the spring received its dedication during the Roman period, but there are few other alternative explanations as to why this site bears the name of a saint who was popular only during the early years of Christianity in Britain.

The Romano-British population seem to have also felt that there was a connection between certain wells and the otherworld for at three sites there is evidence of burials adjacent to springs. At both Hobbs Well, Farmborough, and Ludwell, Hutton, Romano-British interments have been found and mention was made earlier, in the description of Iron Age associations, of the Romano-British cemetery in Nemlet field which lay next to Haswell and the Locksbrook stream in Bath. However none of these sites can compare with the sheer dominance of the hot springs at Bath which were the setting for the greatest expression of Romano-British water worship in the British Isles.

Roman Bath

When the Romans came to Bath, probably soon after their conquest of southern England in 43AD, they found the hot springs were already the focus of native religious activity. Realising the potential of the site they enclosed the three hot springs and erected a temple and bathing complex around the largest of the springs—the so-called Sacred Spring, later to be known as the King's Bath. The smaller springs—the Cross Bath and the Hot Bath—were outside the main temple complex, but had their own smaller, associated structures with a number of altars and evidence of cultic activity.

The temple, dedicated to the goddess Sulis-Minerva, was the focus around which the small city of *Aquae Sulis* (the Waters of Sulis) developed. The city was probably never much more than a spa town for there is little evidence of industrial or commercial activity beyond that required to service the needs of pilgrims and local people. Nevertheless, *Aquae Sulis* was one of the most important religious and curative sites in the northern Roman Empire and, from the evidence of tombstones and altar dedications, attracted pilgrims from even further afield.

The structure of the temple complex was centred on the Sacred Spring, with the temple building immediately to the north and a suite of baths to the south ranging from the Great Bath, which was fed directly by water from the Sacred Spring, to smaller tepid pools

*Bronze head of the Goddess
Minerva from the temple of
Sulis-Minerva*

and cold plunge pools. Following almost a century of intermittent excavation most of these are visible today, incorporated within the Roman Baths Museum. Excavation has not only demonstrated the structure of the temple complex, but has also led to the discovery of the use of the Sacred Spring as an interface with the Otherworld, a liminal site where supplicants could ask the Goddess for favours or simply offer their devotions. Thousands of coins along with jewellery and pewter vessels were excavated from the spring, where it is thought bathing was not permitted due to the great sacredness of the site. However, it is the curses inscribed upon sheets of lead and pewter, and thrown into the spring by aggrieved parties, which allow the greatest insight into the nature of those drawn to the spring, for these are pleas to the goddess to restore lost or stolen property and to bring down curses upon those who have offended the supplicant.

Thus the Romano-British baths had many uses—as sacred votive pool, cultic temple site and curative bath complex. The maintenance required on the site meant that with the collapse of Roman civic society and the departure of the legions at the start of the 5th century, the infrastructure of the complex inevitably decayed and within a century it appears that the site lay in ruins and few inhabitants populated the old city.

The Post Roman and Early Medieval period
With the disintegration of Roman civic society there were fewer opportunities for the deposition of datable offerings or identifiable structures associated with sacred waters. It is thus much harder to

describe the use of holy wells in this period and much of the evidence is circumspective. Archaeological and documentary evidence is scarce during this period of the development of Anglo-Saxon kingdoms, when Bath acquired the twin names of *Bathanceaster* (Roman town of the Baths) and *Akemanceaster* (Roman town of the sick men). The latter name suggests that those seeking a restoration of health were still visiting the hot springs as their Romano-British predecessors had done, but whether the healing waters were being visited as part of an unbroken tradition or whether there had been a gap for a century or two is unknown. There is evidence in support of the latter theory, for during the 1880s excavations of the bath complex the nest of a wetland bird was found amongst the rubble of the Roman buildings, suggesting that the site was so undisturbed that wildlife could re-establish itself after an interruption of some 400 years.

Some time during the 7th and 8th centuries the temple well at Pagan's Hill was again being used, for a fine piece of early Anglo-Saxon glassware was deposited there, which could suggest that the site was once more being used for ritual purposes. Elsewhere the early Saxon kings were establishing monastic houses adjacent to important springs: in 675 Osric, King of the Hwicce, granted land around the Sacred Spring at Bath for the establishment of a nunnery, and about the same time a monastery was being established at Banwell next to the powerful spring.

Another minster church was built during this period at Congresbury, allegedly on the site chosen by the semi-mythical St Congar. Congar was reputedly a Byzantine prince who sailed west to escape from the worldly pressures of court life and to fulfil his religious destiny, part of which was achieved by bathing in cold water whilst saying the Lord's Prayer, perhaps in what later became the Southwell.

Congar is one of only a handful of early saints who have associations with the region's holy wells. St Kew is another, said to have crossed the sea on stilts to reach the area north of Weston-super-Mare, later known as Kewstoke. The ruins of a small cell, said to be the chapel of St Kew, stood next to a votive pit that may once have held water and into which a variety of objects were thrown dating from the Iron Age to the Middle Ages. Just over the border into the county of Somerset, St Ern, traditionally a companion of St Congar, left his mark at St Ern's Well in the parish of Weare. St David is said to have visited Bath and by the fall of his tears into the hot waters sanctified their use for Christian believers. The Welsh connection is further enhanced by the belief that St Keyna, one of the holy children of the legendary Welsh king Brychan, came to north Somerset seeking a holy place in which to live and pray. After turning local serpents to stone, she caused a curative spring to burst forth, an action which may have been the legendary genesis for Keynsham's 'Hawkswell'. Equally unsubstantive a figure is Thornbury's St Arild who suffered martyrdom by beheading at the hands of a spurned pagan suitor and whose site of execution became St Arild's Well. Arild was duly canonised and achieved a local cult status during the Saxon period, for when the Normans took control of the area they allegedly removed her remains to Gloucester Cathedral as part of a process of centralisation to ensure her devotion did not inspire local rebellion.

It is not clear whether Arild was a Celtic or a Saxon saint; if the latter then she joins a number of more historically reputable figures who are associated with local holy wells. The most notable of these Saxon saints is Aldhelm, or Aldam, who is commemorated in a holy well at Pucklechurch, reputedly the site of a miracle cure effected by the saint. Aldhelm became Abbot of Malmesbury in 666 and was later created Bishop of Sherbourne, ending his days at another sacred spring which also bears his name, at Doulting in Somerset. Renowned for his itinerant lifestyle he would preach widely and it may be Aldhelm who is commemorated in the Bishop's Wells at Yatton and Churchill, although this is again pure speculation. Another local man who rose to prominence within the church was St Alphage, a native of Weston near Bath, who established a hermitage in the area, only to be elected Abbot of Bath and later become Archbishop of Canterbury, before suffering martyrdom at the hands of the Danes in 1012. The hermitage of this holy man may well have been in the hills above his birthplace, for in the parish of Charlcombe we find St Alphage's Well, a renowned healing well and still a site of power and beauty.

Other Saxon saints, though not necessarily with a local pedigree, are recorded in holy well dedications throughout the region—St

Eanswyth at Cold Ashton, Sts Werburgh, Winefred and Swithin at Bath, St Oswald (possibly) at Alderley, St Chad at Midsomer Norton, St Edith at Bristol, and St Winefred (again) at Chew Magna. These 'national' saints reflect an evolution in well dedications away from the local devotion granted to obscure saints in Wales, Cornwall and Ireland, and glimpses of which are seen with the handful of local Celtic/early Saxon holy well dedications. The phenomenon of 'national' and later 'international' saints being adopted for both holy well and church dedications is well documented and becomes particularly apparent during the Middle Ages as old dedications are replaced by more popular, and more fashionable, ones.

Before leaving the subject of early saints, there is the phenomenon of St Bridget and the Bridewells to consider. St Bride or St Bridget was an historical Irish religious figure who is believed to have lived during the 5th century and to whose life many qualities of the pagan Irish deity of 'Bride', daughter of the high god the Dagda were added. Both modern Christians and modern pagans claim St Bridget for their own, pagans frequently adopting her as one of the most important representations of 'the great Goddess'. With so much faith invested in Bridget-the-goddess, modern pagans are keen to identify sites associated with the saint as sites which were once demonstrably pagan and, given the perceived antiquity of all holy wells, Bridewells and St Bridget's Wells are seen as prime pagan sites. Thus it is important to look at the documentary evidence of the Bridewells to try and ascertain which refer to the saint/goddess and which may have other derivations.

A site which one would presume would be ideal for the existence of a Bridewell is Chelvey in the parish of Brockley. Here the medieval church dedicated to St Bridget is built upon a site believed to date from at least Saxon times and where a number of powerful springs rise close by to the west. However, there is no indication that any of the adjacent springs was ever considered holy let alone dedicated to the saint. That the church's dedication is very ancient is beyond doubt, and it is almost unique in this area—the only other instance being the parish church at Brean over the border in the county of Somerset. Brean itself takes its name from a wider district name, also preserved in the hill name of Brent Knoll, which ultimately derives from a form of *Brigantia*, a goddess of the pagan Celts. As such it has been suggested that Brean's church dedication is an ancient echo of this fact: nothing less than a Christianisation of a pagan goddess. It is thus not too far removed to see the Bridewells as part of this tradition, but each case must be examined in turn to see if the argument remains tenable.

There are six Bridewells recorded within this region, one of which, at Pucklechurch, was also known as St Bridget's Well as late as the 18th century and is thus a fairly safe bet as an early site, given the saint's later wane in popularity and lack of later dedications. From its earliest written form (an Anglo-Saxon charter of 972AD) another of the Bridewells, at Dyrham and Hinton, is believed to mean 'surging, swelling and gushing stream'. However, this reference—*bryde wyllan*—has also been translated as 'bride's well'. If this second explanation is the more accurate then it has much in common with the folklore surrounding the Churchill Bridewell where the site is a bride's place of death, still haunted by her ghost. The Banwell Bridewell is first recorded simply as 'Bridewell' in a late Anglo-Saxon estate charter and offers little evidence of its true meaning, and little is known of the origins of the other Bridewells at Barrow Gurney and Cold Ashton. It is also important not to confuse corruptions of 'Birdwell', a relatively common spring name whose Anglo-Saxon spellings, *e.g. bridwyllan* can be alarmingly similar to those for the Bridewells described above. It is therefore likely that the region's Bridewells come from a number of sources and none should automatically be assumed to be pre-Christian on the basis of their name alone.

Churches and Holy Wells
Throughout the period of Christianity in Britain there has been an association between churches and holy wells. In the minds of some clerics this relationship sometimes tipped precariously towards idolatry and throughout the period up to the Reformation edicts were issued by the church hierarchy declaring devotions at certain wells to be unchristian and calling for certain notorious sites to be either destroyed or rendered less attractive. However, within a generation of the Reformation it is rare to find such proscription, and it would appear that by the 17th century the established church,

in England at least, felt that visiting a holy well no longer held the same spiritual or devotional appeal, and thus potential threat, that it once had.

Nevertheless, the church-holy well association survives to this day in the many holy wells which have strong geographical connections with parish churches. There are at least 22 churches, chapels and monastic sites in this region which can boast such connections, whilst another site, the Bewell at Bristol, was accompanied by a medieval cross. The proximity of church to well varies considerably, from the 30m at Winford to 400m at Keynsham; beyond 400m the connection becomes harder to establish unless both well and church share the same dedication or the current church building is on a different site to its predecessor.

The relationship between church and holy well can be seen from a number of perspectives. A popular argument is that the early church adopted the sites of pagan holy places, thereby encouraging the newly-converted to attend Christian services at a traditional and familiar location. Following this line of argument it is assumed that pagan sacred wells, themselves foci for pre-Christian ritual activity, were thus the determining factors for the positioning of many an early Christian place of worship, which through time became the parish churches we are familiar with today. Exorcism of the wells would be seen to de-paganise them and render their powers at the service of the church. Tales of holy men and women confounding evil spirits at wells are found throughout Europe, and also in Islamic countries, and in this region there is the example of St David's tears falling into Bath's Sacred Spring and rendering it fit for Christian use.

Such an argument is very appealing and may well account for many of the sacred springs associated with churches. However, it does verge on the simplistic and there is at least one other way in which the church-holy well relationship could have developed over the thousand or so years in which the Celtic and Catholic churches flourished. In his book *The Living Stream*, James Rattue notes the possibility that a large number of England's holy wells and their associated cults were actually created by the early medieval church once it had overcome its uncertain ambivalence to the phenomena. So popular were holy wells as an outlet for religious devotion that,

'St Mary's Well near Bristol'. This is an intriguing 18th century print for, despite several St Mary's Wells near Bristol, none of those known fit the topography shown here. Is this a well now lost to us? (Bristol Museum & Art Gallery)

he argues, it was only prudent to manage demand and ensure that new sites were created as and when the need arose. Furthermore, holy wells adjacent to churches would be more amenable to church control than those in isolated or sparsely inhabited regions where unbridled paganism and debauched revelry could occur.

Whichever theory is nearer to the truth, church holy wells provided one very important service—baptismal water. Indeed, so attractive was a constant supply of fresh water to the needs of a church that it is possible that a third strand to the siting argument can be entertained, namely that some churches may have been built near a dependable water supply which became holy by association. In the Bristol region there are five wells which are known to have been used as traditional sources of baptismal water: St Mary's Well, Charlcombe; St Julian's Well,Wellow; the Backwell, Backwell; the churchyard spring, Winford; and the Timsell Well at Blagdon. At Blagdon there are still people in the parish who were baptised at the font of St Andrew's Church with water brought the 200m from the Timsell Well. The water was collected in a large ornate jug, (still on display at the church), and only one person was entrusted with this

17

job: one of the most recent holders of this post—then an old woman—is still remembered in the parish as carrying out this duty less than 60 years ago.

It was not just the established church that used natural springs as a source of baptismal water, for a spring in the St George area of Bristol, now under Plummer's Hill Road, supplied the local Baptist church for many years, and it is likely that further research would yield many other similar scenarios. Amongst some parts of the modern Catholic church there is also an interest in using holy well water for the baptismal font—witness the parishioners of St Alphage in Bath who, until recently, made an annual visit to St Alphage's Well at Charlcombe to take away a gallon of the holy water.

The Monastic connection

Mention has already been made of the proximity of some holy wells to monastic sites, and the wells at Keynsham and Kewstoke (Woodspring Priory) are two good examples which are still flowing to this day. Mention was also made of St Aldam who may have caused the Bishop's Wells at Yatton and Churchill to acquire their names. However, there are other examples involving religious figures such as the lost Anckerswell which once rose in Cromhall parish. 'Ancker' is an archaic form of the word 'anchorite', a hermit, and it is said that the Cromhall well took its name from a much-respected recluse who lived in a cell nearby. Monks gave their name to three wells in the region and abbots to one—both monks and abbots also have fish ponds named after them. In the majority of these cases it is likely that the names refer to ownership rather than to the presence of an adjacent monastic community, although in the case of Charlcombe's Monk's Well (also known as St Mary's Well) there is a persistent tradition that a monastic community lived on the site when Christianity was first established in the area.

Folklore has both monks and nuns bathing at Hutton's Ladies Well—presumably not at the same time!—whilst more reliable accounts tell of the monks of Glastonbury stopping at the Holy Virgin's Well at Wick and Abson to bathe their eyes as they made a procession around this detached Glastonbury estate in south Gloucestershire. Bath Abbey owned and controlled access to the

Sacred Spring / King's Bath until the Reformation, and the Carthusian monks of Hinton Charterhouse Priory owned Ela's Well in Friary Wood. Indeed, if folklore is to be believed, the monastic presence has yet to be fully extinguished at this last site for the ghosts of monks are occasionally seen standing round it.

The High Middle Ages

Following the Norman Conquest, a number of important developments occurred in the evolution of the holy well. One of the most important was an upsurge in the rededication of holy wells to more fashionable, and usually international, saints: both St Mary and St James were popular amongst the Normans and are poorly represented in holy well dedications before this date. Thus perhaps it is to this period that Bristol's Jacob's Well (Latin: *fons Jacobus*) can trace its roots, as could the eleven local wells dedicated to the Blessed Virgin Mary.

The Virgin Mary is the single most popular holy well dedication in the region, and as such reflects a trend found throughout Britain. Many neo-pagans with an interest in holy wells see the Virgin as a rather clear-cut Christian adaptation of 'the Great Goddess' whom many believe to have been the overarching deity of pagan holy wells. There are many fascinating and undoubted similarities between the Christian Virgin and a great many of the goddesses of the Classical World and the Middle East but few scholars have found many convincing arguments to link her with a 'Great Goddess', a deity which, it must be said, is largely a product of late Victorian academic research with many of her attributes taken from not only European paganism but also Eastern and Native American traditions. As such the 'Great Goddess' venerated today is essentially a modern creation, but is none the less a reality for many people, for whom she represents a genuine outlet for spirituality.

The historical Christian Virgin, despite her complex origins, was the focus for a phenomenal level of devotion during the Middle Ages and not only were many existing holy wells re-dedicated to her during this period, but also new holy wells were 'created' to satisfy the demand.

In three parishes: Bathford, Chew Stoke and Wick and Abson there is a curious phenomenon, not known in other areas, where a

St Mary's Well is closely paired with a St Anthony's Well. Such a pairing presumably dates from the High Middle Ages when the cults of both of the saints were at their height, but why they should be paired in this manner is a mystery. These three St Anthony's Wells are the only confirmed dedications to the saint in the region—a fourth possible dedication at Blackswarth Hill, east Bristol, remains unproven. There must therefore have been a popular association between these two saints at some point in the Middle Ages.

Another curious saintly geography is shown by the spatial distribution of St Anne's Wells, the four proven sites at Brislington, Frenchay, Siston, and Cold Ashton, and a fifth, unsubstantiated, site at Horfield, all fall within a relatively narrow belt of land running north of Bristol and east to the edge of the Cotswolds. The cult of St Anne was late in achieving widespread appeal in England, arriving in the country in the 12th century and taking a long time to gain devotees, so it is very likely that the St Anne's Wells represent one of the last bursts of holy well (re-) dedication in the area. All this is very far removed from R.C.S. Walters' assertions in *The Ancient Wells, Springs and Holy Wells of Gloucestershire*, where he championed the arguments of a Canon Bazeley who argued that 'St Anne' was in fact a corruption of the name of a pagan god!—an argument very much in keeping with the spirit of the late 19th and early 20th centuries.

From the mid-14th century onwards there is a slow trickle of references to local holy wells appearing in deeds and charters and also a rare topographical account. From 1389 comes the first reference to the Henbury Pennywell when it appears as *Pennywell fontem*. Other Bristol wells receive a mention a century later in the *Itineraria* of William Worcester where the author describes the main features and the boundaries of the late medieval city. Described here are St Vincent's Well, later to achieve fame as the Hotwell, as well as boundary wells such as the *Begereswelle* at a site now in St Paul's, and the important quasi-ritual site of the Bewell. The Bewell, which rose at the top of St Michael's Hill, was more than just a boundary spring for it was accompanied by a high cross and what is believed to have been a prehistoric tumulus—Bewell Tump. Worcester tells us that a gallows stood here on which 'traitors and thieves' were hung, and later at this site, during the reign of Queen Mary, Protestant martyrs were burnt at the stake. Even though these grizzly details were played out in the late Middle Ages and the Early Modern Period they do echo the ancient use of wells as liminal sites, portals between this world and an Otherworld, places where sacrifices were made to the presiding spirits, and a dominant theme in much animistic belief.

The Conduits

When settlements grew to such a size that the natural springs and excavated shaft wells could no longer satisfy demand, landowners, institutions and parish authorities had to look elsewhere to bring water to those who needed it. Monastic communities had long been in the practice of bringing water from afar to their buildings. Where they owned land on hills or along a spring line the water could be capped and transported many miles via a primitive but effective system of wooden and stone pipes known as 'conduits'. Locally, the earliest record of a conduit—that bringing water from the Huge Well at Knowle into the Bristol suburb of Redcliffe—dates from 1190 and was intended for the monks of St John's Hospital, but soon supplied other sites owned by landowner Robert de Berkeley.

This pattern of distant springs supplying discrete areas within medieval Bristol eventually led to a complex network of conduits or 'Pipes' disgorging their load at fountains or troughs, known as 'castellettes'—so-called from their ornate architecture. Springs on Kingsdown, Brandon Hill, Knowle and Pile's Hill at Totterdown fed into this system as did the Pamiwell or Pennywell at St Werburgh's. The conduits were essential to the survival of the medieval urban population and branch pipes known as 'feathers' ran off from the main monastic pipelines to supply the population *en route* although access to these 'feathers' was in theory the prerogative of monastic tenants.

The monastic conduits of medieval Bristol were the most extensive in the region and supply a wealth of fascinating insights into the workings of the medieval city as recorded in great detail by the Temple Local History Group in their 1984 monograph *An account of St John's Conduit—Bristol's Medieval Water System*. Medieval Bath was similarly endowed, and both the abbey and the parish of

21

St James were supplied by conduits running from Beechen Cliff to the south of the city, and there were at least five fountains in the northern half of the city fed from St Swithin's Well at Walcot. The St Swithin's system may be of considerable antiquity, for a large cistern, which took in the spring water before supplying it to the fountains, once had an oratory built above it which was dedicated to St Werburgh. This dedication suggests that the cistern dates from at least the late Saxon period, and if this is indeed the case it is interesting to speculate that the St Swithin's system could have been adapted from a Roman predecessor.

However, the conduits and castellettes were more than just a water supply. Like the springs from which they flowed they were regarded with respect and veneration. In Bristol, there were ceremonial dressings of the conduits on New Year's Day and on Ascension Day when they were adorned with 'greening boughs and woodland flowers', and in pre-Reformation times there was the 'Ceremony of the Blessing of the Waters' where the following prayer was offered:

> May the Blessing of God Almighty,
> the father, Son and Holy Ghost, and
> all the saints, be upon these springs,
> and those who use them, and those
> who tend them for ever more

Following the Dissolution of the Monasteries, ownership of the conduits was transferred to the city parishes who were supplied from them and throughout the next three hundred years they remained the main source of drinking water for many of the inhabitants of both cities. Furthermore they maintained their position as community foci. In Bristol, when Queen Anne was proclaimed in 1701, it was said that 'the conduits ... were adorned with flowers and gilded branches', whilst some forty years earlier, in Bath, the ascension of Charles II was marked by a grand civic procession to the conduit outside St Mary's Church where, instead of water, the fountain 'began to run with claret', and it was here that the assembled company 'drank a health to his majesty'. To mark this event in Bristol a Maypole was erected next to St Edith's Well.

At least some of the conduits were believed to carry medicinal waters. At the Carnwell conduit in Bath the water had a powerful reputation for curing eye complaints, whilst the water which issued from the Key Pipe in Bristol was visited by those suffering from gout and rheumatism, who would bathe their legs in the fountain.

A surprisingly large amount of the old conduit pipework still exists beneath Bristol's streets, mostly post-medieval it must be said, and has been mapped and described by the Temple Local History Society. Above ground little remains to be seen today: the 19th century fountain head of St John's Conduit is built into the wall of this city church, whilst a grilled iron fountain in the form of a lion's head at the side of Redcliffe Way is the only visible evidence of the Redcliffe Pipe. A shrine, believed to have stood above a 'feather' of Bristol's Carmelite Conduit, was still *in situ* until 1936 when it was removed to the City Museum. The most visible reminder of the Conduits lies in the names of city streets such as Conduit Road and Pennywell Road, both east of the city centre and both marking the course of the Key Pipe.

Other aspects of holy wells in the Middle Ages
Away from the cities there is little structural evidence of medieval holy wells. Many old structures have been rebuilt over the past 450 years, leaving only a scattering of sites which can display some indication of their medieval origin. One of the best preserved is the so-called 'Hameswelle' on private land at Cold Ashton, where a drystone revetment wall surrounds a small wellhouse that has carved stonework typical of the late middle ages. The Merriwell at Easton-in-Gordano is another interesting structure, despite its medieval credentials being not accepted by all. Here, a canopy wellhouse straddles the former boundary of the old Manor House with the public road; a gate on each side allowed separate access for both villagers and those in the Manor. A medieval wellhouse also once existed at St Anne's Well, Frenchay, but was removed piece-meal earlier this century until by the 1940s only a small pile of stone remained. Many other wells which appear to be ancient are almost impossible to date; the stonework around Ela's Well at Hinton Charterhouse, for example, may be contemporary with the

Carthusian Priory, but the lack of carved detail or mortar makes this site essentially undatable.

One of the few 'rural' holy wells in this region for which there is contemporary medieval detail is St Anne's Well at Brislington, now a Bristol suburb. A 13th century chapel once stood by the well and both sites were a great centre for pilgrimage until the Reformation. Pilgrims here included members of the nobility and two royal visitors—Henry VII and his wife Elizabeth of York—in the late 15th century. Many of the records of St Anne's dwell upon the chapel where many expensive and ornate offerings were made, especially by mariners, the Cordwainers and the Weaver's Guild. However, the well was still the essential focus of the pilgrimage, demonstrated by the medieval coins excavated from the site in the 1880s.

Although archaeological and documentary evidence is frequently lacking, it seems probable that many of the holy wells venerated during the Middle Ages continued to be the objects of localised pilgrimage, albeit shorn of its overtly religious nature. Thus the holy wells which were recorded by the early topographers, dedicated to saints or which maintained reputations into the modern era as places of healing, divination, wish fulfilment and supernatural activity, are likely to be those sites where medieval pilgrims came centuries before. But in the post-medieval period there emerged a new class of 'holy well' which did not necessarily owe anything to previous medieval veneration—the Spas.

The Spas
Many people with an interest in holy wells, and most writers upon the subject, tend to see Spas as an entirely separate phenomenon, more mechanistic and less 'mysterious' or romantic perhaps than the 'true' holy well with its roots lost in the swirling mists of time. Others, however, see the Spa phenomenon as a logical progression in the continuing evolution of the veneration of water. The religious and superstitious overtones of an earlier age may have been replaced with the rationalism that so enveloped the Age of Reason, but people in their tens of thousands were still putting their faith in the curative and life-transforming waters. The contemporary chroniclers of this new age were as likely to be physicians as romantic

topographers, more intent on discovering the chemical composition of the water than marvelling at its miraculous powers, and often keen to prove their spa's legitimacy by lists of potted case histories, but they were as much convinced by the powers of water as any medieval peasant.

Some of our spas had former lives. Thus the hot springs at Bath have a history of veneration from at least the Iron Age with their waters used for curing illness from Roman times, whilst Bristol's Hotwell Spa started life as the highly regarded medicinal spring of St Vincent's Well. Many of the others enjoyed a much more recent, and frequently short-lived, fame during the golden age of spas in the mid to late 18th century. The development of spas occurred throughout the country from the 16th century through to the early years of the present century, and whilst all regions can boast their own spas, the Bristol region is particularly blessed with what were two of the most prestigious spas of all—Bath and the Bristol Hotwell. These sites were pre-eminent in their day and attracted visitors from both Britain and abroad. Each year thousands of sick people would travel to Bath in the hope of finding relief from a whole suite of ailments, from infertility and lead poisoning through to digestive problems, broken bones and jaundice, indeed so many conditions that there were very few problems a trip to the spa could not cure. The Hotwell was similarly infallible in its reputation as a cure-all with particular credit given to its powers over diabetes, a wealth of internal complaints and, in later years, tuberculosis.

The two spas were engaged in fierce competition throughout much of the 18th century although the Hotwell's unfavourable location—sandwiched tightly between cliffs and the river—prevented it from offering the range of facilities available at Bath, and thus it tended to attract fewer of the glamorous and sophisticated clientele that made the much more expansive spa at Bath so fashionable. This social differentiation further exaggerated the disparity between the spas and prevented the Hotwell from having the same importance to the local economy as that of the spa at Bath.

The development of Bath as a spa is a case of seamless progression from its popularity during the later Middle Ages. Royalty had long been taking the waters here, both Plantagenet and Stuart monarchs being particularly enthusiastic and regular visitors. With such a degree of patronage, speculators could afford to erect the great crescents and terraces which came to surround and later define the city in Georgian times. The character of the whole city was fashioned in a rapid evolutionary development, medieval streets and houses were swept away to be replaced by fashionable boulevards and avenues, all of which served to emphasise the paragon of style and innovation which Bath had become.

Bath's success faltered during the Napoleonic Wars when the country experienced a more straightened financial climate, and once peace resumed fashionable society looked for a rather more exotic spa treatment in continental countries that war had long made inaccessible. Further decline set in with the fashion for sea bathing as a health tonic, but nevertheless Bath's spas continued to adapt to changing circumstances and, albeit with considerably reduced glamour, the waters were still being used until the 1970s. Bristol's Hotwell suffered a more severe decline, and despite brave attempts to resurrect its fortunes the spa was effectively defunct by the end of the 19th century.

The presence of the great urban spas in the Bristol region encouraged the development of smaller, more rural spas; without the 'overspill' of patronage provided by visitors to Bath and the Hotwell it is hard to see how many of the smaller sites could have survived purely on their own merits. In the accounts which remain of these frequently ephemeral sites we read of those with acute medical problems who had yet to experience relief at the main spas, but who were lured by advertisements, tea gardens and touts to visit a site that was little more than a short carriage drive out of town. At least nine minor spas once operated in the region, some like the Bladud Spa at Larkhall, Bath, survived until the 1930s but the majority were very short lived. Lyncombe Spa in Bath was typical in its demise, for within 60 years of its discovery the site was described as 'long since disused' and the spa buildings converted to a residence. Some spas, such as that rumoured to have existed at Nailsea, have vanished so completely that their very existence cannot now be verified.

Throughout the history of spas there was a determined scientific effort to establish the physical properties which lay at the heart of the curative waters. Physicians would boil the water until it had evaporated and then examine any powdery residue that might be left. Those who could no longer accept the medieval notions of 'miraculous cures' needed rational explanations for the powers of healing water and detailed papers were written proving that such-and-such a mineral was the true elixir, the water itself merely a medium which held the true medicine in solution.

This all seems a long way from the 'mystery' of holy and healing waters which had prevailed since prehistory. In the Age of Reason the educated and religious élite could take the waters and recommend their use without any fear of being accused of superstition or ignorance. However, it is clear that for many ordinary people the holy waters of their ancestors continued to exercise that 'mystery' which their educated countrymen had thought well and truly banished by the application of science and reason.

Holy wells in modern times
Much of the evidence for the existence of holy wells in this region comes from the writings of 19th century historians and topographers. The 18th century had seen a flowering of topographical literature and an appreciation of the picturesque, and within this milieu many features of an idealised and lost age were romanticised and treated as relics of a world filled with mystery. Being objects of irrational superstition, holy wells easily fell within this sphere, they were seen as medieval leftovers and those who venerated them or sought cures from them were held to be character actors from a timeless play, anachronisms in an increasingly rational and industrial world.

Although some of the accounts of 19th century holy wells can be viewed as somewhat patronising with the educated élite commenting on the quaint ways of the peasantry, without them many a well would have been lost to us and another corner of the land deprived of a site of awe and veneration. Great social and economic changes were transforming Britain throughout the 19th century and many holy wells were experiencing a loss of importance in the local landscape. This period has been termed 'the great change' and marks a time when many old relationships between people and the land were being radically refashioned. A declining rural population meant that many holy wells could no longer be guaranteed a visit from those in need of its help and as a consequence many sank into obscurity.

The growth in universal education further undermined local belief in holy wells, for with more people exposed to rational argument and the advances in scientific understanding, reliance upon faith and miraculous powers was in decline. Those who kept such beliefs alive were increasingly those who had not received a formal education or who were by nature more inclined to accept the existence of the unexplained.

Whilst indigenous support for holy wells was falling away, salvation for some came in the form of an increasing Roman Catholic population. Fuelled largely by Irish emigration and centred mostly around towns, cities and other industrial areas the Catholics still belonged to a culture where the veneration of holy wells was a living reality. Spared the complete Protestantisation of landscape in their native land that had so drastically altered the English relationship with the holy well, the Irish rediscovered sites which had been sacred in medieval times and reinstated pilgrimage and devotion at wells which had been effectively secular for over three hundred years. It was the strength of Irish Catholic pilgrimage for example which helped secure the future of St Anne's Well at Brislington when its owner attempted to exclude public access.

Many wells were still spoken of as holy, healing or haunted throughout the 19th century and most appear to have retained a degree of local allegiance, but the mere fact that a well has been accorded special status at one time does not guarantee its survival. Throughout the 19th century certain wells achieved popularity, peaked and then fell into obscurity whilst other wells took their place. Many of the accounts of 19th century wells emphasise the healing qualities, indeed it is rare to find examples of pure devotion or superstition. When these factors do occur it is usually as an aside to the well's healing powers.

It may never be possible to know how many holy wells went unrecorded during the 19th century and so have become 'lost'. Those whose fame allowed them to enter the 20th century were to experience an even greater erosion of influence than that evidenced in the preceding one, and a less romantic generation of historians and topographers tended to exclude holy wells from their accounts, preferring instead the more analytical and rigorous pursuit of conventional history. In a sense historians took themselves more seriously in the early 20th century and found discussion of superstitious practices something of an embarrassment. This is a great shame, for the inclusion of less academic material would have enlivened and enriched many a turgid and dry parish history.

Visits by indigenous local people to holy wells continued well into the 1920s, and there are accounts of sizeable numbers visiting some wells such as St Catherine's Well in the southern Cotswolds. Coalminers from made an annual pilgrimage to the Rattlespring at Marksbury in north Somerset until at least the mid-1920s, bathing their eyes in its waters and taking bottles of the curative fluid home for those too ill to make the journey. However, from the 1930s onwards those visiting the wells appear to have principally been from the older generation.

Fearing that local holy wells would be lost completely, some enlightened scholars took to recording as many wells as they could find and published their findings in books and the local press. During and immediately after the First World War the Somerset Benedictine monk, Ethelbert Horne, compiled *Somerset Holy Wells and Other Named Wells* published in 1923. To date this remains the most complete study of the wells of that county but only touches on the wealth of holy wells to be found in Somerset; for example of the 108 holy wells and notable springs with folkloric associations in the area of Somerset covered by the present work only 10 appear within Horne's book! Nevertheless Horne's work was indispensable in preserving records of several wells that would otherwise be completely lost to us.

In Gloucestershire the civil engineer Skyring Walters was engaged on a similar scheme, publishing *The Ancient Wells, Springs and Holy Wells of Gloucestershire; their legends, history and topography* in 1928. Walters' publishers, *The Bristol Times and Mirror* also provided a regular outlet for another holy well afficionado—Frederick Creech Jones. Jones was a Bristolian with a great passion for the history of his city and stands out from others of his time by his fascination for the local and the personal, describing minor aspects of local history, the characters, folklore and vernacular buildings of the city that were even then passing into memory. Jones, being an engineer with the Bristol Waterworks Company, had a particular interest in holy wells and recorded many obscure facts and beliefs associated with the wells of the city and its suburbs. The parlous condition of St Anne's Well at Brislington particularly concerned him and he led a campaign to restore its dignity, declare its surrounds a public park, and re-instate an annual pilgrimage and religious service at the well. Aided by Ethelbert Horne, and with the support of many Bristolians who were regular readers of his weekly newspaper column, Jones eventually persuaded Bristol Corporation to buy the site, restore the well and open the area as a public park. In doing so Jones provides an example, rare at the time, of someone determined to arrest the decline of their local holy wells; it is to his credit that St Anne's is still there to this day and not lost to enclosed ownership or urban development.

From the mid-1930s until the 1970s holy wells continued to experience a gradual and inexorable decline, despite the work of Horne, Jones & Walters, as those who frequented or remembered them became increasingly old or died. Local histories would occasionally make mention of wells, but the most significant contribution during this period was the call to local Women's Institutes in 1952 to enter parish histories into a national competition. These histories were the work of the women themselves and are remarkable for the contrast they provide to the dry and academic works usually provided at the time by those studying local history. Within the WI local histories there is frequently a wealth of folklore and incidental historical information and it is from such sources that we gain our last real insight into the living traditions of local holy wells at a period when much living knowledge was on the point of being extinguished. Even so, it is notable how frequently reference to local holy wells is made in the past tense, contributors recalling conversations with their elders or beliefs held as children.

In 1965 more information on Somerset's holy wells was provided by the publication of *Somerset Folklore* by Ruth Tongue, a prolific author and compiler of local lore. Tongue's work on holy wells borrows heavily from Horne, but she does supply much previously unrecorded material, some of which is of relevance to the Bristol region. During the late 1960s there was a revival of interest in what can loosely be described as the mystical and romantic tradition of landscape and history. Enthusiasm for the notion of ley lines (originally invented in the 1920s) gained favour once more and there developed a complex set of ideologies about ancient sites, especially those which appeared to offer a link to our pagan past. Holy wells fitted well within this new approach and throughout the next two decades to the present day they became part of the burgeoning belief systems of the New Age, Earth Mysteries, Women's Spirituality and Celtic Spirituality. Each group adopted holy wells to suit the needs of their own beliefs, and it must be said that wishful enthusiasm rather than measured study has played a key role for many modern holy well enthusiasts. The publication of *Sacred Waters* by Janet and Colin Bord in 1985 gave a considerable impetus to the renaissance of holy well studies and encouraged readers to consider the magical nature of these special sites.

It is within this background that holy wells survive in the modern landscape. Many wells remain utterly obscure, even to those who own the fields and woods they rise in, let alone a new generation of neo-pagans, though some of the more celebrated and accessible wells, such as the Chalice Well at Glastonbury, receive a constant stream of pilgrims and curious visitors. More conventional and established groups are once again adopting some of the abandoned holy wells; annual pilgrimages to St Arild's Well, Thornbury, and St Anne's Well, Brislington, are co-ordinated by local church and history societies, whilst well-dressing was briefly introduced by Paulton Women's Institute in the 1980s upon restoration of the Paulto' Spring.

Many local holy wells still draw people to throw in coins as they make a wish, and it is probably in this guise, as wishing wells, that most people are familiar with holy wells. Water from St Alphage's Well, Charlcombe, was recently used in baptisms and a number of wells still provide opportunities for those with health problems to improve their condition. A number of wells are actively cared for and several have been restored for present and future generations by a group of holy well enthusiasts, 'The Source', who provide free labour and expertise to prevent local wells deteriorating any further.

However, it is in terms of mysterious and ancient places of wonder and awe that the majority of holy wells in the Bristol region are thought of today. Too often their waters are either too polluted or too reduced in flow to provide a hygienic and reliable source of holy and healing water for local people. However, to know that they exist, and to know of the veneration and legends which once surrounded them is perhaps as much as we can expect. Many of these sites exert a considerable power, even though that power may be hard to quantify; to acknowledge and protect them is an act of respect for the memory of generations past and for our environment and wellbeing today.

CHAPTER III
Rituals and Cures

Holy wells stood out from other springs and bodies of water by the uses to which they were put. When going to the holy well a person essentially had one thing in mind—to improve the condition of their life. Frequently this improvement was in the physical realm and was manifested by seeking cures for long-standing or acute illnesses or by seeking an enhancement in their fortune, perhaps attaining a longed-for goal. However it is rare to find local accounts which suggest any indication of an outright religious or spiritual motivation such as we find into the present century in Ireland or in the other Catholic countries of Europe.

This loss of a conscious religious awareness is a product of the Reformation, for within two generations of the official adoption of Protestantism as the state religion great swathes of popular ritual devotion had been discarded by all levels of society. Many of the religious holidays were abolished, to be replaced with state sanctioned alternatives; the cult of the saints, so tied in with the Catholic veneration of the well, went into decline; and the diffusion of Renaissance ideas on the structure of the universe and the nature of life itself provided a more functional and methodical belief which did away with the more spiritual Catholic philosophies that had once held sway.

Many would like to believe that deep down the rural population kept to their old beliefs, sullenly guarding the rituals of old; spiritual guerrillas fighting a long and slow-burning war against an imposed orthodoxy which only the élite themselves espoused. Such a romantic notion has long prevailed within the study of indigenous folklore, and students of holy wells have frequently been to the forefront of this thinking. As attractive as the notion sounds, all evidence points in the opposite direction; those studying the nature of religious and ritual life in the period following the Reformation have demonstrated the surprisingly rapid abandonment of the old ways within a couple of generations of Henry VIII's edict. Keith Thomas in *Religion and the Decline of Magic* and Ronald Hutton's *The Stations of the Sun*, two of the most important works in this field, chronicle the eager adoption of the new ways, with Catholic observation, in all its forms, an increasingly marginalised force in society.

Within such a period of rapid and dramatic social change one would have expected the whole phenomenon of holy wells to have been swept away along with monastic estates, rood screens and the relics of saints but, despite the odds, holy wells survived. People still visited them in the hope of effecting a cure or of seeking the fulfilment of a wish. Shorn of ecclesiastical sanction, people still made offerings to sacred waters, much as they had done for a thousand or more years. Now, however, the visits appear to have become more superstitious than spiritual, forms of pagan and Catholic well ritual may still have been followed, but the belief that such activities were intercessionary had died.

Cures
There were very few ailments for which the holy and medicinal waters of the Bristol region could not offer a cure. For those bitten by a mad dog, rabies could be kept at bay by journeying to the parish of High Littleton and drinking water from a well at Hallatrow, whilst warts were treated by the rainwater collected within the trough of Chew Magna's Tun Bridge Wishing Well. Leprosy was cured at Bath by immersion in the Cross Bath and the Hot Bath, the disease having been treated here since at least Norman times, and if we are to believe the legend of Prince Bladud, from prehistory! For blood poisoning the afflicted needed to go no further than St Anne's Well, Brislington, a site where medieval mariners also found solace for one of their specific ailments— scurvy.

A great many wells offered cures for a full suite of illnesses and dysfunctions, the King's Bath at Bath perhaps holding the record for treatable ailments, so many in fact that one wonders whether

A less-than glamorous portrayal of the King's Bath at Bath and its clientele by J.C Stadler in 1801 (Bath City Library)

there was anything it could not cure. Frequently a holy well was said to have 'general' curative properties, or that drinking its waters was conducive to long life and good health. General purpose healing wells may go back a long way if we are to believe the etymology of the east Bristol place-name 'Soundwell' which derives from the Old English word *gesund* meaning 'healthy'.

At one time all holy wells may have been non-specific cure-alls only providing specialist treatment after a number of years, perhaps after a spectacular cure and word spread to fellow sufferers. It may have been by this process that scrofulous disorders were cured at Adam's Well, Banwell, and consumption became the speciality at Yatton's Bishop's Well and Holwell. Gout was relieved by bathing in Bath's Locksbrook stream and the conduit head of Key Pipe at the side of Bristol's old docks. The Key Pipe was also sought out by sufferers of rheumatism who would bathe their legs in the water as it poured out of the pipe, indeed Bristol waters seem to have been particularly suitable for rheumatics for there was also a Cold Bath

35

Fashionable society on display at the Pump Room, Bath c.*1825*
(Bath City Library)

near the site of the castle and St Anne's Well at Brislington. The
cure of lameness and sprained feet is a widely acknowledged holy
well speciality, with St Alphage's Well at Charlcombe and the
churchyard spring at Winford achieving fame as two of the best
springs in the area for the treatment of these conditions. Indeed at
Winford it is said that a gypsy boy, whose leg was terribly injured
and who faced the real prospect of amputation, was taken to the
well and bathed; within days the leg had brought about a miraculous improvement and the boy completely recovered.

Internal complaints were also catered for at the holy well. In the
16th century the petrifying spring at Stowey was believed to cure
those with 'the stone'—kidney stones. Perhaps it was the medieval
'doctrine of signatures'—which ascribed like curing like—which
led to this conclusion, for the spring was known to cover everything
which came into contact with it with a hard lime crust. Kimber
Combe at Bitton possessed a 'purging' spring whilst the hot springs
at Bath were famed for their cure of digestive maladies, the King's
Bath helping to relieve 'The vayn appetite of going to stoole, when
a man can do nothing when he cummeth there', whilst in 1760

Richard Russell wrote that regular bathing at the Cross Bath 'will commonly give two or three stools extraordinary'!

Skin conditions were also alleviated, with the hot springs of Bath again proving of multiple use, whilst many of the 'Cold Baths' which were in use across the region during the 18th and 19th centuries specialised in skin conditions. If a woman were not content simply with a healthy skin and instead sought a more beautiful and softer complexion, then there were wells which would satisfy her wish. The Virgin's Well at Tortworth was sought out for this reason as was the Maiden's Well at Wraxall whose water, incidentally, was also believed to render young boys more feminine and for this reason was liberally used by the governesses of Clifton! Gender bending wells have also been noted in Ireland; for example if a couple in Co. Mayo wished to change the sex of their child all that was needed was for them to visit St Brendan's Well at Kilmeena where the unsuspecting infant would be dunked and emerge a different gender!

Eye Wells

Of the wealth of cures to be found at holy wells there is one which is paramount, not just in this region but throughout the British Isles: the curing of eye complaints. Of the 69 recorded healing wells in the Bristol region (excluding 9 spas with no history prior to the mid-18th century) 36 (52%) are eye wells. Only six of these have other curative properties recorded for them. Many who have commented upon holy wells have attempted to offer explanations for this imbalance, but a thoroughly convincing argument has yet to be found. The commonest and most mundane explanation has been to suggest that the dark, smoky interiors of poor people's homes — a situation which has only been alleviated during the past century — was to blame. The argument is that such conditions could cause much inflammation and eye strain, and, with no accessible optical health care, a simple wash in the pure water of a holy well would bring considerable relief, especially if one takes into account the possibility that dissolved minerals and trace elements will be present in the water.

An alternative line of thought is that in the washing of eyes we may be seeing the vestige of a holy well ritual. But there is no record of an eye washing ritual in the Catholic church, the only link with Catholic ritual might be making the sign of the cross with holy water, but then there is no direct contact with the eyes. If Catholic ritual is unlikely to be the explanation, the possibility is that bathing the eyes may be a vestige of a pagan well ritual. This opens up a number of tantalising possibilities, chief of which is the Germanic legend of the god Odin. Odin wished to gain omniscience and knew that the only way to achieve this was to drink from a well at the foot of the World Tree. However, to do so he must make a sacrifice to Mimir, the keeper of the well. Odin thus ripped out one of his eyes as an offering and only then was he able to drink of the sacred waters. Odin was a god worshiped by both the Anglo-Saxons and the Norsemen, who between them had a profound impact not only upon England, but also over large tracts of land popularly thought of as purely Celtic, such as Scotland and Ireland.

It is not known whether pagan Germanic well ritual involved an acknowledgement of Odin's sacrifice, indeed any evidence of pre-Christian activity at sacred springs is extremely rare anywhere in northern Europe. Even if the legends of the pagan Germans provide a link between eyes and wells, what evidence is there of similar associations in Celtic areas? In Ireland it was believed that St Bridget, an historic figure whose *Life* may have incorporated elements of a similarly-named pagan deity, plucked out one of her eyes to rid herself of an unwanted suitor. An equally severe rebuff was delivered by the virgin, St Caolainn, who, upon being told by a man that he admired her eyes, gouged them out and threw them on the ground saying 'there, they are for you'. Irish legend has a number of eye gouging tales, but as all Irish documents were written by Christians, frequently several hundred years after the supposed events, it is impossible to say which parts are pagan, which Christian, and which are just pure fiction.

A further investigation of pagan Celtic mythology suggests that wells were seen as the 'eye' of an earth deity, a idea supported by one of the suggested derivations of the name of Sulis, the Celtic goddess worshiped at Bath's hot springs, being that of 'eye'. This derivation, if accepted, adds weight to the idea that springs and wells, and holy wells in particular, could have been seen as places to commune, face to face, with supernatural beings. Further support occurs for this theory in Wales where the word *Llygad*, which means 'eye', is used to denote the source of a river or stream, an idea supported by Janet and Colin Bord in *Sacred Waters*, who also note the saying 'you must not look into running water, because you look into God's eye'.

Francis Jones notes a particularly interesting tradition at the Carmarthenshire holy well of Ffynnon Gwenlais, where the virgin Gwenlais was beheaded and a spring of water welled up. Here it was said that 'The Spring has two eyes ... of a very different nature', a situation also found at Mother Pugsley's Well in Bristol where two springs and two basins were once found, one for domestic use and the other to be used only in the bathing of the eyes. At Mother Pugsley's it was believed that the waters received their virtue from the tears of the virgin widow who sat by its side lamenting the loss of her husband. The tears of a virtuous, and saintly figure are said to have caused wells elsewhere to become blessed, indeed a medieval tradition held that it was the tears of St David which gave the hot springs of Bath their great sanative powers.

A rather more primitive belief, common in north Somerset, was that all wells which rose to face east, towards the rising sun, were useful in eye complaints. Likewise those which gave rise to streams that flowed in an anti-clockwise direction were perceived to be powerful eye wells.

It could be thought that once medicine had progressed, the ophthalmic properties of holy well water would have been consigned to history. This is not so. There are several instances of modern doctors prescribing holy well water for those with eye complaints. Perhaps we can forgive the Victorian doctor in Nailsea who sent local coalminers to the Sunnyside well to bathe their sore eyes, and an indulgence could also be extended to the physicians associated with the Thornbury Union Workhouse who sent for water from Rockhampton's Penny Well when one of their residents needed eye treatment. But what do we make of the Bristol Eye Hospital requesting water from the Virgin's Well at Tortworth or the Olveston doctor who persisted, even up to the foundation of the National Health Service, in sending patients to the healing waters of the Miles Well?

A view of Bristol's Hotwell

Animals

An interesting sideline of the holy well was in the cure of animals. The legend of the discovery of Bath's hot springs, where the outcast and leprous Prince Bladud found that the leprous pigs in his charge had cured themselves by bathing in the mud around the springs, is widely known. There are a number of mythological elements to the Bladud story, such as the role of the pig as a totemic animal and a creature of the Celtic Otherworld, and these themes are examined in greater detail in R.J. Stewart's *The Waters of the Gap*, a book which explores the fascinating myth and symbolism which have become woven around the hot springs. Apart from the Bladud swine, Bath can boast the only other instances of animals being cured by holy well water in this region. Horses were at one time bathed in a pool called 'the Horse Bath' formed by run-off from the Hot Bath. However this treatment of sacred healing waters for use with animals did not find universal favour, for in 1730 John Strachey records a magistrate advising 'not to profane so sacred a Water to ye Use of Beasts'.

Less than a mile to the south-east of the city centre, in the suburb of Widcombe, Rosamund's Well, used for the cure of human eye disorders, was also used in treating eye complaints in dogs; it is not known what the human users of the well thought about this!

A similar depiction of Bristol's Hotwell

Fertility

Throughout the world holy wells share one particularly basic function—to provide barren or newly wed couples with children. The holy well as a reproductive aid may seem bizarre and ridiculous to an educated people but for millennia those desiring children would visit their local wells or travel to distant and highly regarded fertility springs in the hope of speeding conception.

This was not just a silly superstition practised by an ignorant and desperate peasantry—royalty would make tours of noted fertility wells, hoping to ensure the birth of a son and heir. In 1485 Henry VII's Queen, Elizabeth of York, came to St Anne's Well at Brislington, and after praying at the well offered up 2s 6d at the nearby chapel in the hope that she would conceive a son; within a year she had given birth to a boy—Prince Arthur. In her actions the Queen was but part of an ancient tradition of despairing and aspirant mothers who visited St Anne's Well, a tradition which was still followed here up to the early years of this century. Another Queen—Mary, wife of James II visited a number of Bath's holy wells in 1686 in the hope that her devotions would allow her to conceive an heir.

Bathing at the King's Bath, the Cross Bath and St Winefred's Well, her wish was granted within the year when Charles James Stewart, the Old Pretender, was born. All the wells Mary had visited claimed the honours, though the Cross Bath was so sure of itself that a large commemorative cross was erected within it to replace a medieval structure which had formerly stood there.

Fertility wells are found throughout the world—people would visit them to bathe or drink, and perhaps take a bottle of the water away with them. So desperate were some women to conceive that they would make pilgrimages, like the Queens noted above, travelling great distances. At one time the King's Bath at Bath was one of the most renowned fertility wells in the country; the Tudor physician William Turner noting in 1562 how it relieved 'Barunnes of man or woman'. So many women visited Bath in the hope of relieving their infertility that their ailment was described as 'The Common Cause' and great pride was shown by the city in the reputation of its women, who resorted to the bath when pregnant, of never being known to miscarry. The hot steam rising from the baths led contemporary wags to suggest that it was perhaps the release of other pent-up steam in the lewd bathhouses of the city which caused so many miraculous conceptions. Even now the steaming hot wells of Jerusalem are visited by childless women who believe that the 'djinn' or 'spirit' who caused the vapours was 'capable in a definite and physical sense, of giving them offspring.' In Germany it was once widely believed that babies originated in wells, ponds and rivers, being brought by storks to human mothers. In the north German province of Schleswig-Holstein there were two 'baby wells' administered by women who, if asked, would wake a baby from its watery sleep and ensure its delivery to a would-be mother. In Australia certain Aboriginal groups believed that the spirits of unborn children lived in the rocks and trees around special wells. If a woman desired a child she went to these wells and whilst there a child-spirit would jump from its rock or tree into her womb. No such direct explanations are given for the powers of our own fertility wells, but such beliefs may once have existed here too.

The few details we have of the ritual involved in procuring children via the holy well suggest that the offering of pins, frequently bent or twisted, was of central importance. So-called 'pin-wells' are recorded at Wrington, Siston, Portishead and East Harptree, all sites with other powers of healing or divination beside their role in fertility. The offering of bent pins is a reminder of the damaged goods, such as bent spears and broken pottery, found in Bronze Age and Iron Age ritual pools and sacred rivers. Such decommissioning of valuable material is thought to have been a way of demonstrating that the treasured goods were now out of circulation in our world, but capable of being used by the deities to whom they were offered.

It must be noted that in nearly all accounts, both British and foreign, it is the woman who must seek restitution for barrenness. The relative paucity of male fertility rituals associated with holy wells suggests either a sexist arrogance that it is not the man's 'problem', or that women were somehow more receptive to the powers of the well. In this region William Turner's note that 'Barunnes of *man* or woman' could be cured at the King's Bath, is an almost isolated instance of men seeking relief for their condition. However, there is an oblique reference to male infertility in an account of St Alphage's Well, Charlcombe, where, apart from the 'blind and the lame', 'the impotent' also sought relief at the sacred spring.

Ceremony at the Well
To gain the maximum benefit from the power of the well it was not just sufficient to visit it and drink or bathe, something more was required of the visitor, something which suggested that a deal was being made between the supplicant and the nebulous power of the water. In pagan times set rituals were probably followed at holy wells, the benefits gained from the waters being the gifts of the well deity, and an acknowledgement, or admission of respect, for the deity was required before anything could be gained. Thus a prayer, an offering or a sequence of prescribed actions would be made to ensure that the deity would be willing to dispense their favours.

This can be said with some certainty for such sequences of events have been recorded from 'pagan' societies throughout the world. With the diffusion of monotheistic religions, principally Christianity and Islam, there is no place for minor deities or well spirits and so the ritual involved with holy wells is directed to the one god, although frequently this is through the intercession of saints. There has been much conjecture about whether holy well saints are reconstituted pagan deities or whether they were distinct and genuine figureheads of the new religions; people who really did exist, but whose biographies have become mythologised with time so as to appear now as truly mythical entities. In truth this discussion may never be answered with complete satisfaction as sufficient documentary and archaeological evidence does not exist to prove either argument. What can be said, however, is that there appears to be room for both arguments as well as a suggestion that within folklore fusions occurred between accounts of pagan deities and monotheistic saints to produce hybrid figures to whom people would pray or make offerings. As noted earlier the people who visited British holy wells within historic times were there as Christians and were using the holy wells to communicate with the Christian god. When asked by antiquarians or surveyors what they were doing, many were adamant that their actions were entirely Christian. This is an important point to reflect upon, for although well ritual may have retained a considerable amount of pagan influence, once converted the bulk of the population ceased to see their actions in pagan terms.

The manner in which people made their devotions to the well could either reflect a wider ritual context or be in a fashion unique to a particular well. Common themes are found throughout, however, such as the best time to visit, the number of prayers or actions to be repeated, the sequence of actions to follow, and ways in which the water was used.

The Time

Wells could be visited at any time of the year, but were widely believed to be most effective on particular dates. In this region, and indeed throughout the British Isles, May Day was the most popular choice. This is a day with a great deal of mythological association and is essentially the most unreconstituted and most pagan of festive days with its roots stretching back well before the Christian era. Of the seven wells in the Bristol region where a specific visiting day is recorded, four are associated with May Day whilst another, St Winefred's Well at Bath, may also once have had a May association though all we are told is that 'spring' was the time to visit. However, it was not just that any time on May Day would suffice, for where more detail is recorded it seems that the early hours of the morning was when the powers of the water were at their most favourable. In other areas the time is specified even more precisely to the hours between midnight and dawn, a belief echoed in the assertion that Chew Magna's Tun Bridge Wishing Well should be visited by 'creeping down at midnight'. In Wales certain holy wells were used for divination during May and it is frequently recorded throughout Britain that young women were guaranteed beautiful complexions by bathing their faces in either the dew or the water of a holy well before sunrise on May Day—an activity recorded at Tortworth's Virgin's Well.

The other favoured time to visit the well in this region was Easter. Water from a well in the parish of Wraxall was used by Methodists for brewing tea on Good Friday and there is the Marksbury 'Easter Well', a field name associated with a spring in the west of the parish. Some have suggested that the Marksbury name is a reference to the spring's geography, *i.e.* lying east of some notable feature but its position does not support this idea, and furthermore the use of the term 'easter' in a geographical context is extremely rare in this region.

Ritual
Once at the well, and at the right time of year, what was the next step? This is a complex area where evidence is scanty and general-isations are tempting, the documentary record is meagre and archaeology even poorer. Nevertheless, a number of themes can be discerned in the Bristol region, all with parallels elsewhere.

Procedure. Accounts of holy wells in Wales, Ireland and Scotland are frequently detailed in their descriptions of how the supplicant was to approach the well, what was done there and what was to be done afterwards. In this area there are few accounts with which to make a comparison. One of the most bizarre, however, involves the Southwell at Congresbury, where on the eve of May Day, women would gather at the well to dance around it barking like dogs. Ruth Tongue, who first noted this tradition, speculated that it was connected with an account that witchcraft used to be practised on the nearby Cadbury Hill on this same date, and that the ritual at the well may have been associated with this. The other evidence which we have for the form of ritual comes from the procedures followed at the wishing wells of Conkwell at Winsley, and King's Castle Well at East Harptree. At the Conkwell, a visitor would crawl to the well on their hands and knees, cup their left hand in the water, make a silent wish in their mind and then drink the water from their hand. At King's Castle Well, the water was again gathered in the hand, but the silent wish had to be made three times to prove effective.

Apart from the use as baptismal water there is rarely any unambiguously religious activity recorded at holy wells in this region, indeed the only instance appears to be the soot deposited on the roof of the well chamber at St Alphage's Well, Charlcombe, said to have been caused by generations of pilgrims lighting candles within the chamber as they came to take the water.

The Roman artefacts excavated from the Sacred Spring / King's Bath at Bath present a fascinating variant on the ritual involved with the wishing well. Amongst ritual objects associated with healing and the cult of the goddess Sulis-Minerva there were found a number of curses which were thrown into the spring, most inscribed on thin sheets of lead but some on stone. An analysis of the personal names associated with these curses shows that the majority, and nearly all those associated with the lead sheets, were Celtic, whilst a minority, and most of those associated with the carved stone, were Roman. Thus the more expensive stone curses were probably associated with those of greater wealth and higher status, whilst the cheaper lead curses were the realm of the poorer, indigenous population. The nature of the curses themselves relate mostly to thefts, the victim asking the goddess to reek vengeance upon the guilty, with the stolen property or stolen persons to be either returned or promised as an offering to the temple. Cursing wells are rarely encountered but the fear they inspired was quite remarkable. Francis Jones, writing of the holy well of Ffynnon Elian in North Wales notes how people would pay to 'put someone's name in the well' if they had caused the individual offence. The fear of being 'put in the well' was acute, and some individuals who had suffered this treatment could in turn pay a large sum to have their name 'taken out of the well' and the curse upon them lifted. Although this account seems to represent a starkly ancient and pagan tradition Jones notes that there is no record of the well's cursing reputation prior to the later 18th century, indeed before this date it is noted as a benign healing well. The Ffynnon Elian story suggests that a tradition of sacred wells having the power of cursing was alive at that time, but that a well could independently adopt this tradition.

The belief in cursing wells could thus have been alive from at least Roman times to the early 19th century and, although there are hints of this practice continuing at a well in Anglesey in the 1940s, it does not generally appear to have been a common attribute of the holy well nor a practice which has survived as strongly as others have done.

Offerings. The curses thrown into Bath's Sacred Spring were accompanied by ritual metalwork, carvings and a great number of coins, and a visit to the Roman Baths Museum will offer conclusive proof that the sacred waters still have a power over visitors to shower the water deity with precious offerings. In excavated pools throughout the Baths complex vast quantities of coin (as well as bank notes!) are thrown into the waters by tourists, few of whom would probably be aware of the origin or the antiquity of the tradition they are following. So ubiquitous is the notion of throwing coins into a 'wishing well' that sham wells, with story book well housing and windlasses, are still constructed by charities or fundraising ventures to encourage people to donate money, appealing to a light-hearted and innocent superstition that it is 'lucky' to throw coins into a well and make a wish. Bath's international status may further encourage the leaving of coins, for across the world prominent water features in major tourist centres have taken on the role of wishing well, often with the romantic association that the person offering up the money will one day return to that place.

Coins are the most frequent offering made to holy wells. Small, low value coins seem to be preferred, with one and two pence pieces the most popular amongst modern people. In the past, of course, the bulk of the population were too poor to offer more than small coinage on a regular basis and this may be the origin of the modern preference for low denomination copper coins. The names of some wells actually record the offering of coins, thus the six Pennywells in our region were most probably wishing wells where the appropriate offering would achieve the desired result and a Farthingwell in south Bristol may have got its name too from the use of that particular coin.

Where holy wells were thought to aid fertility, pins were often left as offerings to the spring. Pins appear to have been almost entirely a female form of offering and may once have served as a symbol of womanhood that would be immediately recognised as such by the well spirit. One of the more remarkable finds from the excavation of Bath's Sacred Spring was an ivory-carved female torso of Romano-British date, and probably indicates that in this case it was the breasts which were felt to be in need of healing. In pre-Roman Bath a pair of Celtic spoons was deposited at the side of the Locksbrook at the edge of a field called Haswell. Pairs of spoons are normally associated with votive sites, and the fact that two spoons were found, rather than one or three, suggest that their placing was deliberate. Could the Locksbrook spoons have been offered to the stream whose waters were believed to be medicinal even into the 19th century, or were they offered to the now-lost 'Haswell'?

Deposits of coins and precious objects during the Roman period have often been interpreted as the actions of a populace panicked into hiding wealth during times of instability. However, a number of Roman coin hoards have been discovered in similar situations to the Locksbrook spoons. In the latter 19th century coin hoards were found at Filton (north Bristol) and Filwood (south Bristol) along the banks of streams near ancient trackways. Roman coin hoards have also been found at a spring in Hanham (east Bristol) and at the site of a now lost dolmen in Wraxall parish. Perhaps these sites were simply convenient and memorable markers for those fearing robbery or persecution. However, it may be equally true that these sites were considered sacred and the coins not a cache but a votive offering.

It may have been memories of valuable offerings that led to the belief that some wells conceal treasure and in the Bristol region there are four sites where treasure is said to lie hidden. The Abbots Fishpond at Abbots Leigh, is said to be the site where the last abbot of Bristol's St Augustine's Abbey threw his most treasured and most valuable possessions into its depths to prevent agents of the Crown seizing them. The origins of the treasure motif are less obvious at two of Bristol's holy wells: the Bucklewell at Shirehampton, and St Anne's Well at Brislington, but at Culverhay Castle in the parish of Englishcombe a large stone-lined well within the ruined motte would suggest that the lost fortune of the de Gourney family was the prize. The belief in these treasure tales was so strong that from both Englishcombe and Abbots Leigh there are stories of treasure seekers attempting to drain and go to considerable lengths to excavate the sites in a bid to win the hidden prize.

Some have seen the traditions of holy well treasure as the last vestige of the water hoards of prehistory—the pools, springs and rivers into which precious objects were thrown during times of need. If so, this is a tradition with roots stretching back to at least the Bronze Age when there was a great flowering of ritual involving bodies of water, not just in Britain but throughout Europe.

Well dressing. For many people the famed Derbyshire well dressing pageants where great floral displays are placed over village holy wells are the limit of their holy well knowledge. Derbyshire well dressing occurs throughout the spring and summer and is the focus of good natured rivalry between neighbouring villages, each trying to outdo the other in the beauty and complexity of their designs. Without exception the displays are strongly Christian in their subject matter, a feature which comes as a surprise to many who expect strong pagan undertones. Throughout the world wells are dressed with flowers or other colourful items such as religious prints, beads or cloth and it can be safely said that the need to decorate a well is a universal and very ancient aspect of human spirituality. Thus, although the Derbyshire wells are firmly Christianised by their dressing, they are the descendent of a tradition which is decidedly pagan in origin.

In this region traditional well dressing was practised until the 1920s. On May Day morning in the parish of Wrington, young women would climb the hill to the Waterstone—the great capstone of a collapsed Neolithic dolmen that sits in a field just south of Lulsgate Airport. Here they would pour offerings of milk into a depression on the surface of the stone which was said to always hold water no matter what the vagaries of climate. Once this action was complete they would then dress the stone with garlands of Primroses. Folklorist Ruth Tongue noted how primroses were flowers with strong fairy associations in Somerset, and as there is evidence that the area around the Waterstone had other fairy associations, it is tempting to speculate that the garlands were originally intended for the fairies or another resident spirit. Primroses were also the favoured flowers used to decorate Tortworth's Virgin's Well, also on May Day morning, when young women of the parish would visit the well as part of an annual ritual to ensure fine complexions and good husbands.

Bristol's conduits were decorated during the medieval period: F.C. Jones records a ceremonial dressing on New Year's Day and Ascension Day when 'greening boughs and woodland flowers' were used, a practice which continued into the 18th century, though shorn of its pre-Reformation context, when the conduits were adorned with 'flowers and gilded branches' to celebrate the ascension of Queen Anne in 1701. Similar festivity is recorded from Bath when St Mary's Conduit was part of the festivities marking the ascension of Charles II in 1661, here 400 young women walked from a church service to the conduit bearing 'crowns and garlands, bedecked with all manner of rare and choicest flowers.'

The last of the traditional well dressings in this region took place in 1919, with the final May Day visit to the Virgin's Well at Tortworth. However, well dressing has continued, as a revival, in Gloucestershire at the Seven Wells at Bisley and there was a short-lived attempt to create a tradition at the Paulto' Spring in Paulton following restoration of a series of spring-fed troughs along the roadside in the 1980s.

Festivity. Visitors to the holy well would often be lone individuals visiting the site for personal and specific reasons, but once or twice a year large numbers of people would converge on the holy well in an act of communal intent. Merry-making would often ensue and the event become a public holiday. 18th and 19th century Irish commentators frequently write of the bawdiness and heavy drinking associated with these days, known as 'paton days' or just simply as 'patons', a name deriving form the 'patron' saint to whom the well was dedicated and upon whose feast day the crowds would gather. In England these days were often know as 'wakes'. Contemporary accounts of patons exist for much of the British Isles but tend to be fewer in number and less colourful in their description than the Irish, but it seems that they were once widespread and well-supported especially before the Reformation.

The dressing of wells were communal celebrations, and indeed those in Bristol and Bath which were held to mark royal celebrations were preserving both the spirit and the tradition of pre-Reformation saints' days, but in a new and secularised context. Furthermore, there are hints that boisterous holy well wakes took place in the countryside around Bristol for the Thrubwell at Nempnett Thrubwell was described in the early 19th century as 'formerly of some notoriety' and there are also records of 'May Day festivities' taking place at Olveston's Dropping Well, whilst another of Olveston's holy wells—Miles Well—once rose at the foot of Eastcombe Hill which was renowned as the site of yet more village festivities. Another debased vestige of the old wakes was the drinking of sugared water or the eating of special cakes; the former is recorded at St Winefred's Well, Bath.

The Rag Wells. One final and archetypal holy well tradition remains to be explored: the tying of rags to trees and bushes around certain curative wells. As with many holy well traditions, the use of rags is a universal phenomenon and is therefore of ancient, and pagan, vintage. However British rag wells are not common. Francis Jones' study of Welsh holy wells could supply only ten instances out of 1,179 wells covered by his work, and in this region only two authentic examples are known: the Rag Well at Compton Martin and the Shingle Bell Well at Limpley Stoke, just over the border into Wiltshire. A third, possible, rag well was St Mary's Well, just over the Gloucestershire border in the parish of Boxwell with Leighterton.

Rag wells may always have been rare and even within the select band of known rag wells each had its own idiosyncrasies—in Ireland Patrick Logan noted wells where the rags had to be of a certain colour. Nevertheless, the general procedure with all rag wells appears to have been as follows: the supplicant went to the

51

well and bathed the afflicted part of their body with a piece of cloth, frequently representative of the part of the body in need of healing, such as part of a shirt or blouse for a chest complaint. The rag would then be tied to a nearby tree or bush, or whatever was available. Once tied the rag would be left to gradually decompose, in the belief that as the rag decayed so the illness would abate.

Modern ritual

Celtic holy wells appear more interesting and colourful than their English counterparts largely because the Celtic lands retained a more traditional social structure for a longer period of time. In the Bristol region, the forces of cultural modernisation started long before they did in Ireland or the uplands of Wales and Scotland. Nevertheless there are still people in this region who practice some of the old customs, visit wells for curative purposes, or resurrect holy well pilgrimages.

The Well Pilgrimage. The local resurrection of well pilgrimage can be traced back to the 1880s with the revival of the tradition at St Anne's Well, Brislington. Bristol's growing Catholic population, mainly emigrant Irish, found the well to be of similar virtue to many they had known in Ireland, and consequently they treated it as an Irish well would then have been treated. From this period to the present day, albeit with a number of interruptions, the tradition has continued although with an increasingly Anglican face. The worshippers at Brislington's parish church, St Luke's, hold an annual service on St Anne's day and then form a procession to the well where a short service is held involving the blessing of those assembled with water from the well.

A similar, though smaller and more private, pilgrimage is held at St Arild's Well, Thornbury on the saint's feast day. A procession leaves St Arild's Church in Oldbury-on-Severn and walks along the lanes and footpaths to the well where prayers and hymns are offered, and a communal meal partaken followed by drinking of the well water.

A slight variation on this theme is the annual Pipe Walk from the city church of St Mary Redcliffe to the Huge Well at Knowle, south Bristol. This follows the route of the medieval Redcliffe Pipe—the conduit takes water into the city and terminates in a fountain at the side of the churchyard. Although essentially a secular act, preserving a tradition of routine maintenance, the Pipe Walk has many of the trappings of a holy well pilgrimage, especially at the Huge Well itself where participants are invited to inspect the sparkling water at the springhead.

Another striking practice was until recently followed by the parishioners of the Catholic church of St Alphage in Oldfield Park, Bath, who would make an annual visit to St Alphage's Well at Charlcombe to take a gallon of water for their baptismal font, whilst in the parish of Backwell the eponymous grotto-like spring was recently used in an Easter celebration as the cave in which Christ's body lay after his crucifixion and from which he rose from the dead. New religious uses are thus being found for holy wells which might otherwise sink further into obscurity.

Modern healing. The desire to not appear old-fashioned and superstitious prevents many people from talking openly about topics, such as visiting a holy well, which might appear ridiculous to others. As a result it is very difficult to find modern first-hand accounts of people visiting wells for curative purposes. The great exception to this rule is found where the waters have been transformed into spas where either science or reputable history provides an excuse to allow people to bathe and drink the waters to their heart's content, safe in the knowledge that they will not be ridiculed. Indeed, so popular is the belief in the therapeutic value of spas that at least one of Bath's hot springs will shortly reopen as a functioning sanatorium.

However, away from prestigious sites there are only fleeting glimpses of local belief, such as the farmworker who requested water from the Abbot's Well near Hawkesbury, not less than four years ago, believing it would help fight a serious heart condition. To find such an acknowledgement of belief from within modern rural populations is rare; it is within the educated, largely urban, population that there is most evidence of modern holy well devotion. Here, a search for meaningful ways with which to express personal spirituality, a fascination with ancestral themes and what has been called 'the aching alienation of the modern mind' have given holy wells a new reality to a population many generations removed from ancestors who visited the ancient wells as part of a continuum of genuine folk tradition. A new generation of holy well devotees tie rags to trees around wells, leave offerings of food, or light candles and sticks of incense, or just simply make silent prayers to the deities or spirits they feel are resident at the site. Within this modern tradition there is frequently a fusion of ideas and practices from a number of cultures and religious beliefs, although the tradition often sees itself as carrying on from Celtic, and especially pagan Celtic, antecedents.

Whatever the nature and historical authenticity of the new generation of holy well enthusiasts their actions, along with those who throw coins into wishing wells, help maintain the notion of the 'otherness' of our holy wells, as special places of singular power within a landscape that is frequently perceived as demystified and mundane.

CHAPTER IV
The Spirit at the Well

A further strand to the rich tapestry woven around the sacred well lies in the realms of the supernatural. In this region alone there are 32 haunted wells and pools, half of which can claim exclusive association with their ghost, the other half sharing their spectre with other features in the landscape.

Well ghosts have received relatively scant attention from historians and mythographers. A number of authors have acknowledged the classical heritage of water nymphs, minor elemental spirits who were believed to live at, and guard, sacred springs and pools. The nymphs were to be treated with respect and their favours sought by offerings freely given to the waters which they guarded. Honouring the nymphs was believed to ensure the constant flow of pure waters, avoiding extremes of flood or drought, a vital insurance when human endeavour was so tied to the vagaries of nature.

This association of nymph/spirit and water sources may be an ancient and universal archetype, for the motif is found across the world and in many cultures. There are a number of ways of exploring the realm of the well spirit but two of the most illuminating are via the folklore of fairies and goblins, and then the belief in ghosts.

Puck and pals
The most primitive and elemental well spirit was Puck. Those familiar with the works of Shakespeare will be aware of the mischievous reputation which this nature spirit has acquired. Throughout the centuries Puck, also known as 'Hobb' and 'Robin Goodfellow', has become an archetypal trickster. One of its

commonest tricks was leading weary travellers astray and into danger, as he often appeared as a bright and welcoming light to those lost in a night time wilderness.

The name of this spirit is ancient and appears in slightly variable forms in many Indo-European languages, with the universal meaning of a goblin, demon, woodland spirit or minor devil. With so many cultures sharing a recognition of Puck the ancestry of this uncanny and otherworldly creature can be placed at least as far back as the time of a common Indo-European language, over 5,000 years ago.

Throughout Europe Puck is frequently associated with water, his favourite haunts being springs, bogs and waterfalls. But it is the association with springs that is particularly of relevance to the Bristol region, where the relationship is attested by such names as *Pucanwylle*, or Puck's spring or stream, a placename recorded in the Anglo-Saxon estate charter for Weston near Bath, and probably referring to the spring and stream near Dean House, Kelston. Part of the Bath suburb of Fairfield Park is built on a field which, in 1742, was called Poke Piece. It lay adjacent to a series of fields called Well Acre and was just to the south of the Whitewell, a noted spring that lay on the boundary between the parishes of Walcot and Charlecombe. The Pucklewell at Dyrham and Hinton may also originally have been named after the elemental creature, for the first part of this name 'pucela', meaning 'little Puck', has been recorded elsewhere in Britain in direct association with the sprite. Puckwell on the borders of Rockhampton and Ham with Stone parishes is also of note, especially given the haunted reputation of the lane running past it. Of similar vein is the field name Puxpitt in Flax Bourton parish where the suffix 'pitt' may stem from the Norman French *puit,* meaning a shaft well, a term which holy well historian James Rattue has noted being used during the Middle Ages in association with a number of proven holy wells, and which may be the origin of Bristol's 'Pithay'. Puxpitt's credentials are further enhanced by the arrival at each Halloween of a female ghost which would appear by an ancient oak tree that once stood by the side of the field. It is of note that three of these Puckwells are found on parish or estate boundaries.

Puck's alternative name of 'Hobb' cannot be used with such confidence because the name may simply be that of a landowner or farmer. However, with this caution in mind, there are still two possibilities: Hobwell in Long Ashton, and Hobb's Well (alias Hobb's Wall) at Farmborough. The former is the name of a field through which the Failand to Long Ashton corpse path ran, and adjacent to it is a field called Spirts, a name believed to derive from the local dialect term for 'Spirits'. The Farmborough site is more commonly called Hobb's *Wall*, but its alternative spelling of Hobb's *Well* suggests the commoner name may be a rare Somerset instance of a linguistic pattern more frequently encountered in the Midlands where *Wall* is often used instead of *Well*. As if in support of the holy well argument a curative Cold Bath was once recorded here, Roman burials have been excavated and the site was believed to be haunted.

Puck and Hobb are frequently equated with the fairies, although the two orders of supernatural being are quite distinct in folklore where Puck is usually a lone spirit and the fairies are usually encountered *en masse*. However, what was seen at Barrow Gurney's 'Fairy Well' remains a mystery for not even the oldest parishioners can remember how the fairies came to be associated with it. Equally puzzling is the derivation of Fairy Pit at North Stoke—is the second half of this name one of Rattue's *puit*-derived holy wells, or is it simply just a reference to a quarry where fairies were once seen?

The modern perception of fairies is one of delicate, lacy creatures flitting about like butterflies, but our ancestors frequently described them as brightly coloured creatures, often about 18 inches high and usually seen in groups. Frequently they were said to be just tiny flickers of light—red and green being favourite fairy colours. As such these descriptions have many similarities with the natural phenomenon of Earth Lights—just as fairies 'dance' around, appear to display an interaction with observers, move at impossible speeds, suddenly appearing and just as suddenly disappearing, so some forms of Earth Light behave in a similar manner. It is only recently that Earth Lights have come under the scientific spotlight and tentative theories have been put forward to explain them. Their origin is believed to be as forms of energy released through the earth's crust at times of geological stress such as when the crustal plates move, when earthquakes and tremors are felt and volcanoes become active. The effects of these violent geological events can be felt many hundreds of miles away and it is believed that Earth Lights are particularly frequent just before these events happen. Geological fault lines are believed to be where Earth Lights first appear, and certainly when reports of sightings are plotted on a geological map there is an undisputed correlation with faulting. So it is possible that where a well issued forth on or near a fault line Earth lights would be seen, and to our ancestors they could only be spirits, supernatural beings who lived in the well.

Occasionally there are reports of 'lights' being seen at wells without any connection with Puck or the fairies. At Englishcombe, for example, the appearance of 'Lights in the Night Time' recorded in 1765 as hovering over the well within the mound of Culverhay Castle, were described as simply something uncanny as was the incident involving Queen Anne, wife of James 1. Whilst the Queen was bathing at the King's Bath, the most important of Bath's hot springs, 'there arose from the bottom of the cistern, by her Majesty's side a flame like a candle, which had no sooner ascended to the top of the water, than it spread itself upon the surface into a large circle of light, and then became extinct.' The Queen was so alarmed by this incident that she immediately decamped to the adjacent bath' which thenceforth became known as the 'Queen's Bath' and refused to enter the King's Bath ever again!

Ghosts

Dramatic and amusing as the antics of Earth Lights, Puck and the fairies are, they pale into insignificance compared to the number of ghosts associated with wells, pools and other bodies of water.

Well ghosts are recorded throughout the British Isles, their presence frequently related to a legend of murder, suicide or despair at the well. Death by throwing oneself down a wellshaft or into a deep pool was a common form of suicide in rural areas well into the era of living memory, and there are still strong feelings of distaste and trepidation towards wellshafts for this reason, especially amongst the older members of the farming community.

This concentration on the darker side of the human experience is frequent throughout all aspects of ghost lore, but holy wells have a number of distinguishing characteristics not shared by ghosts in general. In their book *Sacred Waters* Janet and Colin Bord devote a chapter to 'Ghosts at Wells, Lakes and Rivers', running through a catalogue of predominantly female apparitions and elemental spirits. This gender bias is supported by evidence from the Bristol region where, excluding the 'Puck' wells, 16 of the haunted waters have female ghosts, 3 have both female and male, 5 are of no specified gender, 2 are elementals and only 6 are solely male.

Almost without exception our female ghosts are young. 'Long Anne', the ghost of a young woman who drowned herself in a field well at Farmborough, also has some of the characters of a mermaid, for like the siren she sits above the waters tempting passers-by to come and join her in her watery grave. Long Anne's direct communication with the mortal world is exceptional, for more often the ghost at the well is oblivious to our presence. Thus at Long Ashton village the spirit of a young maidservant appears at noon during midsummer, at one time startling a gang of builders who were renovating the house where she had once worked. The ghost came up the driveway to the house, walking by the men, and proceeded to a spot on the lawn where a shaft well had once existed; here she folded her hands as if in prayer and disappeared into the ground, much to the concern of her audience. The men later learnt that her appearance was annual and that the well was where she had committed suicide a century before, after she had been jilted in love.

A spirit with a more modern ancestry is the 'white lady' that appears by the fountain which is Barrow Gurney's war memorial on the A37, Bristol to Bridgwater road. It is said that during the 1960s a young woman was killed here as she ran for help following an accident. Her ghost is frequently seen standing by the fountain or crossing the road, an action that is believed to have caused a number of accidents here within the past 30 years! Sometimes, however, the ghost is reported as that of an old man in flat cap and raincoat. One motorist who had driven through the 'old man' rang the local police station to inform them that he thought he had just killed someone, but that there was no body to be seen. The policeman who dealt with this enquiry had dealt with many similar incidents at this spot and informed the driver that he was but one of a long and continually updated list of alarmed motorists. Although this female ghost is said to date from the 1960s the area has had a haunted reputation for at least a hundred years: old accounts describe a phantom horse and cart being driven off the road at the site of a former crossroads less than 50m from the fountain.

It is not just those using the roads who experience alarm at the site of a holy well ghost, for a forester, driving through Friary Wood, Hinton Charterhouse late one winter's afternoon, was terrified by a brilliant white female apparition that stood above the medieval stonework of Ela's Well. 'The hairs on the back of my neck stood on end,' he claimed, 'and I pulled the throttle back and drove out of the wood as fast as I could.' It is tempting to speculate that this ghost is that Ela herself, Countess of Salisbury, who stopped to drink at the well on her way to found the nearby Carthusian Priory in 1232. As at Barrow Gurney, male ghosts have also been seen here—phantom monks standing around the well.

In the neighbouring parish of Wellow a species of phantom unique in the Bristol region was the white lady associated with St Julian's Well, for she was a harbinger of doom for the Hungerford family, Lords of the manor of Wellow until the mid-18th century. Like the banshee of Irish folklore whose frightful wail warned of the imminent death of a member of the family to which she 'belonged', the white lady of Wellow forecast the death of a Hungerford whenever she appeared by the edge of the well on St Julian's Day. 'Mourning by the crystal stream', she was believed to have been a Hungerford who had suffered a gruesome murder centuries before. However, despite her intimate association with the family, the white lady was not restricted to St Julian's Well for, although the holy spring was her base, she would also be seen 'walking' the district. It is of note that Combe Hay, the parish to the north of Wellow, has a White Lady's Well—was this another haunt of the Hungerford ghost?

The Wellow ghost, although resembling an Irish banshee in her gruesome task, is a rather tame version of the supernatural death messenger. Banshees had many forms, often showing distinct regional variations; a form found in parts of Scotland was 'the washer at the ford'; a creature which would be seen washing the bloody clothes of warriors about to die in battle. Banshees could also be associated with burial mounds, and in the light of both these qualities it is interesting to speculate on the nature of the female ghost which was seen at the Barrow Well, Compton Martin, somewhat incongruously washing cabbages!

Although the description of the Barrow Well ghost does not specify colour, the appearance of most female well ghosts is white. Two of these 'white ladies' have already been described, and there are at least six more recorded for this region. These are of mostly tragic, and sometimes headless, aristocrats haunting pools and wells throughout the region and whose legends are all somewhat poignantly Romantic. However, one rare instance of a non-aristocratic white lady comes from the parish of Churchill, where a brilliantly white female apparition appears beside the Bridewell. This ghost is said to be a 'bride' who left St John's Church on her wedding day and walked the short distance to the small spring-fed pool at the northern foot of Windmill Hill. Finding matrimony a daunting prospect she threw herself into the pool to drown, and to this day her ghost is still said to appear beside the silted-up pool, dressed in her radiant white gown.

What is one to make of this 'white lady' phenomenon? The only study of any significance on the association of white ladies with holy wells is that of Coleman O. Parsons, who wrote a monograph on the subject which appeared in the journal *Folk-lore* in 1933. Pursuing a number of themes, Parsons noted that although white ladies had always been part of Britain's supernatural landscape, in the popular mind they became particularly associated with wells following the publication of Sir Walter Scott's *The Monastery* in 1820, where a white lady well ghost is described in a rather Romantic fashion. Parsons claimed that once published *The Monastery* helped create a culture whereby white ladies became increasingly associated with holy wells—a fulfilment of a pure fiction becoming fact. Furthermore Parsons suggested that the 'Lady Wells' of post-Reformation times, which were derivatives of 'St Mary's Wells', 'Our Lady's Wells' etc, were equally responsible for the development of the 'white lady' tradition, as the religious spirituality of the Catholic church was mutated through time into a vague female supernatural presence.

Whilst acknowledging the undeniable power of popular fiction and its role as a primer in creating a perception within the public mind, there remains a fundamental problem in Parsons' theory, and that is that there are so few accounts of holy well ghosts of any description prior to the publication of *The Monastery* that it is impossible to judge just how influential Scott's work was in this field. Indeed if *The Monastery*'s white lady had an influence, it may perhaps have been more in the romantic and tragic life stories which attach to the white ladies. The phenomenon of a ghost perceived as a white lady may well be thus a genuine tradition to which fiction has become attached to make the tales more acceptable for later generations.

Although white ladies dominate the role call of holy well ghosts there remain a fascinating variety of other phantoms which haunt the local wells. To accompany the legion of distressed ladies, a pool at Northwick in the parish of Pilning & Severn Beach is the haunt of a man hanged nearby. There is a male suicide ghost at Paddy's Well in Stoke Bishop, north Bristol. A monk is seen by Hanham Court's medieval fishpond in east Bristol hurrying away with the ghost of a young woman, whilst other monks have been noted at Ela's Well, Hinton Charterhouse. A cursed member of the medieval de Gourney family occasionally haunts East Harptree's Kings Castle Well. Most male ghosts, however, appear in a more heroic guise—as mounted knights or gentlemen of distinction such as the 18th century figure seen to ride over the surface of Tortworth Court's lake, whilst Dick Whittington rides past Cold Ashton's Hameswelle on foggy November nights *en route* from Hamswell House to Toghill Barn. Perhaps the most dramatic of our male equestrians however is the knight who sallies forth from King John's Hunting Lodge in Kingswood, east Bristol and gallops across country to the lost Forest Pool where he and his mount suddenly vanish.

Yet more phantoms fit within no particular mould, like the 'evil spirit' said to haunt Cox's Well at Winscombe, or the 'ghosts' at Cold Bath, Farmborough, and Stancombe Spring, Flax Bourton. The phantom funeral procession seen at East Harptree's 'Spring Ground' is in a league of its own, as are the black demonic beasts which vanish at Stonystyle Pool, West Harptree, creatures which depart from this earth after haunting the lanes of Fair Ash crossroads, a site where suicides were once buried.

Other Legends

Ghosts, strange lights and nature spirits are the most commonly encountered legendary holy well motifs, but they are not the total picture. A belief in hidden treasure, lying at the bottom of pools and wells has already been mentioned. Some legendary associations are perhaps unique to holy wells. Some wells were believed to be prophetic, the vagaries of their flow read as indicators of future events. Thus when Brockley's Pots Hole, a shallow limestone depression normally dry from one year to the next, would suddenly erupt as a seething pool of pure water forming a powerful and fast-flowing stream, local people would be dismayed for this was a sure sign of war. When the Bristol Hotwell suddenly turned blood red and a field well at Plummer's Hill in east Bristol turned black in 1755, it was seen by many as an omen of the Apocalypse. At the Hotwell 'All flew to the churches, where incessant prayers were offered to avert the apparent approach of their destruction, and to appease the anger of heaven.' It was not until several days later that the cause of the well's disturbance was made clear when it became known that the event happened at the exact moment of the great Lisbon earthquake. That which was seen as an act of God's vengeance was but a symptom of enormous geological power.

In some parts of the country, most famously Northamptonshire, there are 'drumming' wells where a distinct drumming sound can be heard from time to time coming from within the well. These wells were believed to prophecy great events—wars, invasions, royal vicissitudes, crop shortages etc, and their activity would be closely monitored to give the population advance warning of things to come. No prophetic 'drumming wells' as such are known from the Bristol region, but there are a couple of interesting sites where drumming can be heard at certain times of the year. The intriguingly named Drumhill Spring in the parish of Stowey-Sutton is a powerful spring where, at a distance of about 20m, a distinct tattoo can be heard. Upon approaching the well closer the sound can be very impressive and somewhat disconcerting! Also in North Somerset, at St Alphage's Well, Charlcombe, putting one's ear against the well chamber can produce a similar, if slightly subdued, result. The drumming is caused by pockets of air being trapped inside the rock as the spring water forces its way to the surface, and cavities within the rock amplify the sound. The power of the emerging water can be quite spectacular, and the noise emitted by a spring in the parish of Hutton could be heard up to half a mile away, leading to it being called Ludwell, 'the loud well'.

Both the noisy wells and those that suddenly erupt after years of dormancy are dependent upon heavy rainfall to supply the water necessary for their spectacular displays. In some parts of the world the weather itself is said to come from a well. In Mexico's Oaxaca State the wind is said to live in a well, sallying forth to blow round the world before returning to the well to lie quiet for a while. The nomadic San people of southern Africa have a similar belief in the rain living in a sacred spring. With these instances in mind what can be made of the belief once prevalent in the southern Cotswolds that the source of a continuous rain brought on by an easterly wind was a pond in the parish of Tormarton? Is this just rural humour or is it part of a wider and particularly ancient archetype?

Luck is another attribute possessed by several holy wells. St Julian's Well at Wellow was thought to be so beneficial that drinking from it would guarantee luck to any that went there, and over time it developed the alternative title of the 'lucky well'. Popular folklore holds that the Luckwell in Bedminster, south Bristol, got its name from a troop of Cromwellian soldiers stumbling upon the spring after a long and dusty march. Overjoyed, the men exclaimed 'What a lucky well.' This derivation is imaginative if somewhat trite and an alternative origin is simply 'St Luke's Well'. A Luckwell in east Bristol and 'Hopewells' in both the north and east of the city may have once been associated with good fortune, or alternatively may have had their names mutated from words which have not been recorded in earlier placename material. The granting of wishes, and good fortune in general, is part of the wider theme of interaction between people and the wells, frequently involving offerings, and as such is explored in greater depth alongside wishing wells on page 47.

Belief in witchcraft was once a powerful aspect in many people's lives. The fear of being cursed by a black witch was very real and the means by which people would protect themselves from spells or the evil eye were myriad. Where possible, those who felt themselves to have been cursed would visit a white witch who, usually for a fee, would identify the black witch and either lift the curse or offer advice on how the victim could lift it themselves. In this region particularly powerful white witches were recorded up to the late 19th century in both Bristol and Wells. One method of lifting a curse, recorded in the Mendip parish of Winscombe, was a particularly hazardous manoeuvre known as 'Crossing the Waters of the Gulf'. The Gulf was a natural formation within the limestone of Sandford Hill, described by the topographer Rutter in 1829 as a 'prodigious cavern'. The cursed person would enter the chamber through a fissure on the western side of the hill and the manoeuvre which followed was to be accomplished alone and at midnight when the moon was full. Once inside the cavern the person would find their way to a narrow rock bridge which spanned a pool of water. Once across the bridge the curse would be lifted. Although not strictly speaking a holy well, The Gulf is a body of water used to counter witchcraft and thus can be classed with the small number of wells and pools across Britain where witchcraft was either enacted or countered. Elsewhere in this region our only other witch-craft-well connection was in the parish of Congresbury where Ruth Tongue noted the tradition followed by women of the parish who would gather by the Southwell on May Eve, the Beltaine of Celtic lands and also the feast of the parish's titular saint—Congar—and once at the well the women would proceed to dance around it barking like dogs! Tongue connects this activity with a record of witchcraft being conducted in the mid-19th century, on the same day, at the nearby Cadbury Hill.

Witchcraft certainly exercised the 19th century mind but the fear it inspired was a degree below that engendered by the presence of Satan who is recorded at two watery sites in north Somerset. At Farmborough a pool near Crossways was believed to be the site where a man named Bridges was repeatedly dragged through the water by the Devil. Similar tales may once have hung around the Devil's Hole at Tickenham, a small scrubby pool that once stood in the north-west angle of a minor crossroads. Were these Satanic presences evolved forms of water spirit, such as the 'nicor' of Anglo-Saxon times, a water monster believed to reside in pools and keen on dragging victims into its watery lair to be devoured at its leisure? Supernatural water creatures are rare in this region, but from the Somerset parish of Timsbury comes a belief that in a certain well near the northern boundary of the parish there once dwelt a mermaid. Little is known of this creature except the advice given to children to keep away from the well for fear of being enticed into it by the winsome creature. Landlocked mermaids are not unknown but are more frequently encountered in the north of England and Celtic lands, indeed in Wales one of the few unequivocal pagan well deities—Gwenhudw—is sometimes described as a mermaid. The Timsbury creature is thus a rare and possibly unique feature in this part of the west of England.

Wells and Heads

Human heads are frequently linked to holy wells. In Irish and Scottish folklore the association of certain holy wells with severed heads is not uncommon; the association is less common in Wales than one might at first expect, but is widespread in England with at least two instances in the Bristol region.

Over the past forty years work by Celtic scholars such as Drs Anne Ross and Miranda Green have attempted to show the importance of a 'head cult' among the pagan Celts, using ancient Irish and contemporary classical accounts of the pagan Celts' enthusiasm for collecting the heads of enemies as trophies. The occasional discovery of human skulls from sacred well sites has been used as corroborative evidence, especially in the implication that human heads were used as votive offerings to the presiding deity of the well. When the beheading traditions of British holy wells are taken into consideration as well, with the suggestion that such a 'primitive' motif could only be pre-Christian, the evidence appears conclusive. The idea of our ancestors engaging in such dramatic and savage activity has had a particular resonance for recent generations who no longer feel the embarrassment that such notions caused for their elders. Indeed, the search for pagan, earthy and 'ethnic' roots among the indigenous British population has encouraged such ideas of raw, primal paganism to become almost mainstream and allowed the Celtic head cult to become fact for many people with an interest in prehistory and native spiritual traditions.

However, over the past decade or so there has been an increasingly critical analysis of this cult with a number of scholars questioning the very evidence for such a tradition. In his seminal work *The Pagan Religions of the Ancient British Isles*, Professor Ronald Hutton assesses the available data and concludes that there is 'no firm evidence of a "cult of the human head" in the Iron Age British Isles,' calling into question the emphasis placed on the poor archaeological record for such a practice. Hutton does note, however, that during the Roman period specially constructed shaft wells, some of which appear to have strong ritual associations, did have human heads deposited in them, usually during their excavation, or infilling when rendered redundant. But there is no evidence that this was a pagan Celtic trait adopted by a Romanised population, instead it appears to be a novel Roman tradition. The *cause célèbre* of the head cult hypothesis was the fragment of human skull found in Coventina's Well, a ritual site along Hadrian's Wall in Northumberland. The bone was believed to be proof positive for a head cult continuing from the Iron Age into the Roman period, as it accompanied a rich array of ritual objects and a considerable number of coins. However, a recent analysis of the finds, the most thorough to date, casts considerable doubt upon the idea of a head cult at the well and there is also the suggestion that the votive deity, Coventina—far from being part of the native pantheon—may just as probably have been imported by German legionaries stationed on the wall. Thus the best that can be said for the head cult hypothesis is that it remains 'not proven'.

In the Bristol region the heads and wells connection, whatever its true origin, is attested by two sites: the Cross Bath in Bath, and St Arild's Well at Thornbury. At the Cross Bath there is a record of a human skull being found during clearance work in the 1730s. The skull apparently came from deposits beneath the medieval floor of the Bath from whence later excavations found Roman altars, a possible ritual cup and other objects indicative of the spring's sacred status during Roman times. It is not known to what period the skull belonged, but its existence certainly implies some form of ritual activity involving the human head. At St Arild's Well there is a rare local instance of a classic holy well motif—the beheading of a pious virgin and the subsequent emergence of a spring of pure and holy water. The beheading of devout Christians is the most common manifestation of this motif, frequently the victim is a pious young women, usually beautiful and the object of devotion of some hot-blooded pagan sex-pest. A standard account is usually given of the virgin resisting her suitor's advances, fleeing him, being caught and beheaded in a fit of frustrated rage, whereupon a spring of water emerged from the spot where the head fell or came to rest. The most famous of these martyrs is St Winefred who suffered this chain of events, but whose uncle, St Beuno, managed to re-attach her head and thereby give her several more years of virtuous living. The place in north-east Wales where her severed head fell, and where a spring had bubbled up, became a great medieval shrine and site of pilgrimage, ultimately giving rise to the town of Holywell.

With St Arild, or Arilda as she is also known, we are told that 'a cruel pagan tyrant' called Muncius came to woo her, but was rebuffed. In a rage he cut off her head and was immediately carried away to hell, the saint's head falling to the ground where virtuous and healing water welled up to produce the copious spring of today. Stones which lie in the shallow pool at the foot of the well are covered in a red substance, locally called 'St Arild's Blood' but known to naturalists as the alga *Hildebrandia rivularis* which is also found at other holy wells with beheading traditions and notions of 'Saint X's blood'. By a further twist to the tale the water from St Arild's Well leaves a stickiness on the palate when drunk, much as blood would do. Thus by two natural coincidences the legend of St Arild has been much enhanced in local minds over the years. However, it is hard to say whether the alga and sticky water helped generate the legend or merely offered irrefutable proof of the truth of the legend to the uneducated mind.

Wells and Trees
The worship of trees is a universal phenomenon in pagan cultures, but it is, to say the least, unexpected within a Christian context. In this region alone there are many accounts of individual trees that were believed to possess special powers and were treated with veneration. Moreover, a number of these trees were associated with holy wells.

Just why sacred trees could exist alongside Christianised sacred springs is a question posed by many who have studied holy wells.

The most frequent answer given is that they are either physical survivors from the pagan era or that they are part of a tradition of sacred trees which transferred from paganism to the wilder edges of Christianity. In the Bristol region, with the possible exception of some churchyard yews, there are no known trees which pre-date Christianity, though there are three explicit references to holy well trees and as many as eleven other possible contenders. Perhaps the most famous of the region's holy well trees was St Aldam's Ash which stood by St Aldam's Well in the parish of Pucklechurch and was said to have begun life as the saint's staff, planted in the ground by the holy man when a crowd gathered to hear him preach, but were suffering from the lack of shade. The tree is long gone but its name is preserved in St Aldam's Ash Farm. The Ash was again the favoured tree at a site on the Wiltshire border near Bathford at a place John Wood described in 1746 as Mars Well, a site where he claimed the pagan god was worshiped; it must be said, however, that Wood's reference is somewhat bizarre and it is not clear whether he was interpreting the site or reporting a genuine phenomenon. Another interesting site is in the parish of Norton-Radstock where the place name 'Holywater Elm' was recorded in a 17th century property deed, but the precise location of the tree is unknown. John Wood supplies another interesting account in his *Essays Towards a Description of Bath*, when he writes of the Bel-tree which stood just south of the hot springs and which he unconvincingly associates with Belinus, a solar divinity.

Many people assume that certain species of tree were held to be sacred by our pagan ancestors, and through a selective reading of popular books on the Celts it has become accepted wisdom that ash, hazel, oak and hawthorn were sacred across the Celtic world. However, an examination of original texts and surviving folklore suggests that different species attracted devotion in different areas and only ash and possibly hawthorn can claim anything like a widespread sacredness in the British Isles. Many species of tree had their ritual or superstitious uses but only these two possess something more which elevates them above the rest. It is therefore of note when 'Ashwells' are mentioned or found as these may, perhaps, have some connection with the tradition of holy well ashes. There are four 'Ashwells' recorded in this region, two of which have survived only as entries on Anglo-Saxon estate boundary charters. Few other trees are associated by name with wells: a Rowan tree (N. Somerset dialect—'wriggle') is recorded at Chew Magna's 'Wriggleswell' and Hazel is recorded in the Anglo-Saxon estate charter of Westbury-on-Trym as *haeslwellan*. No 'Thornwells' are recorded in the region, which perhaps suggests that there was not a strong local association between hawthorns and holy wells.

Great and once-venerated trees may also be recorded in the name 'Stockwell' which appears four times in south Gloucestershire and north Bristol. The 'Stock-' part of the name refers to a tree stump, perhaps that of an ancient specimen felled by age or disease, but we will probably never know whether this is just idle speculation or a step closer to identifying our local holy well trees.

Secret Tunnels

Legends of 'secret tunnels' are rarely studied by either folklorists or historians. Such a lack of interest has been to the great detriment of folklore for there are many strands to their existence, all of which should be considered. Essentially, secret tunnels, or 'secret / hidden passageways' are believed to link sites of some importance, usually one site is given as the start point and another as the destination. Distances covered by these 'tunnels' can be a matter of metres or many kilometres through topography that would defy even modern engineers with advanced technology. It is the physical impossibility of their routes which prevents most people from believing in them.

A small number of 'secret tunnels' have been proved to be genuine, these are usually of short length and frequently associated with moneyed estates where the tunnels provided shelter and privacy, often leading from one building to another. However, the bulk of secret tunnels have never been proven. Some have been found to be the remnants of elaborate drainage systems, especially if there are or were large buildings close by; worked-out mine shafts or an *aide memoire* reminding later generations of ownership links, for example between a former monastic site and its granges. Failing these explanations there are more esoteric possibilities such as the idea that the tunnels may be connected with routes which ghosts were believed to follow on a traditional basis. The latter idea is not as bizarre as it may at first sound, for in the Mayan regions of Central America there are traditions of spirits being seen following the routes of underground 'roads' — indeed, in the Bristol region there are several such examples. One involves the Forest Pool, a large pond which once existed in east Bristol. The pond lay on the course of a 'secret tunnel' running between the medieval foundation of King John's Hunting Lodge and Staple Hill House. Along this route and at the stroke of midnight a mounted warrior would gallop from the Lodge until he reached the Pool where he would disappear into its depths.

The other 'secret tunnels' in this region that have connections with wells or pools, link up with prosaic sites such as a pub in Banwell, a 19th century house at Clevedon, and occasionally a site of some greater historic or folkloric importance such as Weston-super-Mare's Iron Age hillfort on Worlebury Hill; a former monastic building at Abbots Leigh; Saltford Manor House; and the gallows site of Brockley Elm. In one isolated instance, at Nempnett Thrubwell, the 'secret tunnel' goes beneath the pool in question and then carries on for a further half a mile.

Bath

The hot springs of Bath are probably the most famous holy wells in the country. They attract over a million visitors every year and are at the heart of the modern city which has grown up around them. Pilgrims, invalids and pleasure seekers have flocked to them since Celtic times and each of the springs has its own history and character. There are also cold water holy wells and smaller, more obscure spas which once enjoyed their own fame in the hills around the city; indeed it was once said that Bath had seven healing wells, to match its 'seven hills', and that the old parish of Weston—now a suburb of Bath—was known as 'the city of seven springs', truly an area of sacred waters![1]

The Hot Springs

> For feeble folke, and crazie good they are.
> For bruis'd, consum'd, farre spent, and very old,
> For those likewise whose sicknesse comes of cold.
>   'Dr Hackwell', quoted by Dr Edward Jorden in *A discourse of naturall bathes and mineral waters*, published in 1631

Throughout the centuries many have wondered at the origin of the jets of hot water that rise at Bath. Modern hydrologists explain that through a complex underground drainage system, water which fell as rain thousands of years ago and seeped into the earth was heated, and then thrust upwards again when the water met the fractured rocks of the Carboniferous limestone deep beneath Bath. It is thought that the waters have been getting gradually cooler over time as the ancient stored hot water is pushed out by cooler, younger waters, although it will be thousands of years before any significant drop in temperature is noted.[2]

The hot water rises as three springs: the **King's Bath** or **Sacred Spring**, the **Cross Bath** and the **Hot Bath**, all now enclosed within Georgian spa buildings. Human activity around them goes back to at least 5,000 BC with the remains of a Mesolithic encampment by the Sacred Spring. Until the Roman period the springs were probably left in their natural swampy condition, although a number of silver coins of the local Celtic tribe, the Dobunni, found in the Sacred Spring, show that offerings were being made to the waters and that the site was undoubtedly seen in a supernatural light.[3]

The Celts are believed to have worshiped a goddess called Sulis at the springs, whose name is thought to mean 'gap' or 'eye', probably in reference to the site as an interface with the Otherworld. When the Romans arrived they identified Sulis with their own goddess Minerva, it being their commendable practice to tolerate and assimilate the religions of conquered peoples and find parallels between 'new' deities and their own pantheon. Of Celtic Sulis we know little, so to understand her the qualities of Minerva must be sought, a virgin goddess from whom came wisdom and good health, the invention of numbers and wind instruments. Sulis may also have been associated with the Celtic belief that all life was formed within a boiling cauldron, a very apt metaphor for the sacred hot spring.[4]

The Romans drained the marsh around the springs and built stone walls around them. A temple and bathing complex was then built around the Sacred Springs: a healing centre dedicated to Sulis-Minerva. The 3rd century Roman writer Solinus described a sacred eternal flame which burned in the temple of Minerva at Bath, fed by local coal the flame symbolised the undying sun which defeats the darkness of winter and death. The famous Gorgon's head from the temple pediment may be a representation of the sun in triumph; alternatively it could be the young solar deity known as Prince Bladud.[5]

Bladud appears in the fictitious genealogy of the British kings as son of Lud Hudibras and father of King Lear. Much of his story comes from the historically unreliable 12th century cleric Geoffrey of Monmouth, although the chronicler Bale is another significant source, telling us how Bladud went to Athens to learn the 'Art of Magick', the first Briton to do so. Legend then tells that on his return he contracted leprosy and was banished from court, becoming a swineherd in the lower Avon valley; his pigs caught the disease from him, but they cured themselves by wallowing in the steaming mud of the hot springs. He too bathed and was also cured, returning to court to claim his title and then dedicate a temple over the springs that had saved him.[6] This legend is somewhat variable and one version has Bladud encouraging his son to bathe in the mud rather than taking the plunge himself.

Bladud (from a print after W. Howe)

In *The Waters of the Gap*, R.J. Stewart places this myth, of the maimed or blemished king cast into the wilderness, in the light of the solar myth of the sun (Bladud) waning and close to death after his long journey, acquiring vigour and vitality from 'the magical cauldron of the Otherworld.' Death and winter are conquered and the sun can return in splendour (to the Court). Moreover Bladud is guided to his destiny, well being and fame, by the pig—totemic animal of the Celtic Otherworld.[7]

Geoffrey of Monmouth tells us that Bladud was also an alchemist, by his own magic creating the springs by burying deep in the earth two tons of burning brass, two tons of glass, 'along with pieces of salt, brimstone and wildfire, the fermentation of which emits a heat that shall last for ever.'[8] This could only be done with the help of Minerva to whom Bladud agreed to build a temple. However, another old Bath legend tells us that the springs derived their healing powers from the tears of the young prince.[9]

Another of Geoffrey's works, the *Life of Merlin*, contains a description of the structure of the universe, at the centre of which were Bladud's hot springs, and, as befits a centre of the universe, the layout of *Aquae Sulis*—as Roman Bath was called—replicated cosmic detail. The ground plan had the city gates facing the cardinal points, two great streets quartering the city as they ran to these gates, and at their intersection were the springs.[10]

On a more mundane level there is another constant thread running through the post-Roman history of Bath—the charity offered to poor travellers who had journeyed from throughout Britain to seek their cure. The Norman bishops built baths and lodgings for those too poor to afford accommodation at the main baths, whilst Bath Abbey oversaw the general care of the poor who had journeyed to the town. Following the Dissolution of the Monasteries however, there was some concern that the poor were being denied access, and an Act of Parliament was passed in 1593 guaranteeing their rights to seek treatment and requiring parishes through which they journeyed to offer them financial support.

Private acts of charity augmented the basic guarantees of the state. Thus, in 1609 Thomas Bellott, who had been steward to the household of Queen Elizabeth, bought land on the southern side of the King's Bath which had once belonged to the abbey, and built a hospital for 'the reception of twelve of the poorest strangers who should come to Bath for the benefit of the waters.' A private bathing cistern was built within the hospital taking overflow water from the King's Bath.[11]

Throughout the 17th and early 18th centuries there was a huge demand placed upon the baths from such 'strangers'. This was exacerbated in 1714 by the extinction of the Elizabethan Act of Parliament. The city worthies realised that the existing facilities were inadequate and in 1742 opened the Bath Infirmary to accommodate the poor during their stay. This building was close to the baths but it was only in 1830 that the healing waters were piped into the building to allow the poor to receive both treatment and shelter under the same roof. The introduction of the water proved a great success and it was claimed shortly afterwards that 'the proportions of cures have greatly increased, while deaths are of such rare occurrence that a whole year has passed without one.'[12] The infirmary later became the Royal Mineral Water Hospital, an internationally renowned centre for the treatment of rheumatic diseases, although it later dispensed with the use of the waters and relied instead on more 'scientific' medicine.

The history and nature of the hot springs are best examined individually. None of them are currently available for public bathing due to fears of infection. Bath was the last of Britain's spas to cease functioning and the lack of native interest in our spa waters is a regrettable, but not necessarily 20th century phenomenon. Lack of investment and initiative was being castigated even in 1631 by Dr Edward Jorden who claimed that 'it hath beene the ill hap of our Country Bathes to lye more obscure then any other throughout Christendome', a situation that was somewhat improved within the following century.[13]

At the time of writing work is underway to create a modern spa facility at the Hot Bath. A public-private partnership, with the aid of lottery money, is creating a spa fit for the 21st century with dramatic new architecture in the heart of the city, a rival to the flourishing spas of continental Europe and a long-awaited revival of Bath's healing waters.

The Sacred Spring
This, the largest spring, rises in the **King's Bath** (ST750647)*: the Georgian superstructure built upon Roman and medieval walling. Its rate of flow is 250,000 gallons per day and its temperature a constant 46°c. Forty-three minerals have been identified in the water and a high iron content causes a characteristic orange staining on the stonework.[14]

It is this spring which has drawn most attention and devotion. The Romans enclosed the site and constructed a temple and bathing complex around it. Their impressive remains are displayed in the

The King's Bath with the Pump Room on the left

Roman Baths Museum; the steps to the temple are *in situ*, visible beneath modern Stall Street, the bronze head of the cult statue of Minerva is here too, along with the sacrificial altar which stood in the Temple precinct. More fascinating sculpture from the Temple buildings displays the facade of the Four Seasons and the Luna Pediment depicting the moon goddess. Facing the Temple, and on a site currently occupied by the west front of the abbey, was an open circular temple: the Tholos, a structure very rarely encountered in western Europe, and the exact function of which remains a mystery.[15]

The centrepiece of the Temple complex remained the spring, enclosed within a vaulted chamber with openings for devotees to offer votive gifts. The offerings to Sulis-Minerva which have been excavated from the spring provide a fascinating insight into both the spiritual and social nature of Roman Bath. Thousands of coins were thrown in as were a large number of curses—sheets of lead on which aggrieved parties would seek revenge or restitution to wrongs they had suffered. A typical example reads: 'Basilia gives to the temple of Mars her silver ring, so long as anybody, slave or free, who knows where it is and says nothing, may be cursed in blood and eyes and have their guts eaten away.'[16] Other treasures were deposited: pewter cups which may have been used for ritual purposes, jewellery, silver dishes and objects such as a pair of ivory breasts which may have represented a diseased part of the supplicant's body which the goddess was asked to restore. The personal relationship between the goddess and the believer can be glimpsed in another of the lead curses: 'Whether pagan or Christian, whosoever ... has stolen from me Anniancis ... six silver coins from my purse, you, lady goddess, are to exact them from him.'[17]

The Sacred Spring is indeed fascinating, but it is for the Roman baths themselves that the temple complex is best known. Due to the large numbers using the facility for curative purposes the baths were of a much greater size than most others in northern Europe. There was a large rectangular bath, (the Great Bath), with smaller baths, sauna and exercise facilities. All these are visible today having been excavated and partly reconstructed; the Great Bath itself, lined with sheets of Mendip lead, still fills with the hot waters of the Sacred Spring, wisps of steam drifting over the surface, through the columns and over the city rooftops providing a suitably mysterious veil with which to cloak the ruins of a past age.[18]

The small city of *Aquae Sulis* grew around the Temple complex, craftsmen and traders supplying the needs of pilgrims and the

The entrance to the King's and Queen's Baths

Temple itself. However, with the departure of Roman rule the town and Temple quickly crumbled and there is little evidence of occupation in the immediate aftermath of the Roman retreat. Swamp reclaimed the springs and Victorian excavators found a wildfowl nest amongst the temple ruins. The curative powers of the water however remained undimmed, the town acquiring two Saxon names: the self-explanatory *Bathanceaster*, and also *Akemanceaster* or 'Roman town of the sick men'.[19]

The religious nature of the site was re-established in 675 when Osric, King of the Hwicce, granted land for a nunnery adjacent to the Sacred Spring. A Benedictine monastic settlement was established soon after by King Edgar and when the monks built their infirmary they chose a site by the spring, reusing much of the Roman walling of the old spring enclosure. Their healing complex, centred on the spring, was known as the Abbot's Bath, later to be renamed the King's Bath.[20]

Following the Norman Conquest the new Bishop of Bath, John of Tours, built a bath for the visiting poor adjacent to that used by monks and townsfolk alike. This was just one instance in a continuum of charity afforded the sick and poor by the institutions of Bath, ensuring that there was always some form of access to the healing waters no matter what one's social status.

During the early Christian period the waters had become newly sanctified to make their use legitimate in the eyes of the new faith — a legend arising that it was from their being blessed by St David that they owed their virtues. Even by early medieval times the King's Bath was offering the cure of a wide range of ills from infertility to broken bones. Like many rural holy wells the Bath also offered cures for eye problems and lameness, but a great number of other ailments were believed especially curable including anaemia, gout, respiratory diseases, jaundice, lumbago, metallic poisoning, neuralgia, palsy, scurvy, sciatica, 'diseases of the head', surgical afflictions and wounds in general. With the development of medicine and pathology, new conditions were constantly being diagnosed and presented as curable.[21] It was even claimed that the age-old human complaint of 'stupiditie' was curable with use of Bath waters![22]

Bath Abbey in 1784, spiritual and temporal successor to the Roman temple. Half-hidden in shadow on the left an invalid is carried by sedan chair into the King's Bath (Bath City Library)

From the Middle Ages onwards physicians had attempted to prove that there was a rational, and later a scientific, basis behind the Sacred Spring's miraculous waters. Early writers contented themselves with explanations like, 'They supply a Want of Spirits' and that they simply warmed up cold, phlegmatic constitutions thereby restoring balance to the body. A compulsion was briefly in vogue for weighing the minute amounts of mineral left when a quantity of water was evaporated, attempting to prove the presence of a unique salutary compound. In the late 19th century the discovery of Radon gas being emitted from the spring led to the belief that Radium was the answer. If this seems like a desperate scramble to prove the unprovable, modern investigation has shown that there is a scientific basis to some of the miraculous claims.[23] The level of Radium, for example, present in the water and air of the King's Bath is such that in some instances it could prove beneficial to the immune system. Audrey Heywood notes that several of the diseases cured at Bath were related to lead poisoning, with lead

81

entering the body by domestic pollution and exacerbating minor conditions, and it has been proven that immersion in water over 35°c encourages the urinary excretion of lead. Further investigation has shown that cutaneous and syphilitic conditions can also be genuinely ameliorated by immersion in a hot bath.[24]

One of the King's Bath's best reputations was in the cure of digestive problems: a visit would alleviate 'The vayn appetite of going to stoole, when a man can do nothing when he cummeth there.'[25] Another speciality was the curing of lameness, described by the historian Coxe who wrote of the King's Bath in 1727: 'In the Middle of it are Crutches as Memorials of the Cures of such as came with them, but joyfully returned without them';[26] one visitor even described this collection of crutches as a veritable 'forest'. Children's diseases were also a speciality of the King's Bath; Dr. William Oliver (1707), listing 'Crookedness, Rickets, Weakness in their Limbs, Big Bellies and Contractions'[27] as conditions being easily cured. Severe dandruff and other flaking skin on the head, along with certain joint conditions, were treated with a poultice of herbs mixed with mud from the bottom of the spring.[28]

However, the most popular cause for coming to the bath was the cure of infertility, so much so that it was known as 'The Common Cause'. In 1562 Dr William Turner listed 'Barunnes of man or woman' amongst ailments alleviated here, but later texts emphasise the female side, women coming to Bath were almost invariably there to 'become fruitful'. Coxe noted that the waters 'are very good for Women that are apt to miscarry, if used moderately, and facilitate Delivery. The Women of the Town ... use them ordinarily all the While they go with Child, and they are observed never to miscarry.'[29] The Stuart queens were noted visitors to the Bath for this purpose. The first to come was Queen Anne, wife of James I, in 1615. In 1644 Queen Henrietta, wife of Charles I came 'for the benefit of the waters', as did Queen Catherine, wife of Charles II, in 1664. In 1686 Mary, wife of James II, came to the King's Bath as part of a tour of fertility wells in the hope of conceiving a son. When the following year she gave birth to Charles James Stewart, the Old Pretender, the King's Bath was one of many that claimed the honours.[30] The Old Pretender's son, Bonnie Prince Charlie, attempted to seize the throne in 1745 but was defeated at Culloden. By a twist of fate he was helped to escape by a man who developed partial paralysis of his limbs through hiding in damp hideaways with his master. All other cures failing him, the man eventually came to Bath to bathe in the waters that sixty years earlier had facilitated the conception of his master's father. However, the blessing bestowed on royalty did not, in this instance, extend to their retainers and the man died uncured.[31]

Royal patronage continued with a visit by Queen Anne, along with her consort Prince George, in 1702, whilst Charlotte, wife of the future William IV 'derived much benefit from her use of the waters' during her stay in 1817.[32]

Treatment at the bath took a variety of forms, and was invariably part of a wider regimen prescribed by one of the many physicians, some genuine others less so, who practised in the town. In the Middle Ages the water was not drunk much but a triangular fountain was later built over the bath's main spring to prevent contamination with bathing water; the fountain then providing a constant supply of drinking water for bathers. Drinking the water was subsequently claimed to 'sweeten the Blood and Nervous Juice'[33], though could take the unawares by surprise: 'They affect some with Sleepiness or Giddiness, almost as if they were drunk.'[34] The amount drunk each day was limited and bathing remained paramount. While under treatment a bath was recommended every second day, usually early in the morning; staying in the water no more than 20 minutes the patients were advised to keep moving about and not let their heads get wet. Over the years a number of ingenious devices were developed to augment normal bathing, most being primitive variations on the shower, although by Edwardian times an arsenal of intimidating steam chests and electric shock baths were on offer to those brave, or desperate, enough to want them.[35]

The social history of the King's Bath is also of great interest. Until the Dissolution, the bath was the property of the abbey and access was ostensibly free to all; an Act of Parliament in 1593 enshrining this right in law. But even by the mid-14th century there was an emergent social division. Mixed nude bathing was the norm, but this was beginning to affect the sensibilities of the more 'civilised' visitors, including Henry VI who found the sight affronted his modesty. Despite the issuing of church decrees little changed until the late 16th century, when decorum started to be observed. However, the suspension of normal social values continued apace and the scorn of respectable society was only gradually brought to bear. In 1631, for example, Dr Jorden painted a less than glamorous picture of England's premier health resort: 'The baths are bear-gardens, where both sexes bath promiscuously; while the passers-by pelt them with dead dogs, cats and pigs.'[36] 'Persons of Quality' removed themselves to the Cross Bath to avoid 'the meaner sort of people.'[37]

The sheer weight of numbers wanting to use the bath posed particular problems of their own and by 1576 it was necessary to build a second bath which was fed by an overflow from the King's Bath. Originally called the New Bath this pool was designed for those who preferred a less intense heat than that experienced next door—the overflow water had cooled sufficiently by the time it reached the New Bath to allow for temperate bathing. It acquired a new name—the Queen's Bath—when Queen Anne of Denmark, wife of James I, who came to bathe at the King's Bath in 1615. Whilst bathing 'there arose from the bottom of the cistern, by her Majesty's side, a flame like a candle, which had no sooner ascended to the top of the water, than it spread itself upon the surface into a large circle of light and then became extinct.'[38] Anne was so alarmed at this that she refused to go in the King's Bath again and decamped to the adjacent bath which henceforth bore her name. The mysterious light may, or may not, be connected with the appearance of a Roman ghost in the adjacent Pump Room—an apparition which is said to appear 'every few years' on a specified day.[39]

The healing waters remained central to the town's existence, but by the 17th century there was a demand for more amusement and distraction to while away months of treatment. A Pump Room was built near the King's Bath in 1706 to add lustre to the act of drinking the waters. It soon developed into a great hall where the wealthy and fashionable would gather to be seen and entertained. The mineral waters of the Sacred Spring were developed into a spa complex in line with similar centres in continental Europe. High society soon came to Bath, and with them money and a great property boom which saw thousands of new buildings erected to accommodate visitors. It is no exaggeration to say that this great social centre of 18th century provincial England owed its origin and wealth to the miraculous waters of its ancient holy well.[40]

Bath's star faded during the turmoil of the Napoleonic wars and the inland spas lost their cachet to the new fashion of sea bathing. The King's Bath complex still drew many visitors, including Charles Dickens who, through the pages of *Pickwick Papers*, described Bath water as having 'the taste of warm flat irons'[41], although much of the glamour of taking the waters had gone. A new spa complex was built on the other side of Stall Street in the latter part of the 19th century and wounded troops were brought there during the First World War, but the King's Bath never regained its past glory. Now the Bath and its Sacred Spring are integral parts of the Roman Baths Museum: the heritage industry and that particularly 20th century form of pilgrimage — tourism.[42]

The Cross Bath

Described by one authority as 'a dainty Bath for young, weake, and tender bodies'[43], the Cross Bath (ST749646)* lies at the end of Hot

The Cross Bath from Bath Street (1829)

85

The Cross in the centre of the Cross Bath
as originally erected in 1688

Bath Street, 200m west of the Sacred Spring. The hot spring that rises here is smaller than the Sacred Spring and in Roman times does not appear to have had any major buildings associated with it, although two Roman altars have been discovered at the bottom of the bath. One of the altars depicted scenes associated with Aesculapius, the god of healing; accompanying this altar was a Roman cup which suggests that the spring may have been used for medicinal drinking. The other altar was dedicated to Sulis Minerva which suggests that Sulis may have been the presiding deity over all the hot springs. Excavations in the early 18th century brought to light a human skull from under the contemporary floor of the bath, from a level with much Roman material, which may indicate evidence for some ritual use of the human head.[44]

In common with its larger neighbour the Cross Bath seems to have recovered from the post-Roman trauma by Medieval times when we find it depicted on topographical maps of the period. The bath acquired its name from a large cross which was erected over the springhead in the Middle Ages, which was later replaced by a more ornate cross which commemorated the birth of Charles James Stewart, in 1688, after his mother Mary of Braganza bathed here for some time in the hope of conceiving a son. The present building consists of a Georgian elliptical wall with a small roofed vestibule. The spring itself is roofless and open to the public on certain days.[45]

The waters of the Cross Bath were once in great demand. The Tudor writer John Leland recorded that it was 'much frequented of people diseasid with lepre, pokkes, scabbes, and great aches.' Leland also noted how efforts had been made to protect bathers from the rigours of the English climate for there were '11 or 12 arches of stone for menne to stande under yn tyme of reyne.'[46]

By the 1630s the bath was in use not only for curing cutaneous diseases, but also epilepsy, urine problems, convulsions and cramps. A particular reputation developed in the cure of 'contractions' and 'flying nervous gout' caused by lead poisoning.[47] However, bathers were warned that their 'fingers ends will shrinke and shrivell, as if we had washed in Soape water.'[48]

This seems a small price to pay for the relief of life threatening maladies and is perhaps more indicative of the relative novelty of soap! During the early 18th century, as social stratification was highlighted, the Cross Bath became popular with those whom John Strachey could call 'ye Quality', those who bathed for pleasure and found the cooler waters and greater privacy afforded by the smaller spring superior to the bedlam of boiling waters that was the King's Bath.[49]

Adjacent to the Cross Bath was the Eye Infirmary, an appropriate site given the reputation of holy wells for curing eye problems. The Bath went into decline earlier than the King's Bath complex for its limited facilities could not compete with the latter's growth, but after several years of closure it was reopened in 1991 by the Springs Foundation, a body committed to the protection and promotion of the healing waters.

The Hot Bath

The smallest, hottest and least known of the three healing springs is the **Hot Bath** (ST749646)*, which rises in Beau Street, 20m south of the Cross Bath. Like its neighbour it is enclosed within a Georgian structure built by John Wood the Younger. The old Hot Bath building was some yards forward of the present structure, the hot spring being left outside Wood's building and standing in the middle of Beau Street where it became known as the Hetling Spring. Its waters were piped into the new spa and into a suite of private baths; at the Hetling Spring itself water was available to

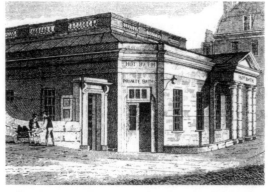

those too poor to afford the facilities of the bath and a small pump room erected alongside an earlier building which had served a similar purpose.[50]

Throughout its history the Hot Bath received much less comment than its neighbours and its

The Hot Bath shortly after its rebuilding in the mid-18th century

virtues are less well documented. It is known that a large bath complex was on the site in Roman times but so far no evidence of a religious association has been found. In the 16th century John Leland wrote that 'at cumming into it, men think that it would scald the flesch at the first, but after that the flesch ys warmid it is more tolerable and pleasant.' In common with the King's Bath it was believed to be a 'strengthening' bath but

Inside the Hot Bath Spa, prior to its current refurbishment

differed in that it 'generally keeps the Body open, while the King's Bath has a Contrary Effect.'[51] The Hot Bath was recomended for those suffering 'rheumes and cold Braines, and in aches of tumors in the feet.'[52] In the early 17th century a 'dry pumpe' was installed whereby a visitor, especially those deemed to have 'hot kidneys' and at risk if fully immersed in the water, could sit fully clothed in a chair and have water pumped onto specific parts of the body. The Hot Bath was renowned for its power to cure digestive problems, a fact recorded by Richard Russell in 1760 when he wrote that regular bathing here 'will commonly give two or three stools extraordinary,' adding that it was the best bath 'for all cold or old Aches' as its temperature caused the patient to sweat profusely. In 18th century medical parlance it was deemed the best for 'cold and moist diseases' such as phlegmatic conditions as well as 'cold and moist bodies.'[53]

The best time to visit the bath was early in the morning in early spring or winter, for summer bathing in the Hot Bath was thought too exhausting. Like its neighbour it too was a refuge for the more sensitive members of society who found the King's Bath too vulgar.[54]

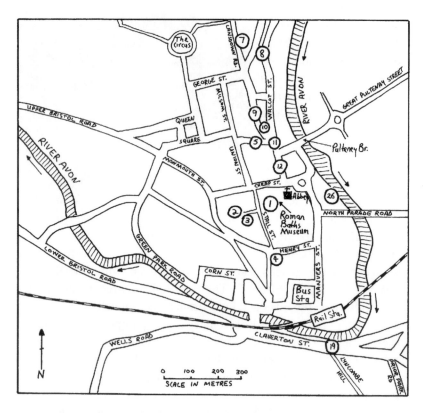

Map of central Bath showing the sites of the following:

1. Sacred Spring / King's Bath
2. Cross Bath
3. Hot Bath
4. Horse Bath
5. Frog Well
7. Fountain Buildings Cistern
8. Carnwell

9. Broad Street Conduit
10. St Michael's Conduit
11. St Mary's Conduit
12. St Peter & St Paul Conduit
19. Claverton Street Cold Bath
26. Cold Bath

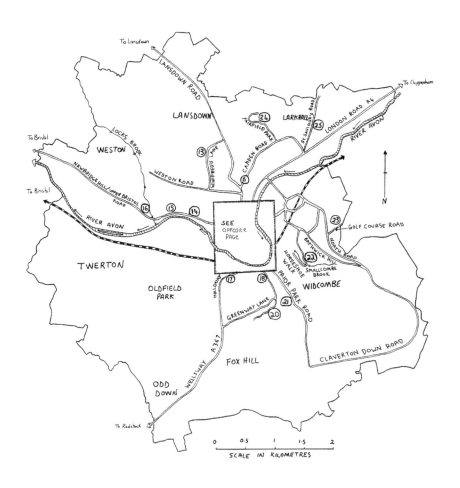

Map of outer Bath showing the sites of the following:

6. St Swithin's Well
13. St Winefred's Well
14. Lower Common Cold Bath
15. Limekiln Spa
16. Haswell
17. Western Beechen Cliff Springs
18. Eastern Beechen Cliff Springs

20. Lyncombe Spa
21. Bagatelle Spa
22. Rosamund's Well
23. Shan Castle Holy Well
24. Poke Piece
25. Larkhall Spa

Lazar's Bath

This bath (ST749646) was fed by the overflow of the Hot Bath and was built by Bishop Robert de Lewes in 1138, as a charitable institution subsidised by the town. Associated with it was Lazar's Hospital, now Abbey Church House, where the poor could find shelter whilst they completed their course of treatment, the two sexes bathing on separate days. Coxe informs us that the bath was one: 'into which none goes but such as the Physicians suppose to have a Leprosy, or something resembling it.'[55]

The Horse Bath

This bath (ST751645) stood in the north-western part of Ham Gardens. It was another overflow-fed pool which took its third-hand waters from the Hot and Lazar's Baths. It was mostly used for the cure of animals but this practice did not find universal acceptance, for in 1730 John Strachey wrote of a magistrate who advised 'not to profane so sacred a Water to ye Use of Beasts.'

Other Wells and Spas within Bath

Cold Bath

In 1704, at the instigation of Bath's most noted physician, Dr Oliver, a Thomas Greenway built a **Cold Bath** on the river bank. The precise site of this bath is not known.[56]

Frog Well

New Bond Street used to be called Frog Lane and in it rose a cold chalybeate spring known as the Frog Well (ST750649), which John Wood informs us acquired its name 'from the great Number of Frogs which used to Harbour' in it.[57] The spring was medicinal and thought useful for inflamed eyes.[58]

St Swithin's Well and the Conduits

Beneath the road in front of the fine architectural sweep of Camden Crescent, just off Lansdown Hill and in the cellar of one of the Georgian houses, there rises **St Swithin's Well** (ST749656). Little

*Camden Crescent. St Swithin's Well rises beneath the road
in the middle foreground*

was written specifically about the well itself, much more attention
being paid to the urban water supply which depended upon it.
Perhaps as far back as Roman times the well had supplied a system
of stone conduits which channelled its waters down into the city
and by the 18th century five conduit heads were recorded, from
which the public could draw water. By the time Camden Crescent
was built in 1788 the conduit system had fallen into disrepair but
the holy well itself was still too important to risk being lost
completely and so it was preserved within the new building.[59]

When the conduit system was operational some water was channelled down into Walcot Street immediately below the well but the
majority was fed down Lansdown Road to a **cistern** (ST749653),
on the site of the present Fountain Buildings, which fed the water
out through the conduit system into the upper part of the old city. In
the Middle Ages an Oratory chapel of St Werburgh stood over the
cistern; the choice of this particular Saxon saint suggests that the
chapel could have been of pre-Conquest date. By the mid-18th
century the chapel had been replaced by an ale house, which in turn
made way for the Fountain Buildings.[60]

Fountain Buildings, built on the site of the ancient conduit cistern and Oratory of St Werburgh

The conduits

Leland notes that 'The city of Bath ... is environed on every side with greate hilles, out of them which cum many springes of pure water that be conveyid by dyverse ways to serve the citie, insomuch that ledde beyng made there at hand many houses yn the toune have pipes of leade to convey water from place to place.'

At the foot of a high stone wall half way up

*The Carnwell in 1876 (above) (Bath City Library),
and recently (opposite below)*

Walcot Street there is a stone trough set in an alcove of polished granite and weatherworn sandstone. This is the **Carnwell** (ST750652)*. The site is at least medieval and has also been variously known as Cairnwell and Cornwell. Much of the character of St Swithin's Well seems to have been transferred to the Carnwell, its particular fame being 'esteemed chiefly for ... efficacy in the cure of Inflammations & Rheums in the Eyes.'[61] The water was thought to be impregnated with some wonderful mineral and people would flock to the fountainhead to take away the healing water. The Carnwell was destroyed in 1740 only to be reconstructed again in the 19th century in the form it exists today. The water however, no longer flows.

Broad Street Conduit (ST750650) fed a stone trough in the middle of Broad Street.

St Michael's Conduit (ST750650) issued at a fountain near the old church of St Michael's outside the North-gate. The fountain was 'A handsome structure, its base a perfect cube ... each front was ornamented with a niche, from which water issued.'[62]

St Mary's Conduit (ST750649) stood inside the Northgate opposite the lost church of the Blessed Virgin. This was perhaps the most impressive of the old city conduits and issued into a fine square reservoir built in the Doric style. St Mary's had a fame and importance which surpassed the other conduits and was dressed until at least the mid-17th century. The Rev. John Collinson wrote in 1791: 'To this conduit the mayor and citizens of Bath, borrowing their practice from days of old when wells and springs had their particular honours, usually made their grand processions, and here they halted.' Collinson then gives an account of one such celebration which marked the Coronation of Charles II on April 23 1661: 'above 400 virgins, most in white waistcoats and green petticoats, going two by two, each bearing aloft in their hands, crowns and garlands, bedecked with all manner of rare and choicest flowers, went to church to the conduit in the market place ... came to the conduit it began to run with claret, where they drank a health to his Majesty.'[63] The time of year, the choice of colours and the use of flower garlands are paralleled in the veneration of many conventional holy wells; may some of the respect once showed to St Swithin's Well have been transferred to the more convenient conduits?

St Michael's Conduit

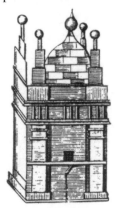

The High Cross Conduit

St Peter and St Paul Conduit (ST751648), alias the High Cross Conduit, stood less than 100 yards south of St Mary's and was built in the form of a cross, commemorating the old High Cross which had once stood at this site.[64]

All the conduits were reputedly useless by 1739 even though St Swithin's Well still flowed strongly. The conduits and their fountains were eventually destroyed in the road improvements and rash of new building which swept through Bath in the second half of the 18th century.[65]

St Winifred's Well

This well (ST742661) lies under the campus of Bath College at Sion Hill. All there is left to remind us of its former presence are the names of the adjacent Winifred's Lane and the old St Winifred's Well Cottage which stands opposite the site. A chapel is believed to have been associated with the well and stood either on Lansdown Road or some yards to the west of the well itself.[66]

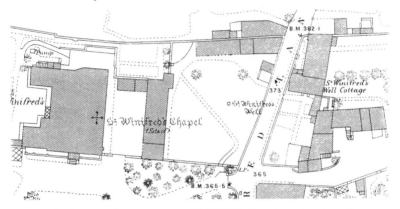

Ordnance Survey map of 1882(?) showing the site of St Winifred's Chapel, well and Well Cottage

The well rose in a field called Great Lydes, but intriguingly less than 10m north of the well was the adjacent field called St John's Piece. Could this field name preserve a previous dedication of the well?[67]

It was often stated that St Winifred's Well was named after the famous spring at Holywell, North Wales, as the particular purity of the water was thought to make the comparison a just one, even though the water here was said to have a hard brackish taste. Spring was the favoured time to visit the well and its waters were often drunk with sugar. The most frequent visitors were women who

St Winifred's Well Cottage

wanted children; those 'with superstitious hopes of maternity' such as Queen Mary, wife of James II, who visited the well in 1686 as part of an itinerary of fertility wells. Mary had grown desperate for a son after 15 years of marriage and a year after her visit she bore Charles James Stewart, the Old Pretender.[68]

The well enjoyed great fame in the second half of the 18th century, but in 1805 a new owner built a house in the well field and barred public access. The top of the new driveway ran past the well, the overflow of which was piped to a stone tank which stood until the 1930s behind the hedgerow opposite the Well cottage.[69]

Lower Common Cold Bath

The overflow from St Winifred's Well eventually formed a stream which flowed down High and Lower Commons. Near where it joined the Avon at Lower Common a Michael Butler built a cold bath house (ST741652) over a small mineral spring. Butler hoped to take advantage of the local fame of St Winifred's Well and catch some of the passing trade; however his bath had been illegally built on common land and he was forced to take it down in 1805 only months after it had been built.[70]

Limekiln Spa

In the middle of Cork Street, Lower Weston, there once stood the Limekiln Spa (ST736652), a transformation of a medicinal spring that had gone by a variety of names; its latest incarnation deriving from an adjacent limekiln.

In 1729 a James Hellier, suffering from diabetes, was advised to drink this water. Hellier 'no sooner began to drink than he found great Relief in his Disease.' Word of his recovery spread to other diabetics who flocked to the well as did those afflicted with other woes, many claiming considerable improvement in their condition. A basin was erected at the spring and the surroundings made more amenable. However, a neighbouring landowner wanted a share in the well's success and diverted much of the water onto his own land where he built a small spa house. Neither 'upper' nor 'lower' wells now held a viable quantity of water and as a result both enterprises failed.[71]

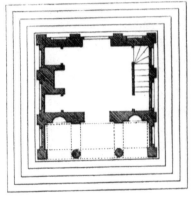

Plan and elevation of the Lime Kiln Spa as first designed

Locksbrook and Haswell

Locksbrook (ST715675 - ST735650) is a small stream which rises on Lansdown above Weston village—'the city of seven springs'. Its source is a petrifying spring and the stream itself was medicinal, for it is said that a man suffering from gout fell into it and never suffered from any ailment again.[72]

Near the brook's conflu-
ence with the Avon is
Locksbrook cemetery which
was created largely from an
old field called Haswell
(ST733640). A few metres to
the north-west was a field
called Nemlett, a name that
might derive from the Celtic
word for 'sacred grove', its
sacred credentials enhanced
by it being the site of a
Roman cemetery. Could
Haswell field be part of this
complex? A 19th century
discovery along the banks of
Locksbrook in the present
cemetery could confirm this,
for a pair of beautifully
crafted Celtic silver spoons
were uncovered here. It
seems possible that they were
a votive offering made either
to the stream or the Haswell
spring itself.[73]

*One of the pair of votive Celtic
spoons found on the banks of
Locksbrook*

Beechen Cliff Springs

The hill of Beechen Cliff, south of the Avon, had a number of interesting springs at both eastern and western ends.

The Western Springs (ST747641)*: Many writers commented
upon the 'faire springs of water' that rose by the part of the Roman
Fosse Way called Holloway. These springs were channelled to the
south of the old city in stone conduits such as that of St James'
conduit which issued by the Southgate, and the conduit which
supplied the monastic community around the abbey. Half way up
Holloway is the chapel of St Mary Magdalene, which was founded
in the 10th century as part of a hospice for pilgrims on their way to

The Chapel of St Mary Magdalene built opposite one of the copious springs of Beechen Cliff

Glastonbury. Almost opposite the chapel there once rose a fine spring, the site of which, now marked by a horse trough within a large alcove, is acknowledged as being the incentive for building the chapel.[74]

The Eastern Springs: There were at least two wells which rose at the eastern end of the hill, one of which was 'much used for

Spring opposite the Magdalene chapel

Disorders in the eyes'[75] and drew large numbers to take its water. In many ways the waters of this spring were believed to be very similar to the Carnwell in Walcot. The other spring was piped into Widcombe to supply a Cold Bath that was built into 26 Claverton Street (demolished in the 1960s). John Wood wrote that the springhead could be found 'at a place where the rays of the sun could never reach till after surmounting the Equinox.'[76] The Cold Bath was once a private institution, but the reputation of its excellent water soon drew the public. However, its fame had waned by the 19th century and its water was then used solely for domestic purposes (ST753640).[77]

Lyncombe Spa

In Lyncombe Vale there was once an ancient chapel, now lost, which may have been associated with a mineral spring which became famous in the mid-18th century as **Lyncombe Spa** (ST753634)*; the private school called Lyncombe House now occupies the site. In 1737 Charles Milsom found some small mineral springs on the land which he rented. The springs soon attracted attention as people came to drink the water and 'found great benefit by it' —encouraging Milsom to build a spa house. Those afflicted with kidney problems were particularly keen on the water, but it was reckoned that 'all victims of pain and sickness' would find relief, despite the water making people giddy! The spa's success was short-lived as the foundations of the spa house caused the springs to dry up and by the 1790s it was described as 'long since disused.'[78]

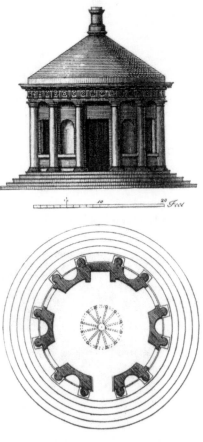

Plan and elevation of Lyncombe Spa as designed in 1737

Bagatelle Spa

To the north of Lyncombe Spa, in the mid-18th century, there was another **mineral spring** (ST756637) which rose in the garden of a Mr Wickstead who realised that it was chalybeate and thus beneficial to health. Wickstead sought to draw the public's attention to the spring, and to supply sufficient water a pump was installed — Wickstead's Machine — which soon rivalled the mineral waters as the chief feature of interest. Sadly Wickstead's venture did not live up to expectations and he converted the site into a pleasure garden. The spa acquired its name from the shape of

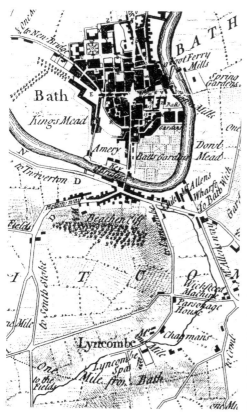

Map of 1742 showing both Lyncombe Spa and Wickstead's Machine south of Bath

Wickstead's house which, in plan, resembled a bagatelle table.[79]

Rosamund's Well

The water of **Smallcombe Brook**, which flows into the Avon north of Widcombe, was once thought medicinal and local people would swear to its power of improving eyesight. Similar powers were held in one of the brook's tributary springs — **Rosamund's Well** (ST759643)*. This hedgebank spring pours out in a never-varying flow into a stone basin at the south-eastern side of Sydney Buildings. Its constant gush of beautifully clear cold water has

Rosamund's Well

never been known to fail and was believed to be good for the eyes—dogs were particularly receptive to its powers of sight-restoration! Until very recently elderly people would visit the spring to drink, bathe their eyes and take bottles of water away to drink with Sunday dinner. The name is thought to be a corruption of St Osmund's Well, the saint being the founder of Salisbury Cathedral, where his shrine can be seen.[80]

Bathwick Conduit

The old village of Bathwick, centred on the ruined parish church near Cleveland Bridge, was supplied with fresh water from a spring on Claverton Down (ST7664), channelled down to the village in an open stone conduit.[81]

Sham Castle Holy Well

Old people in the Widcombe and Bathwick area still speak of the **Holy Well** (ST765650)* to be found on National Trust land north-west of Golf Course Lane and just below the brow of Bathampton Down. The well is marked on the Ordnance Survey 1:25000 map as 'Spring', but it is very difficult to find amidst the fallen trees and dense scrub which almost

Sham Castle Holy Well

envelope it. The structure of the well consists of a stone basin beneath a large stone lintel which is tied into the hillside by iron struts; the stone walls between the lintel and the basin are in an advanced state of decay. The flow of water is slow but constant and the well itself is undoubtedly ancient, sitting as it does beneath an 18th century boundary stone of the Bathwick Estate, a holding which probably maintained its integrity—and its boundaries—from the 9th century when the great monastic estate of Bath Abbey was subdivided.

A haunted well?
The northern suburb of Fairfield Park is partly built on a series of fields called **Well Acre**. Immediately to the north of these fields was another field called Poke Piece (ST754666). This name is almost certainly derived from Puck, the elemental spirit thought to haunt springs, woods and other liminal places. The area would be now roughly between Raglan Lane and Charlcombe View Road.[82]

Larkhall Spa
On the eastern side of St Saviour's Road at Larkhall (ST761669)*, **mineral water** was discovered in 1832 when a man called Blackwin sank a well for his brewery. When he used the water his beer was undrinkable and he sent it away for analysis. The results

Bladud's Spa, Larkhall, at the height of its fame

informed him that he had a strong mineral well, indeed one of the most powerful chalybeate waters known in the west of England. The water was distributed amongst poor people suffering from skin diseases and leg wounds which recovered so well that there was great excitement in the area and large numbers of people came to take the water. Some even declared its virtues as 'not to be surpassed by any others in the kingdom.'[83] A spa house was built around the well in a classical style and continued to cater for visitors until 1930 when the well dried up. An alternative name of Bladud Spa arose in acknowledgement of the old Bath legend.[84]

Bristol

Bristol is one of the largest cities in the United Kingdom and has been so since the Middle Ages, Edward III granting it county status in 1373. Since 1996 the city has been a unitary authority. Modern Bristol comprises the historic core of the old port, 18th & 19th century suburban development around this core, and many small villages and hamlets which have been engulfed by the suburban spread. Beyond the administrative boundaries of Bristol City the urban area continues in the ever-expanding northern and eastern areas of 19th and 20th century suburban development, now technically part of the unitary authority of South Gloucestershire, but in terms of bricks and mortar, very much part of Bristol itself.

The origins of the city lie in the Anglo-Saxon period when a bridging point of the River Avon at its confluence with the River Frome encouraged the development of a small port. There is a considerable amount of evidence to suggest that the area was being exploited by settled communities at least as early as the Bronze Age; there used to be a significant number of round barrows in north-west Bristol. The Romans established a port, *Abonae* at Sea Mills, 6.5 kilometres downstream of the present city centre which, in Anglo-Saxon times, was eclipsed in importance by the Benedictine monastic site at Westbury-on-Trym founded in 720 or 803, and now part of Bristol's northern suburbs.

Many of the holy wells which now lie within the bounds of Bristol were once rural wells, performing the same roles as rural wells have done throughout history. As the urban area spread so the nature and the use of these wells changed; a number were tapped as urban water supplies, their waters carried to the city centre by a complex system of pipes. Other wells remained in use serving local

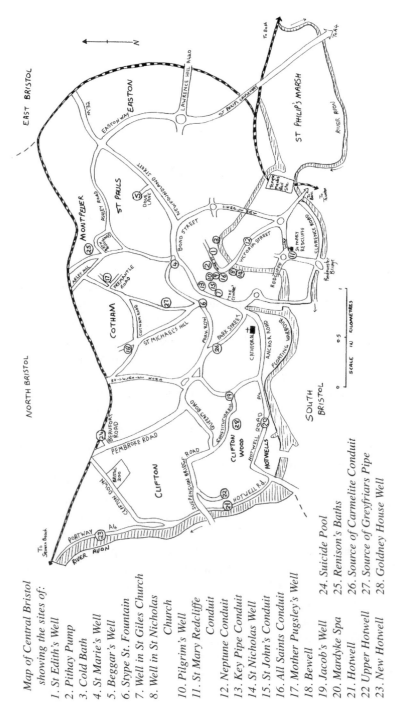

Map of Central Bristol
showing the sites of:
1. St Edith's Well
2. Pithay Pump
3. Cold Bath
4. St Marie's Well
5. Beggar's Well
6. Stype St. Fountain
7. Well in St Giles Church
8. Well in St Nicholas
   Church
10. Pilgrim's Well
11. St Mary Redcliffe
    Conduit
12. Neptune Conduit
13. Key Pipe Conduit
14. St Nicholas Well
15. St John's Conduit
16. All Saints Conduit
17. Mother Pugsley's Well
18. Bewell
19. Jacob's Well
20. Mardyke Spa
21. Hotwell
22 Upper Hotwell
23. New Hotwell
24. Suicide Pool
25. Renison's Baths
26. Source of Carmelite Conduit
27. Source of Greyfriars Pipe
28. Goldney House Well

communities, whilst yet others drew pilgrims from far and wide to take their holy and healing waters.

Many traditions and historical accounts of Bristol's holy wells have survived, perhaps proportionately more so than for any other part of the region. This is partly a consequence of the concentration of topographers and historians resident in the city from the late 15th century onwards, and also the concentration of religious foundations and documentary material relating to property and public health.

In the following chapter 'Bristol' comprises the area of the new unitary authority as well as the adjoining urban areas of South Gloucestershire district.

Central Bristol

City Centre

At the heart of the Saxon settlement, and the medieval core of Bristol, was **St Edith's Well** (ST590731) locally known as St Edywell. A few metres to the east of the well is St Peter's Church whilst the church of St Mary le Port was close to the west. The natural spring was eventually enclosed by a fine stone building, roofed to prevent contamination. When it was rebuilt in the mid-15th century a cross was erected over the well and the site took on a new name of St Peter's Cross or St Peter's Pump. The well was a focus for the community, and the raising of a maypole here in 1661 may hint at a wider appreciation of the spirit of the place. However, both well building and cross were removed in 1766 during a spree of urban renewal, and taken to Stourhead in Wiltshire where they can still be seen. A replacement well, sunk close by, kept the name and seems to have tapped the same source as the old spring, for the reputation of its fine water, its constancy and bright sparkling appearance, continued until 1887 when sewage contamination forced the Health Authority to close it. Today both the old and new wells lie under the flagstones of Castle Park, the site of the old St Edith's Well being marked by a slab laid upside down and of a lighter colour than its neighbours.[1]

*St Edith's Well stands to the left of St Peter's Church in this map
of Bristol made by James Millerd in 1673*

Close by St Edith's Well, in Wine Street, there was once an
ancient and popular draw-well known as **The Pithay** (ST589731),
which also went by the confusing name of **Wine Street Conduit**.
One writer called it a 'hollywell' *i.e.* 'holy well', although no justi-
fication for such a title has survived. A pump was fitted to it in 1625
and 'Wine Street Pump' added to its aliases. In 1643 two Royalists
were publicly hanged here. The name of this well, recorded in 1588
as 'Pyttye Pump', adds strength to the supposition that it was a holy
well for the name 'puit' has been identified by James Rattue as indi-
cating probable holy wells.[2]

Again close by St Edith's Well, but this time to the south-east,
in the area called Castle Ditch, there was once a **Cold Bath**
(ST592730) that was believed to cure rheumatism, nervous disorders and paralysis. In 1772 the bath was destroyed by a landslide
along the bank of the Avon.[3]

On the northern edge of the medieval city centre, in the area
known as the Barrs there rose **St Marie's Well** (*c*.ST590735).
This area is now occupied by the St James Barton roundabout and

110

little is known about the well although it was probably associated with the chapel of St Mary that stood in the grounds of St James Priory which dominated this part of the city during the Middle Ages.[4]

On the north-eastern edge of the city centre **Beggar's Well** (ST596738) was one of the boundary markers of the medieval city. The well was first recorded in 1248 as Begereswelle, a self-explanatory name, and in 1480 was described as being enclosed within a square freestone structure three feet high. Today the site would be roughly on the junction of Ervine Terrace and Dove Lane, St Paul's.[5]

A kilometre to the north-east of Beggar's Well, where Lower Park Row meets Colston Street, there was once a crossroads of six lanes with a public covered well, known as the **Stype Street Fountain** (ST587732) which was noted for a fine cross erected on its roof.[6]

Church Wells

Some of Bristol's most ancient churches once had wells beneath their floors, although it is not clear if they were natural springs or excavated shafts. It seems likely that they provided the churches with both baptismal and domestic water, but we know too little to allow an accurate picture of their function. Most intriguing is the case of **St Giles Church** (ST587730), (which stood at the bottom of Small Street), where there was once a well under the chancel. It has been suggested that this could be the 'holy well of St Giles' patron saint of cripples. The church became redundant during the middle ages and its crypt was then used as a synagogue by the city's Jewish population; did they use the water too? The most curious reference however, comes from William Wyrecestre in 1480, when he wrote that the church was 'first built in honour of a certain Goddess of Apollo or some such Title'![7]

A well exists in the church of **St Nicholas**, (ST589729) and there is also one in the crypt of **Christ Church** (ST 589731) which is believed to be a Saxon foundation. Near the latter there was also a **Pilgrim's Well** (ST588730) at the rear of what is now the Grand Hotel.[8]

111

Cotham

One of Bristol's most famous wells is **Mother Pugsley's Well** (ST587741)*, which has had a variety of other names: Pugsley's, Dame Pugsley's and Gammer Pugsley's Well amongst others.

Until 1845 the field in which it stood, on Ninetree Hill, was essentially a public park with people coming to the well, picnicking and playing games. The well was in the middle of the field, sunk below ground level, with a paved forecourt and reached by a flight of stone steps. There was an archway over two basins which were carved from a single block of stone; the basin on the left being smaller than its neighbour. The smaller basin was solely for medicinal water whilst the larger was for general drinking and domestic use. People would travel miles to take the medicinal water, at its most potent early in the morning; they would bathe one eye at a time in the basin, keeping the other eye open. Many claimed great benefit from Mother Pugsley's 'magic eye water'.[9]

Mother Pugsley's Well from a pencil drawing by H. O'Neill, 1823 (Bristol Museum and Art Gallery)

112

In medieval times, and probably under the influence of the monks of St James Priory, who owned the site and tapped the spring for their conduit, the spring was known as Lady Well, St Mary's Well and also the Virgin's Well. How much this last name inspired the legend of Mother Pugsley and how much of the tale was genuine historical fact is arguable, nevertheless her story has a rare mythic quality.[10]

In 1645 a marriage took place between a young Royalist officer called Pugsley and a beautiful young woman. At the time Pugsley was defending Prior's Hill Fort from a Parliamentarian siege. Immediately after the wedding ceremony he returned to his post and was killed by enemy cannon. His grief-stricken widow buried him by the ancient well on land which he owned below the fort, and from that day wore nothing but her mourning clothes, taking up residence beside the well and rejecting all suitors. She developed a reputation as a wise, kindly woman to whom people could go and seek solace and advice. During these visits people would take the waters of the well which was said by some to have received its virtue from 'the maiden widow's tears'. At her death in 1700, aged 80, she left the well and the field to the people of Bristol.[11]

She also left instructions for a remarkable funeral, the nature of which seems more reminiscent of a pagan celebration than the burial of a devout Christian virgin. From the church her coffinless body was carried on an open cart bedecked with flowers with a fiddler playing before the cart as it made its way through the city. As the body passed through St Nicholas Gate the church bells were rung as if for a wedding, and two young girls walked before the cart strewing flowers in the road. Upon reaching the well she was buried in her wedding dress, next to the body of her husband.[12]

However, Mother Pugsley was not left entirely in peace, for some had thought her a witch when she was alive, and they trampled on her grave. Far greater disturbance was caused in 1845 when a builder bought the field, exhumed the bodies and proceeded to erect houses. Bristol Corporation declined to buy the site as they felt it did not justify the cost, a shameful decision which saw the ancient well disappear under the garden wall which now separates 10 Nugent Hill from 2 Clare Road. At Clare Road there was once a

Mother Pugsley's Well, looking towards Somerset Street,
Kingsdown in 1823 (detail) by Samuel Jackson
(Bristol City Museum and Art Gallery)

magnificent pear tree which was said to flourish because its roots
tapped down into the spring. Remains of a replacement structure
can still be seen in the garden of 2 Clare Road.[13]

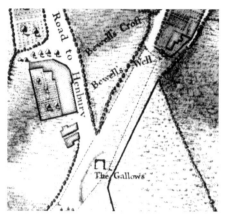

Bewell's Well, a boundary marker of the medieval city as well as a site of execution, as shown on John Rocque's map of 1742

On the other side of Cotham there once rose the **Bewell** (ST580740) which was also known as Bewell's Well and the pump of Cotham. It was the most northerly point on the boundary of the medieval city, at the top of St Michael's Hill, near what is now the junction of Aberdeen Road and Hampton Road. The name means 'well of the bee', an innocent name that was belied by a gallows on which 'Traitors and Thieves' were hanged,[14] and which stood a few metres to the south of the well. By the gallows was a stake at which Protestant martyrs were burned during the reign of Mary; even today some people have an uneasiness at this site. Of greatest antiquity was Bewell's Tump, a large prehistoric mound that crowned the summit of the hill directly above the well, and at the foot of the Tump during the middle ages was a great cross —in all, an important ritual and symbolic site.[15]

Brandon Hill

On the western slopes of Brandon Hill is Jacobs Wells Road, running along the course of the small valley of Sandbrook or Woodwell's Lake which formed the western boundary of the medieval city. At least two springs, one in the grounds of Queen Elizabeth's Hospital and the other at the Old Police Station, rose on the eastern side of the valley. However, **Jacob's Well** (ST580740)*, on the other side of the road, eclipsed its neighbours to become one of Bristol's most important springs.

Jacob's Well is traditionally associated with the Jewish community in Bristol. Before their expulsion by Edward I, Bristol's Jews had to live beyond the city walls. They had a syna-

Jacob's Well, Brandon Hill

gogue in the crypt of the redundant St Giles Church and a cemetery on the slope of Brandon Hill, at what is now the Queen Elizabeth's Hospital. Mosaic Law demanded that cleanliness be an essential part of Jewish life and the spring at Jacob's Well was used to that end. A ritual bath or Mikvah was built, probably in the 12th century, to allow for total immersion. The only medieval Jewish ritual bath to have been discovered in England, the Mikvah still stands today, stone steps leading down to the water which bubbles up through the rock. There may also be another Mikvah, for an unexcavated second chamber was found in the 1980s. On the lintel above the bath is a faint Hebrew inscription which has been variously translated as either 'Flowing water' or 'To give one health and long life'.[16]

After the expulsion of the Jews in 1290 the spring became property of the Crown who granted access to the monks of St Augustine's Abbey, although less than a hundred years later in 1373 the water was granted to the City of Bristol on the condition that a conduit be built into the city and docks. The abbey by this time had secured its own water supply from a number of springs over the road from Jacob's Well and incorporated them into what became known as The Dean and Chapter's Conduit which ran to a large cistern in the abbey precincts.[17] Gaunt's Pipe, a feather or subsidiary pipe, branched off to supply Gaunt's Hospital, a site now occupied by the Midland Bank on the corner of Park and Unity streets.

Throughout the Middle Ages Jacob's Well attracted pilgrims who came seeking restitution from its healing waters, a tradition which continued until at least the 18th century for in 1712 Sir Robert Atkyns wrote that the well was 'much esteemed for its wholesome waters'[18] and it was still in use as a cold bath later that century when it had a particular reputation in the cure of skin conditions.[19]

Throughout its post-medieval history Jacob's Well was leased to a number of tenants who provided a water supply of sorts, including use as a brewery! Its water was bottled for sale and export in bottles of the famed Bristol Blue Glass, and in 1889 was even used to supply neighbouring public baths and wash houses.[20]

The water has a temperature range between 12 and 14°c at source and is said to steam in freezing weather. Its purity has lead to recent, short-lived, attempts at commercial bottling although at present the wellhouse stands locked and unused.[21]

The Conduits

As medieval Bristol outgrew its native supply of springs and deep wells an additional water supply was vital to the health and expansion of the city. Thus springs in the adjacent hills, such as those described above, were tapped and their water channelled down to Bristol in stone, wood and lead conduits known as Pipes. At certain points in the city, usually adjacent to a church, the conduit would terminate at a 'castellette' or reservoir where the water would be accessible to the public. The conduit springs were often on ecclesiastical land and their water would serve a particular religious establishment or a particular parish, although others were gifts from rich benefactors.

However, the conduits and castellettes were more than just a water supply. Like the springs from which they flowed they were regarded with respect and veneration. There was a ceremonial dressing of the conduits on New Year's Day and on Ascension Day when they were adorned with 'greening boughs and woodland flowers' and in pre-Reformation times there was the Ceremony of the Blessing of the Waters where the following prayer was offered:

117

May the Blessing of God Almighty,
the father, Son and Holy Ghost, and
all the Saints, be upon these springs,
and those who use them, and those
who tend them for evermore.[22]

Conduits maintained something of their power after the Reformation and were the venues for proclamations and gatherings. When Queen Anne was proclaimed in 1701 it was said that 'the conduits ... were adorned with flowers and gilded branches, curiously wrought into a variety of figures.'[23]

Two of the smaller conduits have been described in the preceeding pages, but there were six principal conduits serving the city, some with 'feathers' or feeder pipes branching off them to supply other districts. Two of the main conduits were south of the river and the remainder in the north.

South:

1.   **Redcliffe Pipe**. This takes its water from **Huge Well** at Knowle (ST596704) and has its main castellette outside the church of St Mary Redcliffe (ST590723) although a feather once ran off to

Ancient stonework inside the
Huge Well

St Thomas church by Bristol Bridge supplying a couple of minor fountains on the way. The Huge Well, also called Rudge Well, was granted to the parish of St Mary Redcliffe in 1190 by Robert de Berkeley. Originally it was to have supplied the monks of St John's Hospital near the church, and also be for use by Berkeley's prisoners who were held in the parish. Every year since 1190 a Pipe Walk has taken place, in which church

118

officials, local dignitaries, parishioners and spectators assemble at the Huge Well in Glyn Vale on Knowle Hill or at St Mary Redcliffe and proceed to follow the pipe. When starting from the well, the walkers meet at St Barnabas' Church on Daventry Road. In other circumstances the position of this church 100m from the spring would suggest a well chapel. However, this case is one of coincidence as

Inspecting the conduit head at the Huge Well at the start of the Redcliffe Pipe Walk

Pipe walkers inspecting Redcliffe Pipe at St John's Lane, Bedminster

there was no church here prior to 1938. The Huge Well has never been known to fail and rises 100m north-east of the stone well house that marks the start of the pipe, the water being channelled underground to the wellhouse where it is inspected by the walkers and prayers are offered. The procession then cuts through allotments and suburban gardens and on to Victoria Park at Windmill Hill, stopping to inspect the pipe at two manhole covers *en route*. At the northern end of the park, a water maze was built in 1984, taking its design from a roof boss within the 14th century church.[24] Less than 100m to the north, first time pipe-walkers are gently 'bounced' on one of the mark stones that periodically indicate the route of the pipe. This activity is reminiscent of 'beating the

The Windmill Hill water maze, Bedminster, fed by Redcliffe Pipe

The fountain head of the Redcliffe Pipe in central Bristol

bounds' in which parish boundaries were walked by parishioners and young children bumped on boundary stones, dunked in wells or birched to help reinforce their memories of where the boundaries lay. The pipe stone ceremony probably once had a similar function. After a final manhole inspection, the walkers then follow York Road, along the New Cut, as far as Bedminster Bridge. Prior to the excavation of the New Cut, the pipe followed a more linear course up to St Mary Redcliffe. Bomb damage during the Second World War now means that the water flows no further than the bridge. Even so, the procession continues up Redcliffe Hill to the conduit head at the church where water issues from a metal lion's head—courtesy of the mains supply!

The Redcliffe Pipe Walk is the oldest continuously practised well ceremony in the region—a venerable 800 year tradition that has survived where hundreds of others have not.

2.   **Temple Pipe.** This conduit rises beneath the junction of the Bath and Wells Roads at Pile Hill, Totterdown, where there was once a gallows. Here the Ravenswell (ST598718), a combination of several small springs, flows into a large subterranean chamber some 10 to 20 feet high. The water was granted in 1366 by John de Gourney, Lord of Knowle, to the Augustine Friars who had established a small settlement south of Temple Church. The monks wished to ensure the purity of their water and tunnelled 125 metres

Neptune, erected at the end of the Temple Pipe in 1723

into the hillside until they arrived at the springhead. A lead conduit then ran down to the old Temple gate at Spring Gardens where a public fountain once stood; a feather took more water off to the Friary. Later the conduit was extended along Temple Street where a statue of Neptune was erected over the fountain in 1723. The water was later used exclusively by the Great Western Railway at Temple Meads Station, but now runs to waste.[25] The statue of Neptune now graces the dockside, near the Watershed Centre.

Until the early years of the 19th century there was an annual civic visit to inspect the spring and ensure the conduit was in good repair. Money for the upkeep of the pipe and the lavish civic supper which followed the inspection was derived from rents gathered on Temple Fair. However the increasing rowdiness of the Fair led to its suppression and by 1835 there was so little revenue that the Inspection had to be abandoned and the conduit fell into a ruinous state until the arrival of the railway.[26]

The water of the Ravenswell springs remains remarkably pure — when tested in 1986 it was found to be purer than Bristol tap water![27]

North:
1.   The **Key Pipe** was probably the most notable of the northern conduits. Its source was a spring known as the **Pamiwell** or **Pennywell** (ST600751) which rose near what is now The Farm public house at St Werburghs, less than 500m south of the Boiling Well in Ashley Vale. A conduit house was built over the spring in the 14th century and the conduit itself took water to the Frome harbourside in the heart of the city. Its 'very faire castellette' was moved several times in the 18th century but kept to the Corn Street / Clare Street area and saw service in filling the casks of vessels using the port. It is even claimed that it was water from the Key Pipe that John Cabot took with him on his voyage of discovery to Newfoundland in 1497. The conduit served as a focus for the community where the military victories of Queen Anne's reign and the coronations of later monarchs were cele-brated by the cistern being filled with wine. There were also medicinal powers attributed to the conduit water, for until the

1880s old people would bathe their legs in the fountain to cure gout and rheumatism.[28]

A feather from the Key Pipe fed the **Back Pipe**, a conduit that issued forth at the top of Welsh Back. Its proximity to the church of St Nicholas led to the alternative names of **St Nicholas Pipe** and **St Nicholas Well**.[29]

2.   **All Saints Pipe** took its water from 'a pretty sparkling well' that rose in the orchard of St James Priory, a site now occupied by

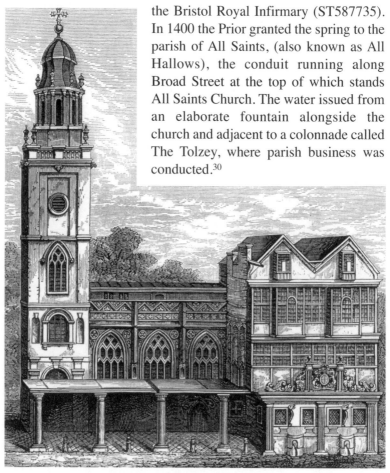

the Bristol Royal Infirmary (ST587735). In 1400 the Prior granted the spring to the parish of All Saints, (also known as All Hallows), the conduit running along Broad Street at the top of which stands All Saints Church. The water issued from an elaborate fountain alongside the church and adjacent to a colonnade called The Tolzey, where parish business was conducted.[30]

Church of All Hallows, showing The Tolzey and conduits

Remains of a shrine which stood alongside the Carmelite Pipe conduit, Frog Lane, c.1920 (M.J. Tozer Collection)

3. **Carmelite Conduit**. The Carmelite Friars had an establishment on the site of what is now Lower Colston Street. Their water supply was a spring that rises in the road outside what is now 81 Park Street (ST582729). In 1267 they built a conduit to pipe this water direct to their establishment; it runs down what is now Park Street then along Frog Lane to a cistern in Pipe Lane over which a shrine was erected: a niche, which held a female statue, probably of the Virgin, surmounted by a winged lion delimiting the boundary of the Hospital of St Mark.[31] In 1376 the Carmelites allowed the construction of a feather from this cistern to serve St John's Church, where a fine castellette was built against the church wall inside the gate. When the Carmelites were suppressed at the Dissolution, the parishioners of St John's took over the responsibility for the conduit, eventually demolishing the old castellette in 1846 and building a new fountain on the Nelson Street side of the church where its stone lions heads and taps can still be seen, the water still trickling out as it has done for over 600 years.[32]

4. **Greyfriars Pipe** had its source at Bedford Place, Kingsdown (ST585735) and ran down the hill to the Greyfriars at Lewins Mead, and then across the Frome into the City.[33]

St John's Conduit in Broad Street, from a drawing of 1825

The Avon Gorge

Mardyke Spa

'It sharpens the appetite, raises the spirits and invigorates the whole frame.' So wrote John Evans in *A Picture of Bristol*, in 1814.[34] In 1786 a well was dug at Tennis Court House on the Hotwells Road, not far from the Mardyke public house. The water that bubbled up from the rock was saline and chalybeate and instantly recognised as medicinal, and the enterprising owner built a pump room in the house with a suite of hot and cold baths. Contemporary writers eulogised the water, cataloguing a vast array of ailments that were believed to be curable by bathing at the spa. The list included scurvy, bilious and rheumatic disorders, skin conditions including 'Scalded heads in children' and 'pimpled faces', scrofula and lymphatic/glandular cases, hypochondria, all cases of visceral obstructions, liver complaints, menstrual problems, piles, rickets in children, nervous headaches, chronic ulcerated legs and 'all other diseases arising from a relaxed habit or languid circulation.'[35] All this did little for the Spa, for by 1810 we find the site had been converted to a coal wharf.[36]

The Hotwell

'Everything conspires to render the thing agreeable.'

Edward Owen in *Observations on the earths, rocks, stones and minerals etc.*, in 1754

Beneath St Vincent's Cliff, at the southern end of the Gorge, a rock jutted into the Avon just south of the Suspension Bridge. This was Hotwell Point (ST565728), a site almost inaccessible on foot as the only land access was a dangerous descent down the cliff face. From the rock a hot spring bubbled up 'as warm as Milk',[37] 24°c, a constant spring that poured forth up to 60 gallons a minute, although this could be reduced in exceptionally dry summers. The spring rose in a zone of geological fracturing in the carboniferous limestone and was fed by water which had been heated by passing through hot crustal rocks; indeed, it shares the same ancestry as the hot springs of Bath. Its situation nine metres below high water and three metres above low water mark meant that the spring was only

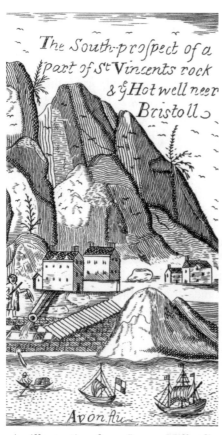

An illustration from James Millerd's An Exact Delineation of the famous City of Bristol and suburbs, *1673, which is possibly the earliest known illustration of the Hotwell*

accessible at low tide and there was a problem with pollution by river water.[38]

The first record of the well is in 1480, when it was called St Vincent's Well from a folk belief that the saint once lived there, having a chapel in the Giant's Cave high up the cliff face. Its inaccessibility meant that sailors were the first to use its waters; they found it worked wonders in curing scurvy, kidney stones, old sores and 'the itch'. They bathed in the water which was held in a brick reservoir and piped down to stone basins, some would let the water splash out of the pipe onto the afflicted part, a cloth was then wetted in the water and wrapped around the area in need of healing. The water had such a reputation that by 1600 it was of national renown and in 1634 it could be described as 'in pretty frequent use, and not without success.'[39]

As more people resorted to the well the list of its virtues increased. In 1650 it was being prescribed for those who have 'hot livers', and 'red pimpling faces'.[40] Behind this lay a general belief in the cure of internal organs and an abundance of skin conditions. This period also saw the well achieve a fame in the cure of diabetes, of which many Bristolians had lately died. John Underhill (1703) records the case of Bristol baker John Gaggs, 38 years old and 'a

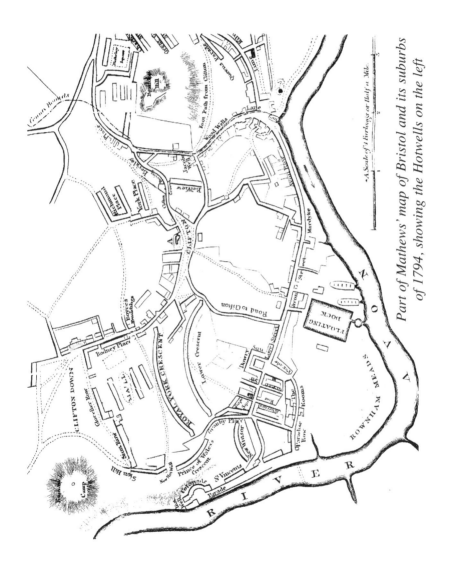

Part of Mathews' map of Bristol and its suburbs of 1794, showing the Hotwells on the left

129

*St Vincent's Rock from a 19th century print. The quarrymen in the
foreground are using the remains of the Lower Hotwell spa house
for shelter and storage. Hotwell House is shown further upstream.
The Clifton Suspension Bridge now crosses the gorge at this spot*

very fat man' who 'made at least three gallons of very sweet urine
with a large quantity of oil swimming thereon every night, and could
not sleep for either drinking or pissing, which in six days so run off
his fat and flesh that he was reduced to helpless skin and bones ...
and given over by his wife and friends for a dead man ... resolutely
cast himself on God's mercy and the Hot-Well water imploring his
friends to support him to the Hot-Well ... he fainting every step and
even in drinking the water, yet to God's glory and their astonishment
his strength so came to him ... he return'd home without assistance
only aided now and then with a sip of his Holy-water bottle, his
trusty friend ... which instantly vanquish's his insatiable thirst and
stopt his pissing ... and by drinking the water for some time perfectly
attained his former state of health.'[41] Accounts such as these were
legion, and by 1690 bathing at the Hotwell was the most popular
prescription amongst local doctors for a patient with diabetes, and it
was not long before diarrhoea and consumption joined the list of
diseases that were miraculously cured at the well.

Such was the astonishing rise in the Hotwell's fame that its owners, the Merchant Venturers, leased the well to an entrepreneur who offered to replace the old reservoir and build a wall around the spring in an attempt to keep the river out at high tide, so as to increase the length of time the water could be accessible. However, the height of water trapped inside the wall threatened to affect the flow of the spring and it was not until 1695 that a satisfactory solution arose in the form of an enclosed pump over the spring which took the water 30 feet up into a spa—Hotwell House—built directly above the spring. Some lamented this change, claiming that the development had rendered the water less effective; others criticised the general abandonment of bathing in favour of internal use, saying that this too rendered the water less beneficial than it once was.[42]

From the early 17th century the Hotwell had attracted the curiosity of a number of physicians who were impressed by its powers. With modern medicine still in its infancy, doctors felt that there was much to learn from medicinal waters and several influential tracts appeared, such as P. Keir's *An Enquiry into the Nature and Virtue of the Medicinal Waters of Bristol and their use in the Cure of Chronical Distempers*, published in 1739. Keir offered his thoughts on mineral contents and the use of a strict regime whilst recovering from illness. Some of his observations seem more poetic than scientific but still offer an insight into the philosophy with which people viewed the well. He writes that the water acts by 'quickening and enlivening the drooping circulation ... in some degree restoring youth.'[43] The historian Coxe felt it 'very good to purge away ill Humours and Sweeten the Blood.'[44] Another doctor, John Underhill, had written in 1703 that the water was 'of excellent use in Slipperiness of Parts.'[45]

More recognisable definitions of the maladies cured by the Hotwell water came to include sterility and impotence, blood poisoning, fevers, rheumatic pains, scrofula, cancer, venereal disease, nervous headaches, painful and excessive discharges including heavy periods, heartburn, colic, bilious vomiting and a wealth of urinary problems, and when brewed into beer it was 'wholesome against the spleen'.[46] Paralytics too were brought to the well, such as Catherine Roberts of Monmouthshire, 'a

The old Hotwell House, c.1824, by Samuel Jackson
(Bristol Museum and Art Gallery)

Mendicant', who Underhill tells us set up home in a hedge near the well one winter: 'All one side being dead with the Palsie, both immovable and quite senseless for above six years before ... in six weeks time by drinking the Hot-Well Water and Bathing her senseless side with the same, and using Friction as she bathed perfectly recovered the Use of her dead Side and remain'd well to her death above five years after her wonderful Cure.'[47]

As befits a true holy well the Hotwell water had a reputation for curing eye problems—relieving ulcers and inflammations and strengthening weak eyes. For the best results the water had to be taken warm from the Pump and applied to the eye with a piece of cloth.[48] Underhill recounts the case of a Mrs Demster of Bristol whose 'Sight was so deprav'd with a painful Inflammation ... that for four months she could not endure the Light, after all other Means us'd in vain, she perfectly recovered her sight ... by bathing her eyes with the hot-Well Water, and sometime drinking the same.'[49]

The taste of the odourless water was agreeable to some whilst others found it astringent and when drunk for the first time it could cause 'a sort of Uneasiness in the Head.'[50] Some made tea with it whilst others mixed it with wine and made it the base for Punch. It kept well when bottled or casked and was taken on board ships due to set sail on a long voyage. A lively bottled water trade developed,

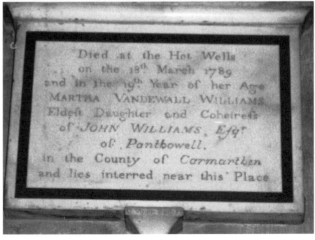

Memorial tablets in Bristol Cathedral of those who failed to find relief at the Hotwell

mostly for the home market, but also abroad. To reproduce the water's warmth at source and reinvigorate its virtues, customers were advised to stand a bottle in a pan of boiling water, and when the contents were warmed, to drink it quickly.[51]

The development of the Spa at Hotwell was restricted by its position, hemmed in between the river and the cliff, but for a while it did offer serious competition to Bath. Large numbers flocked to the Spa between April and October, most were local although a large proportion came from further afield. The regime was to rise early, go to the pump room and drink about half a pint of water, then relax listening to the resident musicians or go for a stroll along the river bank, then drink another glass and at 5 o'clock a final glass. After the first few days three glasses were drunk before breakfast. A service and entertainment industry grew around the Hotwell and it became known as 'one of the gayest and busiest of spas.'[52]

Although internal use now predominated, small private baths were available despite the water having lost its heat by the time they were ready. It was customary to have a five-minute dip before breakfast although most who took a bath were in good health and merely bathed 'in order to cleanse and refresh themselves.' Bristolians had free access to the water, many arriving on a Sunday when a rather festive time was had by all. However, as they were not paying customers they went into the building by a back door so as not to 'interrupt the better sort of company.'[53]

On November 1st 1755 the Hotwell turned blood red, a consequence of the Lisbon earthquake that same day, at the time, however, it was considered as 'an omen of the world's final slaughter. All flew to the churches, where incessant prayers were offered to avert the apparent approach of their destruction, and to appease the anger of heaven.'[54] The water remained foul for some time and an air of panic hung over the spa until its true cause was understood.

In common with its rival Bath, the Hotwell slipped slowly out of fashion after the Napoleonic Wars as a combination of recession, overpricing and the increasing lure of coastal health resorts started to take their toll. Wealthier customers were also able to visit continental spas once more and the allure of Bristol dimmed somewhat.

Even the construction of a new spa house (the Royal Clifton Spa) in 1822 could not revive the Hotwell's fortunes. Further damage was done to the Hotwell's reputation by the mercenary practice of sending terminally ill consumptives to the spa from London, so ensuring that unscrupulous doctors eked out as much as they could from a patient instead of letting them die in peace at home. It furthermore meant a very high mortality rate amongst visitors to the well and as a consequence it was seen as a place to die rather than recover, and it attracted a rather morbid name. By 1867 the decline had become inexorable and Hotwell House was demolished, whilst Hotwell Point complete with holy well was dynamited to make the river easier to navigate. For a while the spring was lost but it later re-emerged right at the base of the cliff. A pump was erected in a grotto in the cliff in 1877 and it remains there to this day, the last vestige of the Hotwell. Even up to 1913 as many as 350 people a day drank from the fountain supplied by the pump although by this time the water had become so polluted that it was declared unfit for public consumption.[55]

Clifton Spa Pump Room was built up on the cliff at the end of the 19th century in a vain attempt to continue the Hotwell tradition with water supplied from the new pump below. Complete with a grand pump room and a furnicular railway the Clifton Spa Pump Room seemed to offer a bright future for Hotwell water. However the age of the spa had passed and the new venture slowly faded into obscurity although the pump room still stands to this day and is the object of much effort by a group of enthusiasts who are aiming to buy and restore the site.[56]

The Upper Hotwell

In the early 1790s a solicitor named Morgan sank a well for his new house at Sion Hill, Clifton. Water was reached at a depth of 245 feet and was found to be the same as the Hotwell water at the foot of the cliff. In 1796, after Morgan's well was proved to have similar medicinal properties to the Hotwell, he built a spacious pump room with bathing facilities as well as providing for drinking the water (ST566728). The well became known as the Upper Hotwell or Sion Spring; its waters which were renowned as 'salubrious and pleasant'[57] were raised by means of a fire engine pump and piped to 340 houses in Clifton and Hotwells as a regular domestic supply. However, despite the Spa's attractions, such as an extensive circulating library and reading rooms, it had become defunct by 1803.[58]

The New Hotwell

A kilometre downstream from the Hotwell another hot spring rose from the base of the cliffs. First recorded in 1702 its constant heat was also 'as warm as Milk when it comes from the Cow.'[59] It seems likely that it had long been in use, perhaps in conjunction with the Hotwell, for it too was renowned for its medicinal properties. A small pump room and lodging house were built next to it, although being even more difficult to reach than the Hotwell there were few visitors. John Dolman lived at the lodging house in the mid-18th century and recorded the visitors to the well in his *Contemplations amongst St Vincent's Rocks* (1755). He notes the tourists who came 'to kill Time', and others who returned year after year to take the waters as a preventative measure to 'keep off Death.' However, 'few there are that come from the feeling Necessity they have of the Water.' One of the latter was John Wesley, founder of the Methodist movement. 'When he first came to the House his once active body, seem'd as if it was near worn out; his Countenance look'd as if a greedy Consumption as determin'd to put a period to his days: But in less than three weeks God so blessed the Water to him (which he regularly drank) that he was enabled to set out on his Cornish Circuit, preaching every Day.'[60]

The export trade in bottled water kept the spa viable for a time, but it failed to thrive and the buildings became storerooms for quarrymen blasting out the sides of the Gorge. In 1894 Bristol Corporation erected a fountain near the original site of the spa and called it St Vincent's Spring.[61] However, even this had to go, in the face of progress, when the Portway road was built at the foot of the Gorge.

North Bristol

Ashley Vale

The **Boiling Well** (ST601756) rises in a tangled and inaccessible willow thicket between a smallholding and the railway line at the end of Boiling Wells Lane. In 1779 Samuel Rudder described it thus: 'Here is a well, whose waters gush out from many places in a perpendicular direction, like a boiling cauldron, and has been used as a cold bath, with great success.' The well was believed to be bottomless and children were warned that if they went into its surrounding pool they would sink and be lost forever.[62]

Less than 500m south of the Boiling Well, and near what is now The Farm public house off Mina Road, rose the **Pennywell** or **Pamiwell** (ST600751). The spring probably still flows but there is now little knowledge of its whereabouts; four hundred years ago however it was the source for one of Bristol's most important water supplies—the Key Pipe (see p.120).

Clifton

Goldney House sits at what was the heart of the old village of Clifton. The house was built in 1720, and is less than 100m south of Clifton's first, medieval, parish church and 250 metres west of Jacob's Well. In the grounds of the house there is a reputed **healing well** (ST574728); its situation so close to the church site is of note, and the two could well have once been associated.

A house in Beaufort Road was built on the site of an old pond called **The Suicide Pool** (ST573742). One set of inhabitants were regularly terrified by the ghost of a woman who glided into a room then disappeared. The next occupant was found dead at the foot of the stairs and the one after that went mad. A similar account of another, presumably Cliftonian, haunted house, tells of the ghost of a hunchbacked, half-witted girl who led a miserable life at the hands of her father and was finally found drowned in a **pool** in the garden. Her ghost haunted the house and drove out its occupants, leaving the place uninhabited for many years.[63]

Map of North Bristol showing the sites of:

1. Boiling Well
2. Pennywell / Pamiwell
3. Pennywell, Henbury
4. Dragonswell, Henbury
5. St Anne's Well, Horfield
6. Magnesia Well, Horfield
7. Hopewell, Lawrence Weston
8. Well, Ashley Vale, Locklaze
9. Hot spring, Shirehampton
10. Woodwell, Shirehampton
11. Bucklewell, Shirehampton
12. Paddy's Well, Stoke Bishop
13. Canopied well, Stoke Park
14. Duchess Pond, Stoke Park
15. Trymwell, Westbury-on-Trym

Filton

A Roman coin hoard was discovered along the banks of a stream in this parish during the 19th century. The precise location is not known but was not far from the Bristol-Gloucester road. The hoard may be the result of a worried person hiding their wordly goods, or it may have been a votive offering to the stream.[64]

Henbury

The parish of Henbury encompasses a great variety of landscapes and sites of historic interest, many of which are contained within the Blaise Castle Estate, a great expanse of parkland which once belonged to the Bishops of Worcester. In one of the wilder, more wooded parts of the Estate, the **Pennywell** (ST556777)* rises at the base of a great ash tree, not far from Hazel Brook. The spring rises within a brick chamber built into the hillside and still partially roofed by a great sandstone slab. The water is cool and clear and runs away as a rivulet with a reputation for petrifying things which fall onto its course although an adjacent stream seems to do this much more effectively. Recorded in 1389 as 'Pennywell fontem'[65] the name suggests that it was probably once a wishing well, and in

The Pennywell

the mid-19th century its 'beautifully clear water' was highly regarded by local people who attributed to it 'many virtues'.[66] The spring is an integral part of the rich mythological and archaeological heritage of the Blaise Castle area, owned by Bristol City Council and freely open for public access.

On the north-eastern side of the parish, in Brentry and close by the A4018 Passage Road, a modern road name—Dragons Well Road—preserves the memory of **Dragonswell Pool** (ST571787), a small pond which gave off steam in cold weather and was believed to be the resting place of the eponymous serpent.[67] The name may be of fairly recent origin for it is not recorded on old maps or documents, neither was it mentioned by the 18th and 19th century topographers who were active in the area.

Horfield

On the northern side of Horfield Common, by what is now Wellington Hill West, there rose a wayside spring which was never known to fail. Its water ran into a basin, a shallow **dipping well** (ST589768) built into a stone alcove with a large flat stone set in front. It is thought that the water was used for baptisms in the parish church some 200 metres to the east, and its position below the site of a Bronze Age barrow is suggestive of an ancient association between the well and the wider ritual landscape. Despite the lack of documentary proof it is commonly thought that the spring was called **St Anne's Well**, the idea being favoured by the presence of an ancient house, St Anne's Cottage, which once stood nearby and which is believed to have been the property of the Augustinian monks of Bristol. The site of the well is now beneath a garden wall.[68]

200 metres south of St Annes Well, near the Pavilion on the Common, there rose a spring called the **Magnesia Well** (ST589764), presumably because it was believed to be particularly rich in this mineral.

Lawrence Weston

The suggestive field name **Hopewell** (ST540795) is recorded in the 1822 Westbury Inclosure Award as lying east of Poplar Farm. Unfortunately the field has largely been destroyed by the recent construction of the M49, and no spring or well is visible.

Lockleaze

Somewhere between Heath House, on the western flank of Pur Down, and the Boiling Well in Ashley Vale, there once stood a small roofed **well** (ST6075), described by Arthur Salmon in 1925 as 'very much like some of the holy wells of the West Country',[69] and a site where a persistent, though unsubstantiated, local tradition stated that the Romans used the water to supply a nearby sanatorium for wounded soldiers. Local people felt it was a strange place and a story was told of a woman who once drank from the well and swallowed an invisible snake which grew inside her, twisting painfully around her organs. She could do nothing to expel it and was doomed to suffer constant torment.[70]

Montpelier

Less than one kilometre north of the centre of Bristol, Montpelier is now a district of dense housing with a wide variety of architectural styles. In the mid-18th century the area was still rural and an attractive stream flowed down the hillside to power a snuffmill at what is now the junction of Cheltenham Road and Station Road. A millpond helped ensure an even flow of water to power the machinery but industrial purpose was superseded in 1747 when the mill's owner, a threadmaker named Thomas Rennison, opened the pond as a **Cold**

Rennison's Baths

141

Bath for public bathing. Cashing in on the region's reputation as a premier spa destination, Rennison realised how the quest for health was not in itself enough to guarantee the success of a spa or bath: having a good time in congenial company was perhaps as important an aspect of the visit as any perceived cure. **Rennison's Baths** (ST591744), as the site became known, grew quickly and by 1765 the old millpond had been transformed into a Grand Pleasure Bath with the later addition of a separate Ladies' Bath. Throughout the baths' existence it was as much renowned for the parties, concerts and 'high reveries' which took place there as it was for the bathing. There is no record of any therapeutic virtues associated with the waters but the bathing establishment, at the foot of a pleasant hillside studded with elegant villas, helped encourage associations with the southern French spa resort of Montpellier, and hence the district acquired its name. In the late 18th century the Old England Hotel was built alongside the baths to provide refreshment and accommodation for the growing number of visitors; the building still stands as the Old England public house. The baths closed in 1916, their site now occupied by the Montpelier Health Centre and the extension of Colston's Girls' School; the only surviving legacy being the adjacent street name of Baths Buildings.[71]

Shirehampton

Three notable wells are recorded for Shirehampton. Little is known of the **hot spring** (c.ST531769) which is said to be under the High Street,whilst another well, the **Woodwell** (ST533765), rose within a brick chamber with steps leading down from Woodwell Lane. The Woodwell was lost when the dual carriageway of the Portway went through the site, and it is not clear whether the sole account of its reputation as a healing well, useful in eye disorders, is not a mistaken allusion to another well which rises 500m to the east.[72]

This third site, the **Bucklewell** (ST538766), was the most famed of Shirehampton's wells, and rises in the floor of a low cave in the steep wooded hillside of Horseshoe Bend, less than 20m above the tidal River Avon. The well is situated below public allotments, with no formal public access, and was once the site of a hermitage. At one time the well was known as the **Holy Well of**

Bucklewell Cave

Shirehampton and people would come and make offerings to the spring, the water of which forms a small pool which is believed to be struck only by the rays of the midsummer sun. Also reputed as a place of hidden treasure,[73] the most enduring belief surrounding this site is that the water was good in the cure of sore eyes. A recent owner of the well, Mr Little, had a problem with excessive blinking as a child, so an old woman told his mother to take water from the well into basin and bathe his eyes. Very soon after, his complaint was cured.

Stoke Bishop

Paddy's Well (ST569758) stood at the south-eastern end of Parry's Lane just as the Lane neared the edge of the Downs. It was said that a man named Paddy, or Parry, had cut his throat at the well and was buried nearby at Cross Elm crossroads; his ghost then haunted the lane and was seen sitting by the well. The water was highly regarded and carted to Clifton where it was sold for a penny a bucket.[74]

Stoke Park

Part of the Pur Down ridge running west of the Frome valley, Stoke Park was a landscaped estate centred on the great house of Stoke Park itself. The house has spent much of this century as a hospital

The Duchess Pond

but once belonged to powerful local families such as the Beauforts. In the 18th century some of the inhabitants were noted for their Druidical excesses, such as the erection of obelisks to pagan deities. It is unclear whether there was once a sacred well on the estate, but on the hilltop near the house there was once 'A very old **covered well** of pure water.' (ST6277)[75]

At the eastern foot of the Down, and hard by the M32, recent landscaping work has recreated the **Duchess Pond** (ST618769)*, the original of which was destroyed during the construction of the motorway. In the 1960s, before the loss of the old pond, rumours of 'an eerie white figure' seen around the pool led a group of sceptical schoolchildren to spend an evening there to prove to themselves that the ghost did not exist. To their amazement they saw a phantom: 'a big white figure of a horse with a woman sitting on it.' The ghost would occasionally disappear and then be seen moving around the edge of some adjacent woodland. It is said that the ghost is that of an old duchess of Beaufort who lived at Stoke House and gave her name to the pond before being killed in a fall from her horse.[76]

Westbury-on-Trym

In Waters Lane, just south of the parish church, an old woman called Betty Waters lived in what is now called **Trymwell** Cottage

(ST573772). From a well in her garden she would sell water which was believed to have medicinal properties and people would travel from many miles around to take bottles of it home with them. The site of the cottage is of note, being close to the site of a Benedictine monastery (founded in either 720 or 803AD) as well as less than 100m distant from the parish church of Holy Trinity.[77]

South Bristol

Bedminster

Bedminster was an early church site established during the formative years of Christianity in this area. There are no remains of the ancient church today but its site may well have been where the now demolished parish church of St John's stood between East Street and Malago Road. No notable wells are recorded within the main urban core of 'old Bedminster' but several are known to the south.

On Bedminster Down one of the fields on the northern slope bore the name **Flowerwell** (ST570700). This name is thought to derive from the Old English for 'floor spring', the first element being often found in association with a Roman tessellated—or mosaic—pavement. Further east along the face of the Down was **Farthingwell** field (ST572701), a name suggestive of the offering of small coins.[78]

Prior to 1906, at what is now the junction of Luckwell Road and Chessel Street, there stood the **Luckwell** (ST576714)*; the well rising at the foot of a slope on which grew a tall clump of Horse Chestnuts. This was once a deep, dipping well with a pointed stone alcove sheltering a stone basin into which the water ran, but after a child drowned here it was enclosed and a pump erected. The well had a good reputation in the cure of weak and sore eyes and it has been suggested that the name is a corruption of **St Luke's Well**. In support of this it is noted that St Luke was patron saint of fairs and the adjacent field was traditionally used to hold local fairs; indeed water from the well was always used by traders when camped nearby. Local folklore offers a more immediate, though less probable origin for the

145

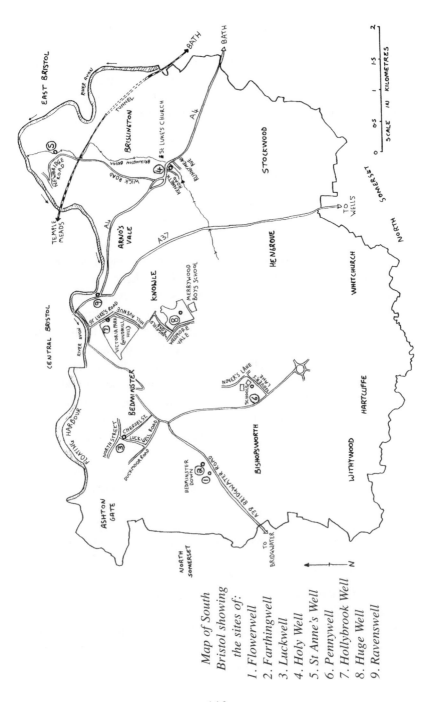

Map of South
Bristol showing
the sites of:
1. Flowerwell
2. Farthingwell
3. Luckwell
4. Holy Well
5. St Anne's Well
6. Pennywell
7. Hollybrook Well
8. Huge Well
9. Ravenswell

146

name, for it is said that during the Civil War Cromwell's army were exhausted after a long hot march and stumbled upon the spring exclaiming, 'What a lucky well!' It may be that 'luck' was indeed the derivation but more in the sense of a wishing well.[79]

Brislington

There were once two holy wells in this parish, one rose to great international fame and is arguably Bristol's most well-known holy well, whilst the other achieved only local fame and is now completely forgotten.

Before the construction of Kenneth Road and Runnymead Avenue there was once a field called Holy Mead, the final gathering point for medieval pilgrims on their way to the well chapel shrine of St Anne's just over a mile to the north. Through this field ran Brislington Brook at the side of which stood the **Holy Well** (ST619705), a circular stone-built structure whose beautifully clear water was said to be good for sore eyes and other complaints. 'Pilgrimages' were made to the well up to the middle of the 19th century, but little is known of it after the 1920s.[80]

In the northern part of the parish, and within the quiet wooded valley of St Anne's Park, a winding track, known as the Pilgrim's path runs by the sacred waters of **St Anne's Well** (ST622725)*, enclosed by railings at the foot of a wooded slope. A 13th century chapel, also dedicated to St Anne, once stood 200 metres to the north-west and together they were one of the great pilgrimage centres of the Middle Ages. Pilgrims and benefactors of high social

status, such as the Duke of Buckingham, were regular visitors. In 1485 Henry VII visited the well and chapel shortly after his victory at Bosworth. Seventeen years later his queen, Elizabeth of York, came to the well and offered up 2s 6d, it is said to help her conceive a son; within the year she had given birth to Prince Arthur.[81]

St Anne's Well

*Parishioners being blessed with water from St Anne's Well on
St Anne's Day, 14 July, 1996*

Bristol sailors were firm believers in the power of St Anne's
Well, visiting it and the chapel before setting out to sea. Foreign
sailors, notably Bretons, would do likewise before their return
home, for amongst her other qualities St Anne was patron saint of
harbours, ports and sailors. The French connection continued into
the early years of this century when Breton onion sellers in the area
would seek out the well before returning home.[82]

Other medieval devotees were the Weavers Guild and the
Cordwainers who made special visits on St Anne's feast day, first
praying at the well and then making offerings at the chapel. In 1542
the Tudor topographer, John Leland, wrote of the site: 'here was
great Pilgrimage to S. Anne', and at the height of its popularity the
St Anne's complex was said to have been in the same league as the
Norfolk shrine of Our Lady of Walsingham.[83]

However, the Dissolution of Keynsham Abbey, which owned St
Anne's, saw the site disintegrate; the chapel was converted for
industrial use and the well decayed to the status of a local holy well.
Local people still came in good numbers, fetching the water for the
sick and the dying, washing their hands in the well to cure scurvy
and drinking the water to cure rheumatism and blood impurities,
and it still retained a reputation for aiding the fertility of barren

women. Bristol historian F.C. Jones wrote of coming to the well as a boy and taking away water for the bathing of weak eyes, and he remarked on its purity: 'It is crystal clear and exceedingly cold.'[84] Around the well were five large stepping stones, known as the Holy Stones worn down by the feet of generations of pilgrims. Money was thrown into the well, a tradition with an unbroken heritage back to medieval times, proven by the excavation of abbey tokens and old Portuguese coins. Coins were also thrown from the bridge carrying the pilgrim path over Brislington Brook. Legends of treasure led children to prod into the well with sticks hoping to find Queen Anne's Ring whilst an inscription above the well once boasted 'Wishing Well' and even today coins are still thrown in. A ghost is also reported to haunt the area immediately around the well, but there is no record of what form it takes.[85]

During the mid-19th century the well enjoyed a considerable revival of fortune as Bristol's burgeoning Catholic population resurrected the annual pilgrimage to St Anne's.[86] However, in the latter part of the century the public were actively discouraged by the landowner from visiting the well for a number of years and a protracted legal battle ensued which eventually saw the whole of the lower part of St Anne's Valley passing into public ownership. As evidence for public access, a Michael Mahoney was called as a witness and asked to explain the attraction and necessity of visiting the well. In his deposition he noted, 'My sight is failing. I got a cataract on my left eye and I used to go up and visit St Anne's Well and got faith in God that by using this holy well the water would do my sight good.'[87] To their credit the jury accepted this argument.

When Bristol Corporation took over the site they erected new stonework with a canopy over the well and in 1924 the annual St Anne's Day pilgrimage was enthusiastically restored. This tradition has carried on, albeit with some lapses, until the present day; some 40 people taking part in the 1996 service of blessing at the well. In this the priest takes water from the well and sprinkles it over those gathered around and thus continues the veneration of this ancient sacred site. A new well superstructure and a statue of St Anne were erected in 1996 by the local holy wells group, The Source, and the site returned to the care and respect it deserved, though the stonework has recently suffered from vanadalism.[88]

Filwood

In 1875 a Roman coin hoard was uncovered here along the banks of a stream close by an ancient road which led up to Maes Knoll on Dundry Hill. The hoard may have simply been buried in reaction to a period of instability or, given its suggestive location, as an offering to the spirit of the stream.[89]

Inn's Court

Novers Lane Infants School is built on a field that once bore the name **Pennywell** (ST582693) a site suggestive of coins being offered up to the spring.[90]

Knowle

Hollybrook Well (ST595716) is shown on an early 19th century map of Knowle, on a site which is now between the north-eastern edge of Victoria Park and St Luke's Road. The name is almost certainly a corruption of Holy Brook Well.[91]

Another notable Knowle spring is the **Huge Well** (ST596704), or Rudge Well, (both names being derivatives of 'ridge well') at Wedmore Vale. It is the source of water carried via the conduit of Redcliffe Pipe into the southern suburbs of the medieval city, and as such is discussed more fully in the section on conduits.

Totterdown

The **Ravenswell** (ST598718), rising under The Three Lamps at Pile Hill, was also tapped to supply a medieval conduit—the Temple Pipe—and is also discussed more fully in the section on conduits.

East Bristol

Frenchay

Along the wooded banks of Begbrook stream, as it nears its confluence with the River Frome, there rises a small spring. Local tradition states that it was once called **St Anne's Well** (ST634772)*, but it was also known as the Begbrook Holy Well. Very little now remains of the stone medieval well house that stood intact until the 1940s; its spring was moon-shaped, lined with fine stone and quite deep with a stone bench around it to allow pilgrims to bathe. It was believed to have been used by Glastonbury-bound pilgrims before their crossing of the Frome and it is claimed that a small ancillary building, either a chapel or a hermit's cell, stood close by. Surmounting the wellhouse was a cross with the inscription: 'Drink weary pilgrim, drink and pray, for the kind soul of Sybil Grey, who built this Cross and Well.' Behind the well was a niche which may once have held a religious statue. Many ghosts have been seen in the riverside woods along this part of the Frome valley.[92]

Hanham

Within the less developed parts of Hanham there are three notable bodies of water. Where the Ring Road has recently cut through the edge of Stone Hill there is a good, though slow-flowing, **perpetual spring** (ST648716). The remains of Roman buildings have recently been found nearby, and in 1953 a hoard of Roman coins were found here; could they have been votive offerings?

South of Stone Hill, and associated with the fascinating complex of Hanham Court and church, there is a **medieval fishpond** (ST649704)* haunted by the ghosts of an old man in a long black cloak and a young girl who he is hurrying away towards the ancient church. Both church and Court were once owned by the monks of Keynsham Abbey.

Further south again, and in a cottage garden along the banks of the River Avon at Hanham Mills, there is a old stone trough filled by a **spring** (ST646701) which rises in steep woodland immediately behind the houses. This well is reputed to be Roman and the cold clear water never varies in quantity or quality.[93]

Kingswood

The area between Staple Hill, Whiteway and New Cheltenham was notable for the clustering of **four sacred wells** which were tradi-

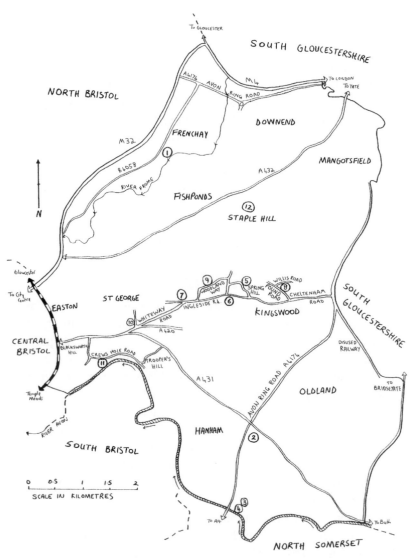

Map of East Bristol showing the sites of:

1. St Anne's Well, Frenchay
2. Perpetual Spring, Hanham
3. Haunted Fish Pond, Hanham
4. Perpetual 'Roman' Spring,
      Hanham Mills
5. Wishwell
6. Hopewell

7. Speedwell
8. Soundwell
9. Forest Pool, Chester Park
10. Plumer's Hill Well, St George
11. St Anthony's Well, St George
12. Dilly Gay's Level (appx.),
      Staple Hill

tionally visited on May Day morning.[94] The exact locations of the wells have been lost but enough clues survive as to offer suggestions to their whereabouts:

Wishwell (ST649748), which gave its name to Wishwell House, Spring Hill.

Hopewell (ST646743), for which all we have is the name Hopewell Hill, very close to Wishwell.

Speedwell (ST635743), which derives from the Old English *gesped* meaning 'success' and 'wealth'. This was probably in the vicinity of the original hamlet of that name near what is now the Speedwell Secondary School.[95]

Soundwell (ST656748), from the Old English *gesund* meaning 'healthy'. This well was probably near the field which bore the name 'At Soundwell' which is now where Randall Close joins Willis Road.[96]

King John's Hunting Lodge at Castle Road, Hopewell Hill, stands close by this cluster of holy wells and can claim to be one of the oldest buildings in the old Forest of Kingswood. It is on the highest point in east Bristol and was reputed to be a lookout tower. Legend tells of a secret tunnel which led from the Lodge to Hill House at Staple Hill, the course of which was taken, above ground, by the ghost of a warrior on a white horse who rode through the gates of the Lodge at the dead of night and disappeared into the **Forest Pool** (ST621747). The pool was directly over the course of the 'Tunnel' and stood on the site of what is now Woodland Way, Chester Park.[97]

St George

When the 1755 Lisbon earthquake caused the Hotwell water to become polluted and be seen as an omen of the Apocalypse, a **field well** in the parish of St George (c.ST624737), which had formerly been very clear suddenly became, 'as black as ink'[98] and remained so for a fortnight. It was also probably this well, now under Plummer's Hill Road, that supplied baptismal water for the old Cloud's Hill Baptist Chapel.[99]

By the site of St Anne's Ferry, near the Avon towpath where Blackswarth Road joins Crews Hole Road, there was once a **spring** of water (ST620730) so pure that a laboratory analysis in 1943 declared it 'by far the best so far examined in the Bristol area.'[100] It was never known to fail and supplied many local people with their domestic and drinking water, but above all it was renowned for its medicinal properties, especially powerful in the cure of weak eyes. Even in the 1920s people were travelling considerable distances to fill bottles with its healing water.

The proximity of this ancient spring, in its covered alcove, to the site of the ancient chapel of St Anthony on the hillside above (now part of the cemetery) drew many to speculate that it may have been called **St Anthony's Well** although there seems to be no documentary proof to support this. The chapel, which stood until the late 18th century, was believed to be connected to Keynsham Abbey by a secret tunnel; the route of this tunnel appears to cross the site of the well.[101]

As with so many of Bristol's wells, St Anthony's no longer exists above ground. Several small streams rise in the area and flow down to the Avon, but their springs are mostly built over; St Anthony's Well is now probably underneath the yard of a builder's merchants.

Staple Hill

East Bristol once had a thriving coal industry and many legacies of this period, from the 17th to early 20th century, remain in the architecture and landscape of the area. Drainage of the mine shafts was always a problem and to help in the extraction of water an intricate system of adits, known locally as Levels, was constructed to bring water to the surface. **Dilly Gay's Level** (c.ST6575) emptied outside the house which, in the latter 19th century, 104 year old Dilly Gay shared with his 102 year old wife. The great age of this couple was seen as proof of the medicinal nature of the 'famous' water which came forth from the level and it was much sought after by local people.[102]

North Somerset

Abbots Leigh

Within this parish lies the woodland beauty spot of the **Abbots Fish Pond** (ST536732)*, a natural pool somewhat enlarged over the centuries. In the Middle Ages the abbots of Bristol's St Augustine's Abbey established a grange nearby and there is a belief that they would come to the pond to fish whilst on retreat. It is also said that stone steps at the side of the pond gave access to a secret tunnel which led to the monastic residence, now Manor House, so that they could travel unseen. When the abbey was suppressed it was rumoured that the last abbot hurried to the pond and threw the abbey's treasures to the bottom of its dark, still depths rather than

The Abbots Fish Pond

surrender them to the king. So firmly was this tradition believed that the pond was once drained to allow the treasures to be retrieved, but, as in so many of these tales, the treasure-seekers found nothing of value.[1]

300m to the south-west of the Fish Pond is **Snake's Well** (ST533731)* in Forestry Commission woodland, and not far from a public footpath. The well is a 12m square and 3m deep pit built of the rare local stone, Quarzitic Conglomerate, a thin band of which is found nearby. The masonry has the appearance of great age and is bedecked with ferns, lichens and great cushions of moss with two shallow pools at the base of the well. There is no recorded folklore for this site, but it is one of a cluster of four similarly named wells in a small area south-west of Bristol.

Backwell

The Backwell

Backwell is derived from the Old English *baec wella*, or 'ridge spring'. An ancient, atmospheric spring near the parish church of St Andrew is the main contender for this title.[2] It lies in the garden of Court Farm (ST494683) and is cut deep into the hillside, a drystone grotto shaped like a limekiln with its sides tapering to an apex 4m above the water below. In recent years it has been the focus of an Easter celebration with the grotto representing the cave tomb in which Christ's body was laid and from where he rose from the dead. Older villagers believe that the water from this well was once used for baptisms although this ceased long ago.

In the south of the parish, at the top of Brockley Combe and

*The ancient stonework, including 19 steps, of Willings Well
is found at the base of the larger tree in the middle
of the photograph*

beneath a flourishing young lime tree in the first hedgerow to the east of Combehead Farm, there is one of the most evocative and mysterious of all the wells in the Bristol region—the **Willings Well** (ST492666). Backwell historian, the Rev. George Matson, believed this locally-famed well to have been a wishing well to which people would come to see what the future held for them, especially whether or not the Fates were 'willing', although the origin of the name is just as likely to derive from the name of a local landowner.[3] The well is buried deep in the earth, and reached by a flight of 19 stone steps. The spring itself rises in a rock-carved grotto with great blocks of stone forming a roof. A square stone basin holds the water and around it a thin bench has been etched out of the rock. The stonework at this lower level is probably medieval, but could possibly be older. Light occasionally filters down to dapple the still waters, but the well is largely divorced from the surface world; a primeval and very powerful place.

One and a half kilometres due east of Willings Well, between Oatfield Pool and Yew Tree Farm, is the **Pennywell** (ST509667); a deep well whose name implies that small coins were once offered up here. Local farmer Mervyn Vowles remembers being brought here as a child to throw small stones into the water. This is interesting because at some holy wells pebbles were sometimes the chosen offering—if bubbles appeared a wish would be granted.[4]

Banwell

The village and parish of **Banwell** takes its name from the 'beautiful and never-failing spring of water which rises near the church.'[5] The first part of the name is probably derived from an Anglo-Saxon personal name 'Bana' although it could also stem from the Old English word for 'slayer', giving rise to the suggestion that the spring may have been used for judicial executions by drowning.[6] This spring is now capped and is a major water supply for the region, rising beneath what is now the village bowling green (ST398591), once a great pond. Eight million gallons of water pour out of this spring every day. Local lore claimed that a secret tunnel led from the pond to the Ship Hotel, whilst local pride asserted that

Banwell Pond c.1910

the proximity of the pond gave the church bells the sweetest and purest tone in the country. Along with Wells and Cheddar, Banwell possessed one of the earliest Anglo-Saxon minster churches in north Somerset. All were dedicated to St Andrew, and all were at or near powerful springs.[7]

Less than 100 yards from the Banwell spring was **Adams Well** (ST398590), a much smaller affair which arose on the north side of the Winscombe Road, and which may indeed still be *in situ* under one of the houses which line the road. In the late 18th century the well was described as 'a spring of excellent water ... most limpid and pure,' supplying villagers with domestic water and 'formerly esteemed for its efficacy in scrofulous disorders.'[8]

On the western edge of the parish a spring called **Bridewell** formed one of the boundary markers of the old Anglo-Saxon Banwell estate. The exact position of the spring is not certain; it may be below the earthwork on Elborough Hill or it may be the small muddy spring that rises in a field south of the Bridewell Lane motorway bridge (ST308582).[9]

Barrow Gurney

Barrow has four wells, the most interesting and accessible being the **Fairy Well** (ST532686)* which rises in a spinney where a footpath crosses the brook west of Wild Country Lane. With the possible exception of the 'Fairy Pit' at North Stoke this is the only well in the Bristol region with an association with the little folk, although even the oldest villager cannot remember how the fairies became connected with this well. All that is told is that people would go to the well to bathe their eyes, for the water was believed to be good in the treatment of all eye complaints. A local woman remembers that her father, who worked the land in this neighbourhood, would always drink from the well using a cup which was never taken away or used for any other purpose.

A drinking **fountain** (ST536676)* at the junction

Barrow Gurney's drinking fountain, also the village war memorial, and additionally haunted by the ghost of a 'white lady'

of the A38 and B3130 is haunted by the ghost of a woman in white who also crosses the main road, much to the distress of motorists.[10] This is one of the region's more modern ghosts, said to be a young woman killed as she crossed the road following an accident in the 1960s. Another motorist reported the ghost as being that of an old man in raincoat and cap.

Further up Barrow Hill, 400 metres north of Freeman's Farm, is the site of the **Bridewell** (ST518672), the old spring now little more than a damp spot in a small scrubby hollow; no folklore is recorded from this site.[11]

On the hillside behind Springhead Farm rises **Cold Bath Spring** (ST525676), once one of the main supplies for the Bristol Waterworks Company. The name implies that the waters were once used for medicinal purposes.

Bathampton

Within the village there is a never-failing **spring** (ST776663)* which issues from the mouth of a stone dog's head and flows into a stone trough. Somerset antiquary and well enthusiast, Ethelbert Horne, thought that the trough may once have been used as a bath for curative purposes.[12]

The spring and possible cold bath at Bathampton

Batheaston

This Cotswold parish, lying 4km east of central Bath was once noted for two sources of mineral water, both of which rose on the south-western side of Banner Down. A **Cold Bath** (ST785680) is shown on Thomas Thorpe's map of 1742—three buildings erected on the northern side of Fosse Lane, behind the modern housing of what is now High Bannerdown.[13] Less than 1km to the west,

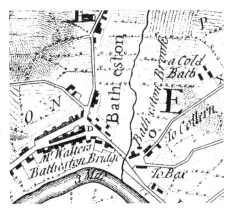

A map surveyed by Thomas Thorpe in 1742 of Bath and five miles around shows 'a Cold Bath' just to the east of Batheaston

at the side of St Catherine's Brook, mineral waters were recorded in the 1870s as rising from an old deserted mine shaft.[14] Neither site achieved any lasting fame.

Bathford

There are a number of interesting wells in this parish, chief of which are St Anthony's Well and St Mary's Well, both in the hamlet of Shockerwick. **St Anthony's Well** (ST803681)* rises in the hedgebank on the north side of a lane, just east of Middle Lodge. It is a stone-sided alcove with water trickling in from under the surrounding field. As recently as the

St Mary's Well, Bathford

1920s there was a complete wellhouse here although now there are only a few pieces of old masonry to suggest this.[15] Coins at the base of the well indicate that it is still thought of as a wishing well, but it was also once believed to be medicinal and was 'Esteemed for its efficacy in the cure of Inflamations and Rheums in the eyes.'[16]

St Mary's Well (ST801687) is the name given to a collection of field springs which flow together into a stone trough in a field called Ladywells on Lower Shockerwick Farm. It appears to have been also called Our Lady's Well, but local people long ago ceased to acknowledge the well and by the early years of this century it had almost faded into obscurity. Indeed, were it not for the efforts of local holy well enthusiast Gerald Grey in the 1920s, who managed to track down a very old man who remembered the well, it would almost certainly have been lost to us. Tradition relates that a chapel once stood nearby.[17]

However, these two holy wells were eclipsed in fame by the **Bathford Spa** (ST791672). Discovered in the 1740s, on the south bank of Box Brook, the curative mineral waters were soon being used by local people and achieved a particular reputation in the cure of wounds and running sores. A pavilion was built over the spring in 1746, but the site was later bought by a Bath doctor who used it for his own pleasure, discouraging public access. The Spa eventually fell into disuse and little remains at the site which was near the Mill buildings north of the village.[18]

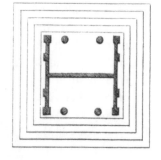

Plan and Elevation of the pavilion for the spring at Bathford Spa (from John Wood's An Essay towards a Description of Bath

Blagdon

In Blagdon Combe there rises one of the great wells of the Mendip Hills: the **Shirbourne Spring** (ST498591)*, which takes its name from the Old English words for 'bright or radiant stream'.[19] The spring is more commonly known as Rickford Rising and emerges from the dark wooded hillside less than ten metres south of Rickford Millpond.

Two more notable springs are found near the parish church of St Andrew. Just north of, and below, the church is the **Lower Well** (ST505590), traditionally shunned by villagers in the belief that it was contaminated from the adjacent graveyard. More wholesome and impressive is **Timsell Well** (ST502589)*, an old stone reservoir-cum-wellhouse with a small basin beneath a defunct tap, and with a couple of stone benches on either side. Most of the water is now diverted into a stock pool, but this was once the main village water supply and was also the source of baptismal water. An old woman would fill an ornate and metal-bound stave jar with water from the well and carry it up the hill for the baptism. This practice continued until relatively recently, for there are people in the village in their early 60s who were baptised with Timsell Well water; the jug is on display within the church, at the foot of the font.

St Andrew's Church, Blagdon, seen from the wall by the Timsell Well

163

Brockley

Towards the top of Brockley Combe, on the southern side of the road, a small tributary valley leads to the remarkable **Pots Hole** (ST483662)* where every seven years, so folklore tells us, 'a stream bursts forth' and rushes down the side of the road with sufficient force to turn a mill. Another folktale says that when the spring flows it is a prophesy of war. With a modern understanding of hydrology it can be said that after exceptional rainfall this normally dry limestone depression becomes a raging torrent. An 18th century boundary stone is set in the wall behind the Hole, marking the division between Brockley and Wrington parishes.[20] An even larger erratic spring, Great Pots Hole (ST485660) rises 400m to the southeast, often in conjunction with Pots Hole.

Burrington

On the southern lip of Burrington Combe, and strictly speaking in the parish of Priddy, there is a field called **Hawkeswell Quoit** (ST484580). 'Quoit' occurs in local placenames as a reference to ancient standing stones, often attributed to the work of either giants or the Devil. At this site, however, no stone or folklore has been recorded, but the juxtaposition of the spring name with a possible standing stone is of note, for in a number of cultures there is a strong association between megaliths with sacred waters.[21]

Butcombe

Cleeve's Well (ST513620)*, once one of the most noted holy wells in north Somerset, rises high above the village, along the roadside of Yew Tree Batch. Its name means 'spring on the steep slope' and so notable was

Cleeve's Well, Butcombe

the power of this well that people would travel great distances in the hope of effecting cures for a whole range of diseases. Its waters were particularly renowned for their powers in curing eye disorders due, it is said, to the spring's rising on the eastern side of a hill, a location thought especially useful for the eyes. 19th century commentators described Cleeve's Well as 'a remarkable spring never known to fail' and, indeed, during the severe drought of 1921 it was the lifeblood for eight local dairy farms who had suffered the loss of their own water supplies. Masonry foundations indicate that there may once have been a stone structure around the spring. A local woman, Mrs Mary Bendall, cares for the well and has erected a sign recording its name for the benefit of passing motorists. Mrs Bendall attests to the well's curative powers, claiming how the many cuts and scratches suffered by her hands in clearing bramble and debris from its surrounds, heal completely within three days, leaving neither scabs nor scars.[22]

Charlcombe

Of the many springs in this parish the most famous is **St Alphage's Well** (ST725681)* which rises amongst a grove of storm-battered beech trees just below the eastern end of Lansdown Race Course. Built into a stone bank, the spring is hidden behind an old wooden

door, flowing into its stone chamber with a musical gurgling and an occasional drumming. A few metres to the west is another spring in a stone wellhouse, identical to that of St Alphage, and it too flows briskly.

St Alphage's Well was a favoured haunt of gypsies, whilst a 19th century poem recorded the virtue of the 'holy stream' being sought by

St Alphage's Well, Charlcombe

the blind, the lame and the impotent, supplicants kneeling before the well and bathing in its waters. The water was believed to be of 'singular purity' and was until recently sought after by the Catholic Church of St Alphage in Bath, who came to take away a gallon of the holy water for use in the baptismal font.[23] At one time there was a deposit of soot on the roof of the well chamber, left by the burning candles of generations of pilgrims.

Legend tells us that St Alphage, a native of nearby Weston, developed a reputation as a holy man and established a hermitage at a lonely spot near Bath, soon attracting a band of disciples. The hermitage may well have been near the well, for the unusual circular boundary around it suggests similarities with the sacred circular enclosures of the early church. The saint was elected Abbot of Bath and later became Archbishop of Canterbury, although in 1012 he was kidnapped by Danes and stoned to death at Greenwich.[24]

600m to the north of St Alphage's well lies Chapel Farm, opposite the Blathwayte Arms and site of the Bath Racecourse stables. The core of the farmhouse is a medieval chapel and hospice that was reputedly much used by pilgrims on their way to Glastonbury. The age of the building has been variously attributed to the 12th

Chapel Farm

166

century although a 15th century date seems more probable.[25] Beneath a cracked flagstone at the rear of the farmhouse in an area that was once the chapel graveyard, there once existed **St Lawrence's Well** (ST726687). This was a shaft well and was filled in with rubble during the 1940s. The family at Chapel Farm have been tenants for a century but do not recall the well or its water having any special virtue. The area immediately adjacent to the chapel has long been reputed to be the burial ground for soldiers killed at the battle of Lansdown in 1643, and there is also a tradition of a secret tunnel running from the battlefield and under the chapel to one of the cottages near the farm.[26]

At the heart of the shrunken village of Charlcombe is the atmospheric church of St Mary. This is said to be the mother church of Bath and may have been the chapel of a small monastic community. A holy well, sometimes called the **Monks Well**, but more

commonly, **St Mary's Well** (ST748673)*, rises nearby. The well originally rose in the grounds of the neighbouring Rectory, but was re-positioned and rededicated in 1989 at its present site when the Rectory was sold. It is in a public garden opposite the church where a modern stone carving of Christ being baptised in the Jordan stands above an elliptical pool, the sacred water being piped underground from its old site. The water was famous for being 'good for the

St Mary's Well at its new site

St Mary's Church, Charlcombe. The figures in the foreground with buckets are probably collecting water from St Mary's Well which rises less than 100m east of the church

eyes' and many people took bottles of it away with them. It was also a wishing well, and supplied the church font with baptismal water.[27]

Chew Magna

There are two wells of interest here, although a third site—**St Winefred's Well**—which was renowned as a 'mother's well' was also said to be found here, but if it ever existed, it is now lost.[28]

East of the village, at Blacklands, is the **Bully Well** (ST580642), the waters of which are believed to be good for the eyes. The cold, clear water rises beneath a three-stemmed ash and flows into a stone basin in the bottom corner of a field.[29]

In the village itself, the fifteenth century Tun Bridge which spans the Chew is the unlikely site of a **wishing well** (ST577629)*. The eastern pier of the bridge terminates in a square trough which has been suggested as a socket for a cross or religious statue. Local lore states that during outbreaks of smallpox, country dwellers would collect their supplies from the trough to avoid the risk of infection. The trough enjoyed greater fame as a wishing well where 'creeping down at midnight and dipping your hand in the water, you get your wished-for-lover, or less romantically, cure your warts.'[30] The water supply at this well is rain-derived and given to periodic drying out.

Tun Bridge Wishing Well

Chew Stoke

The appropriately named Pagan's Hill to the north of the village was the site of one of the most important Romano-British temples in the West Country. On a minor hilltop commanding extensive views, a 6th century BC Iron Age shrine was developed, around 300 AD, into a Romano-British temple complex. The layout of the site displayed a deliberate orientation on a north-west to south-east axis and west of the temple, and on the same axis, was a **sacred well** (ST557626) some 56 feet deep, used for the deposition of votive offerings. Lead curses found nearby may have performed a similar function to those found at the Sacred Spring in Bath—intercessions with deities on behalf of those who felt aggrieved or cheated. Excavation of the site produced evidence of a possible cult in the shape of a finely carved statue of a dog, a motif also found in Roman temples in Bath and west Wiltshire. The well and temple went out of use in the mid-4th century, only to be reoccupied, probably by Christians, in the 7th

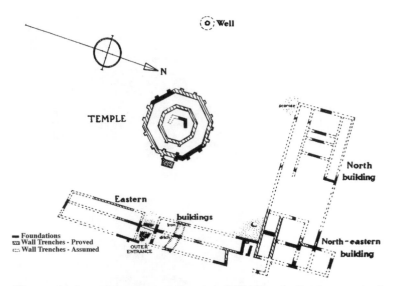

Above: A plan of the Roman Pagan's Hill Temple Settlement made by excavators Philip Rahtz and Leslie Harris, the former seen below at the temple's well (SANHS collection)

and 8th centuries when its use for votive purposes appears to have been revived.[31]

Three-quarters of a mile south of Pagan's Hill there is the wayside spring of **St Anthony's Well**, (ST559614) which has been covered over by a concrete cap since the 1950s. Rising immediately east of the B3114, by Fairseat Farm, and opposite the junction with Breach Hill Lane, the well was less than a hundred metres south of the site of a supposed stone circle that stood by what is now the Methodist chapel. Again, just east of the B3114, near Ben Bridge, there rose **St Mary's Well** (ST557594), now submerged beneath one of the western bays of Chew Valley Lake. There was an ancient crossroads here called St Cross, also known as Moreton Cross, and close by was a cell of four nuns. The well was never known to run dry and a wellhouse or chapel stood near the site from where a medieval pilgrim's token was excavated in the 1950s. Although the spring is now lost it is gratifying to think that its waters now form part of Bristol's water supply and almost a million people are unwittingly drinking the water of an ancient holy well![32]

Churchill

Near the parish church of St John, and in the hedgebank of King Lane, is the **Bishop's Well** (ST438602)* which flows only after periods of prolonged wet weather. It is an inconspicuous spring, but its name hints at a grander past, perhaps associated with one of the great missionary bishops of the Saxon era such as St Aldam?[33]

The footpath north-west from the Bishop's Well leads to the low-lying field known as Bridewell Bottom. The **Bridewell** spring (ST441604)* which gave the field its name is at first sight unremarkable, being a large damp hollow at the crux of two hedges. However, local lore states that long ago a bride left St John's

The Bridewell, haunted by the ghost of a young woman

Church on her wedding day and walked along the footpath to the well where she threw herself in and drowned. The story does not say why this happened, but it is said that her ghost haunts the well, still dressed in her shimmering bridal gown.[34]

On the border with Burrington parish is the **Hylisbrook Spring** (ST466593)*: the 'Great Spring' recorded in the Anglo-Saxon estate charter of 904 AD. One of a number of powerful north Mendip springs, Hylisbrook rises suddenly and spectacularly from within a small wooded grove with a sufficient volume of water to create a sizeable stream. The site, also known as Langford Spring, has yielded evidence of Roman activity including the remains of a small building that may have been a temple or shrine, as well as some Roman artefacts. There is no proof that the spring was ever venerated, but local people will tell of the power and magnetism they feel inherent at this place.[35]

Clevedon

On the northern edge of Clevedon town is Ladye Bay where a **spring** (ST408709)* flows out among the boulders from the base of the northern cliffs. Some have speculated that this was once a holy well although little evidence is offered to back this theory; however it is said to be one of the haunts of the Grey Lady or Dark Lady, a spectral figure who roamed the area between the coast and the old church at Walton-in-Gordano. The adjacent caves have yielded a remarkable carving of what some have claimed is a Celtic head, (similar to one found above the Monk's Well on Steep Holm island). Another cave near the spring is believed to be the entrance to a secret tunnel that led to Old Park House in Walton.[36]

There is also a **spring** (ST409726) which rises by the church-yard wall of St Mary's at Walton and which flows out to sea at Ladye Bay; however its proximity to the burial ground and fears of contamination meant that its waters were little used.

In the early years of this century the **waters** which fed the Baths near the Pier Hotel were said to be a 'sovereign remedy for hair problems.'[37]

172

Combe Hay

In the private grounds of the Old Rectory a landscaped stream cascades towards the road. 20 metres from the driveway a spring rises at the streamside, enclosed by square stone walls but open to the sky. This is the **White Lady's Well** (ST735600). No folklore survives, but from the name it was either owned by Cistercian nuns or may once have had a well ghost, perhaps shared with St Julian's Well in the neighbouring parish of Wellow. The Wellow ghost was believed to walk the district, so it is not impossible that Combe Hay may have been one of her haunts.[38]

White Lady's Well

Compton Martin

On the western boundary of the parish, and on the south side of the A368, is a neglected triangle of shrubby ground. Here, amongst a pile of garden waste is the **Barrow Well** (ST537573)*. At least two springs issue forth here to form one of the headwaters of the Congresbury Yeo. The name of the well is interesting for no barrow has been recorded in the vicinity, despite the adjacent field names being Barrows Orchard and Barrow Cross. Local folklore states that the well was haunted by the ghost of a woman washing cabbages—a more bizarre ghostly activity is hard to imagine!

Could the ghost have been a variant of the 'Washer-at-the-ford'? In Celtic lands, a sight of this otherworldly woman washing her bloody clothes would lead a warrior to believe that his violent death was close at hand. Closely associated with the Washer was the Banshee ('the woman of the mound') a supernatural figure often found near ancient fairy mounds.[39]

800 metres to the east, below the Norman parish church of St Michael, and adjacent to the village pond, is an ornate green pillar-box structure. This is the **Dipping Well** (ST545570)* of which the Rev. Collinson wrote 'Near the church rises a spring, the source of the river Yow.'[40] The Congresbury Yeo is fed by a large number of tributaries which have their source in sacred or remarkable springs. No other river system in this area shows a similar pattern—was the Yeo itself once thought a holy river?

Compton Martin's third remarkable spring is the **Rag Well** (ST547566)* which rises in the eastern hedgebank of the hazel-shrouded Highfield Lane—the old Roman road from Mendip into the Chew valley. This was the haunt of gypsies and the only documented holy well in North Somerset where strips of rags were tied to trees and bushes growing nearby. The leaving of rags at holy wells is a truly universal phenomenon, the rags are votive offerings left to aid the cure of the weak bodies that had been bathed in the well water. The Rag Well was held to be particularly good at curing bad eyes and sprained feet, as well as fulfilling the more utilitarian role of being the village's main water supply.[41]

Congresbury

The village of Congresbury was reputedly founded around the monastery established by St Congar, a shadowy 7th century figure from 'over the seas'. Many legends surround the life and works of Congar, most no doubt historically untenable. However, during the 7th century the local population did move to Congresbury from the Dark Age settlement on Cadbury Hill. The site they left was once home to a Romano-British temple and, until the mid-19th century, a venue for witchcraft on May Eve. May Eve, or Beltane, was also the feast of St Congar, an event marked by the women of Congresbury who gathered at the **Stonewell** (ST437634), south of the parish church, to dance around it barking like dogs. There is a legend which records how Congar would rise early each morning and 'enter the cold water where he stayed until he had thrice repeated the Lord's prayer.' Somerset folklorist Ruth Tongue speculated that there was an association between St Congar and conger eels which are reputed to 'bark', but such eels are marine fish and Congresbury is 8km from the sea. To add even more conjecture, some commentators claim that it was in fact the **Southwell** (ST441641), on the northern side of the village, which was the focus for ritual activity and not the Stonewell. Either way, both wells now lie under modern housing estates and Congresbury is the poorer for it.[42]

Dundry

A field known as **Holywell** (ST560690) is on the north-western boundary of the parish, east of the A38 and only a field away from the southern suburbs of Bristol. No folklore has survived for this site and the well is effectively lost amidst scrub and building waste.[43]

Immediately opposite the parish church of St Michael, a stone alcove built into a roadside wall marks the site of the **West Church Well** (ST557668)*, once a major water supply for the village.

East Harptree

One of northern Mendip's most interesting landforms is Harptree Combe, a wooded gorge which forms the boundary between the parishes of East and West Harptree. Half way along its length the Combe forks at a great spur of rock on which sits the foundations of Richmont Castle, an ancient seat of the de Gourney family. Cursed spirits of the de Gourneys are said to walk the Combe at night, as does the more sinister figure of Satan; a reminder of the Combe's alternative name: The Devil's Batch.[44]

At the western foot of the castle hill, and in the longer, western branch of the Combe, is the **King's Castle Well** (ST560558)*, alias the Harptree Wishing Well. The well sits at the base of a lush ferny bank—a spring rising in a small rockpool, a sharp-edged natural basin which holds the cool, clear water. Elderly villagers remember being brought here as children to throw coins into the well and make a wish which had to be made three times in silence before the water was drunk out of the hand. Barren women seeking fertility would come to the well and drop bent pins into the water, large numbers of which were annually brought to the surface during clearance work. The ghost of the Combe was seen by the well at the turn of the century when a group sitting opposite saw the figure of a man in a long cloak and a large black hat of a kind not in fashion at the time; he seemed to them to have a rather 'displeased' expression.[45]

Elsewhere in the parish a field called **Spring Ground** was the site of a phantom funeral procession.[46]

Easton-in-Gordano

Less than 100m from the church of St George, at 41 Church Road, is an unusual **canopied well** (ST514758)*. Its deep shaft is roofed and enclosed on two sides, whilst the other sides, facing the road and house, are open. Parts of the structure may be medieval and it is thought the design allowed shared access between the Manor House on one side and the public on the other. The modern house

The canopied well

Pill Spout

is called Merriwell; the position close to the church and along the village funeral path, is of note.

In the riverside village of Pill, a spout pours forth water into a stone trough at the rear of the shops along Baltic Place. This is **Pill Spout** (ST525757)* whose waters were once believed to be 'good for you' and never froze over nor dried up in the summer. Local people still remember being sent, as children, to fetch jars of the water to drink on Sundays. Before the construction of the shopping precinct the spout issued some 20m to the south and the water is now deemed unfit for consumption. The spout owes its origins to local magnate Sir William Miles who paid for a pipeline to be constructed between Pill and the Maiden's Spring in Wraxall parish, outbreaks of cholera in the village having shown that the native water supply was no longer safe nor adequate.

Englishcombe

A document of 1609 gives the name **Halywells** *i.e.* 'holy well' as a place in this parish although the exact location is unknown. It may have referred to a **well** (ST719630) in the middle of Culverhay Castle, a former seat of the de Gourney family, and which today is little more than a grassy mound. Until the late 18th century there was a great curiosity about the well. In 1765 John Wood wrote: 'People imagined great Treasures to have been hid (in it), and reported that Lights in the Night time were often seen hovering about the work.'[47] It was furthermore the haunt of a ghost, believed to be that of one of the de Gourneys. A large maple tree grew over the well, but this was felled to allow treasure seekers access. In

Culverhay Castle. What is believed to have been a haunted, treasure-filled well rose within its circuit

doing so they discovered none of the curiosities that they had sought but in their excavation showed the well to have been nine feet in diameter and dressed with finely worked stone.[48]

Farmborough

At the foot of Blackberry Hill, at Crossways, there is a small road-side **pond** (ST646597)*. A man named Bridges claimed that on many occasions he had been led through this pond by the devil, although looking at the quiet, silted-up pool now, it is hard to visualise its former reputation.[49]

Half a kilometre to the north-west, and south of the middle section of Tilley Lane, there is a striking **field well** (ST655603)* where it is claimed that in the last century a woman committed suicide. More than once travellers along Tilley Lane have reported seeing her ghost, known as Long Anne, sitting on the old well beckoning them to join her.[50]

The western end of Tilley Lane is also haunted; white, misty looking objects accompanied by the sound of a running chain being seen at the field known as **Cold Bath** (ST655603), a name suggestive of a healing spring. Nearby is the settlement of Hobb's Wall — alternatively **Hobb's Well** — where Roman burials have been discovered.[51]

Long Anne's Well, Farmborough, where a ghostly figure beckons travellers to join her in her watery grave

Flax Bourton

At the southern end of Bourton Combe a spring rises once or twice a year after heavy rainfall. It is called **Stancombe Spring** (ST507680)* and can be so large that it forms a stream which flows north to flood the surrounding farmland. The area where the spring rises is believed to be haunted and until very recently a field just to the south was where local children were taken 'to see the fairies'.[52] To the north-east of the Combe, on the border with Long Ashton, is a field called **Puxpitt**. In his recent work on holy wells the historian James Rattue notes how the place-name element 'pit' can indicate a holy well, as in the medieval Pylgrimesput in Southampton. Thus in Flax Bourton there may be the well of Puck, the Anglo-Saxon goblin or elemental spirit. As if in confirmation of this there is the folktale of an old oak tree which formerly stood next to the field, along Barrow Court Lane, and by which, at each Hallowe'en, the ghost of a woman would appear.[53]

500m north of Puxpitt field is the spring known as **Snakewell** (ST514693), one of four similarly-named springs in a tight cluster of adjacent parishes south-west of Bristol. The Flax Bourton name

The Romanesque carving of St Michael killing a serpent

may be connected with the Romanesque carving over the doorway of St Michael's Church, 1km to the south-west, which shows a religious figure killing a serpent. For a full discussion on the Snakewell enigma see p.204.

High Littleton

At Hallatrow (a place-name which means 'holy tree') there was once a **well** (*c*.ST6357), the waters of which were in demand for those who had been bitten by mad dogs. It is perhaps appropriate that the churchwardens of Bitton in south Gloucestershire are recorded as having sent for Hallatrow water when one of their parishioners met this fate.[54]

Hinton Charterhouse

Hinton's main interest lies in the ruined Carthusian priory north of the village. The priory (also known as Hinton Abbey) has no holy well, but is intimately connected with **Ela's Well** (ST786590), 1km to the east in Friary Wood. Ela was a 13th century Countess of Salisbury who was renowned for her great devotion and virtue. Many tales were told of her piety, including her founding Lacock Abbey in Wiltshire on the same day in May in 1232 that her husband founded Hinton Priory. It is said that after attending the Lacock founding ceremony in the morning she rode the 12 miles to the Hinton ceremony, stopping on the way to drink at the spring that would henceforth bear her name.[55]

The well was once associated with a chapel which stood in the hamlet of Friary and it acquired a reputation as a healing well, especially for those with eye problems. It is even stated that within living memory a blind woman bathed her eyes at the well and had her sight restored. However, there is more to this well than medicinal powers. Old reports of phantom monks being seen around it gained a greater currency a few years ago. A forester was just completing a winter day's work in Friary Wood and was driving back at dusk towards Friary, on a track just below Ela's Well. As he drove by he looked over towards the well and saw a figure in white standing alongside it, 'The hairs on the back of my neck stood on end and I pulled the throttle back and drove out of the wood as fast as I could.'[56]

The well is difficult to find, is on private land and permission from the landowner should be sought. The easiest route is to take the metalled track from the A36 down to Friary. After 600m on the left a metal five-barred gate leads onto an earth track. Immediately after the gate a small stream runs across the track from the left. Follow this stream uphill for about 20m. This will lead to the well, framed on three sides by what is probably medieval walling. With its pure and cold water, this is a primitive, earthy and powerfully atmospheric site.

In the far west of the parish is the **Ladywell** (ST767574), a series of seepages rather than a spring, which rise in the western half of a lush valleyside conifer plantation. No folklore or historical associations have been recorded for this site.

Hutton

In pastureland to the east of St Mary's Church is the **Ladies Well** (ST355585) framed by a stone lintel and two stone uprights, and looking rather like a mini dolmen. There is an old belief that nuns were once resident in what is now Hutton Court, 200m to the west, and it is claimed that their bath house stood by the well and that they used the well water for all their everyday needs. It is also said that monks used to come here to bathe every night, presumably this was once the nuns had departed![57]

800m north-east of Ladies Well is the hamlet of **Ludwell** (ST358592)*, a name which literally means 'loud well' and which refers to the spring that rises in a private garden. Visible from an adjacent footpath, the spring's flow is dependent on the volume of water in the limestone cave system of which it is a part. After a heavy rainfall the water gushes with such force that on a still night the noise can be heard up to half a mile away. The local Roman population certainly felt the place to have spiritual associations for they buried their dead around the well.

The Ladies Well, Hutton, formerly a 'nun's bath house'

Kelston

Several **medicinal springs** rose on the slopes of Lansdown Hill in this parish although their location is not clear. One may have been at the **Broadmoors Well** (ST702676) reservoir below Coombe Barn.[58]

The stream running west of Dean Hill House was once part of the border of the Saxon estate of Weston and was called the **Pucan Wylle** (ST710666) or 'Goblin's Well'.[59]

Kewstoke

Opposite the parish church of St Paul is a steep flight of steps the construction of which is assigned to either the monks of Woodspring Priory or the shadowy Dark Age figure of St Kew. Roughly half way up the steps a **pit** (ST336532) was found in the 19th Century, associated with a structure that was either a medieval chapel or a hermit's cell. The fact that the pit may have been a votive well is suggested by a bizarre selection of objects found within it, ranging in date from the Iron Age to late Medieval. Unfortunately, both pit and building were destroyed in 1941 by a stray bomb.[60]

The Monks' Steps or St Kew's Steps

In the north of this parish are the romantic ruins of Woodspring Priory, complete with majestic tithe barn. Beneath a walnut tree at the eastern end of the barn is the Woodspring **Holy Well** (ST343662); a stone staircase of 15 steps leading down seven feet in a broad spiral to a slow-flowing spring which takes several days to fill to the top. It is a curious structure which may have been an immersion well, although no folklore has survived to offer any clues. Local lore does, however,

Woodspring Priory

183

Medieval Tithe Barn at Woodspring Priory. The holy well rises at the foot of the tree to the right of the barn

hold that the blackbirds around Woodspring sing differently, retaining in their song the sacred music once heard here. This is remarkably similar to an account from the 10th century Irish text, *The Journey of St Brendan*, which describes how Brendan and his followers came to an island and found a well overshadowed by a tree, the branches of which were covered with birds singing holy music.[61]

Contrary to expectation the Holy Well, now in a private garden and not usually open to the public, is not the origin of the name Woodspring; the name instead comes from an Old English source meaning the 'Worle's coppice wood' — Worle being a neighbouring parish.

Keynsham

Keynsham's holy well is the **Hawkswell** (ST652690)*, 300m to the north-west of the parish church and inches away from the edge of the by-pass which destroyed much of the remains of the Augustinian abbey which once stood between the parish church and the River Chew. At one time the waters of Hawkswell flowed into an old stone basin but the site is now a lush, damp area beneath a flourishing young lime tree. Hawkswell water was reputedly good for the eyes and it is said that when cattle graze this field they always sleep around the spring. The well may be the one mentioned in the story of St Keyna after whom the town is allegedly named.

Keyna was a Welsh holy woman who found solace in a lonely wood near Keynsham and turned to stone a great number of snakes that had infested the area. She then prayed for water and a spring burst forth 'which gave health to many infirm people.'[62]

In Saltford village there is (or was) a **pool** (ST686678?) in the old Park area, to the north of the church, which was believed to be connected to the Manor House by a secret tunnel.[63]

Locking

In the grounds of Locking Manor there was once a **haunted well** (ST364589). It is now under a car park but its legend is one of the most interesting in the Bristol region.

In 1685, the Lord of the Manor, John Plumley, joined the Duke of Monmouth's disastrous rebellion and, after the final defeat at the Battle of Sedgemoor, fled back to Locking. To avoid detection he hid in a cave at the mysterious Locking Head Castle. Unfortunately, the family's faithful dog found him and when Loyalist troops were close at hand he barked at them, inadvertently drawing them to his master. Dragging Plumley from his hiding place the troops then hanged him in full view of his wife who ran back to the Manor. Unable to contain her grief she picked up the dog, ran out to the well which stood in the driveway, and threw herself down. Both she and the dog were drowned.[64]

From that day forward the ghost of a White Lady accompanied by a phantom hound was seen by many in the village. The ghosts followed a regular path through the grounds of the Manor which became known as the Ghost walk ; most frequently they appeared between two ancient yew trees and, if seen, would vanish only to reappear near the well, sometimes jumping up and down the well-shaft.[65] As with so many well ghosts, that of Lady Plumley is said to resemble a bride and in *Old North Somerset* (p.23) the Rev. Alan Holt quotes an anonymous poem on the Locking legend which emphasises this fact:

> And on some evenings, now 'tis said
> She walks the drive just like a bride,
> Arrayed in white and shimmering gown.

Unfortunately the ghosts have not been seen for over a hundred years, not since renovations at the Manor had ripped down a false wall, behind which lay a secret chamber. Local opinion held that this chamber had been the ghosts' home when not haunting the well, and once exposed the ghosts could no longer remain, leaving flight their only option.

Long Ashton

Along Dawsons Walk, in the narrow valley where Ashton Brook flows through attractive mature woodland, there is a waterfall which thunders down after heavy rain. On the left bank of the stream, near the foot of the fall, is the **Drop Spring** (ST544700)*: the protruding end of an old iron pipe, water dripping from it at a slow but constant rate of 2 or 3 drops per minute. I was taken to this spot by Mr Yeo who, 87 at the time, was the oldest native-born resident of the village. Many years ago Mr. Yeo's father would come here if any members of the family had an eye problem, for the Drop Spring water was guaranteed to help those with bad eyes. It was the practice to stand a medicine bottle below the pipe to collect the drops of the oily spring water. The drops came so slowly that it took 24 hours to fill the bottle, although others reckoned that a week was needed and up to ten bottles at a time could be found stood by the spring awaiting their turn to be filled. The spring is alleged to have been discovered in 1892 by a villager suffering from conjunctivitis who found great relief after applying the water to his eyes.[66]

Near the Drop Spring, and along Lynbrook, there was a spring known as the **Snakewell** (ST541701)*. Despite its name being ripe for folkloric association, no legends or beliefs are recorded here.[67]

In the village itself there was a **domestic well** off the driveway of an old house, although the exact site is not clear. Builders were renovating the house one June 13th when, just before noon, the figure of a woman came up the driveway from the road. She was apparently in her mid-30s, wore Victorian dress and walked very slowly with a fixed, glassy stare. Upon reaching a sundial on the lawn she folded her hands and slowly disappeared into the ground. When the owner of the house returned the perplexed builders immediately quizzed him about this woman. 'Oh yes' he replied, 'she always appears on this day—it was the day she committed suicide. It happened about a hundred years ago; she was a maid-servant here, but was crossed in love and threw herself down the well. The well has since been blocked up, but it was there, beneath the sundial.'[68]

HOBWELL LANE

At the eastern end of the village is the district of **Hobwell** (ST550710), probably deriving its name from the ghostly mischievous sprite called Hobb, more commonly known as Puck. On the opposite side of the road is a field called Spirts, a name often believed to be a contraction of 'spirits' and thus a signifier of a haunted site.[69]

Further east again and just below the western pier of the Clifton Suspension Bridge, on the left bank of the Avon, there rose the **Scarlet Well** (ST564728) which issued immediately opposite its more famous neighbour, the Hotwell, and at its peak discharged 100 gallons per minute. In the Middle Ages a hermitage and chapel stood beside it and in later years it was a Cold Bath, used in the cure of disease, before later powering a succession of mills. During the 17th century it became known as The Mill-Spring but its medicinal reputation remained strong for large numbers of people, from both near and far, came to take its waters.[70]

Marksbury

In Hungerford Bottom, 1km to the west of Marksbury village, a spring rises and forms a small stream in a field called **Easter Wells** (ST657621)*. No folklore has been recorded but the name is suggestive of waters held to be at their most efficacious at this time of year.[71]

In the south of the parish, along Conygre Brook, and on the borders of Priston and Farmborough parishes, is a truly powerful well—the **Rattlespring** (ST673612). Until the early decades of the century, the well drew people from as far as Midsomer Norton and Bath to seek its sight-restoring waters; the miners of the Somerset coalfield being particularly convinced of its power, making an unofficial pilgrimage here until the late 1920s. Children were thought to be especially receptive to its curative powers and bottles of water were taken away for those unable to make the journey. The spring rises in a sombre glade on the boundary with Farmborough parish, 100m west of where a footpath crosses Conygre Brook at the head of a small tributary stream. Half-hidden in deep shade is a stone bank, dappled with ivy. At the foot of this bank the spring pours out of an undercut recess in the rock.There is a tangible sense of power here, a timeless setting for the never-failing spring, brooding in its isolation.

A third Marksbury spring is that described in an Anglo-Saxon estate charter of 936 AD: the **Merewelle** (ST6762) or 'boundary spring'. This is believed to have been on the old parish boundary with Stanton Prior.[72]

Nailsea

The **stream** (ST464714)* near Milton's Farm, on the northern edge of town, was resorted to by those suffering from arthritis who bathed their feet and legs at a certain point along its banks. Perhaps this is the site of the vanished and long-forgotten **spa** which reputedly once stood in this part of the parish?

There was also once a 'remarkable well' in the hamlet of West End, probably the never-failing **Gaul Well** (ST451698) which is now under a manhole cover in a muddy paddock. Elsewhere within the old core of Nailsea village itself there was said to be a **well** in a cottage garden which was haunted by the ghost of a witch.[73]

Nempnett Thrubwell

The parish takes part of its name from the **Thrub-well** (ST520635) which the early Victorian writer John Rutter informs us was a spring, 'formerly of some notoriety'.[74] The local place-name Merry Hill may be connected with this and commemorate some celebration, although anything could be hidden by the rather prudish term 'notoriety'. The name is thought to mean 'a bubbling spring', and although the exact site of the Thrubwell is not recorded it is generally accepted as being in the grounds of Thrubwell Farm.[75] Perhaps it is the small, spring-fed pool very close to the Merry Hill crossroads, which is believed never to freeze or dry up. Curiously, this pool lies directly over the line of a 'secret tunnel' that is reputed to run from Butcombe Court to Regilbury Court.

North Stoke

The rather idiosyncratic parish church of St Martin stands near the rising of a number of springs, the largest of which has recently become known to some people as **'the holy well'** (ST704691)*. Not far from the church, on the south side of Pipley Bottom, is a field called **Fairy Pit** (ST707694), perhaps another example of the word 'pit' being used in the context of a holy well.[76]

Norton-Radstock

St Chad's Well rises at the base of the obelisk

At the Island, in the heart of Midsomer Norton, and less than 200m from the parish church, is **St Chad's Well** (ST662540)*. This is a never-failing spring which feeds a small pool within a stone grotto, the water then flowing into the adjacent River Somer. Surmounting both spring and grotto is a large 19th Century obelisk upon which is a tablet commemorating the Crimean War veteran Major Frederick Stukeley-Savage, and stating: 'This memorial is erected by his mother, who in accordance with his wish, has endeavoured to improve the spring for the benefit of the poor of the parish.'

It has been argued that the name 'St Chad's Well' dates only from the time of Stukeley-Savage's improvements, (indeed the name could also derive from the dialect form of 'cold well'), but the folklore of the site suggests that it may have had beliefs associated with it before this date. Old people told of coming to the well when a fair was in town, the fair people asking local children to fetch them water from the well, 'cause they reckoned it was the best water they had ever drank and they wouldn't touch anything else while they were here.'[77] The Somerset folklorist Ruth Tongue recorded 'General Tonic and Curative Purposes' associated with the water, and indeed until the end of the 19th century local midwives considered it a cure for weak eyes in new-born babies. St Chad's also has a reputation as a wishing well.[78]

Paulton

The sight of hard-pressed ponies pulling drays of coal up Paulto' Hill induced 19th century benefactress Julia Hill to build a stone trough for them beside an ancient stone basin that had long held the waters of **Paulto' Spring** (ST658565)*. A metal tank now augments Hill's trough, all three containers holding never-failing icy-cold spring water. There is no recorded folklore associated with Paulto' Spring but its spirit of place was acknowledged for four or

five years in the late 1980s by a well dressing ceremony held to mark its restoration. Although the water is now officially unfit to drink, old people from the neighbourhood still come to the spring on a Sunday and take away containers of the water to use in the making of wine.[79]

Paulto' Spring

A view of St Mary's Church, Portbury, from the in-filled pond by which once stood a standing stone

Portbury

The parish church of St Mary the Virgin is one of the oldest and most interesting in North Somerset. Immediately south of the church there is a monolith bearing a brass plaque to record the stone's rediscovery in 1987 after having been buried for 40 years. Originally the stone stood adjacent to a **field pond** (ST503754)*, immediately north-east of the church, which was filled in at the same time as the stone was buried. The juxtaposition of stone and pond, at the point where dry land would have given way to marsh, would suggest a ritual association as megaliths from the Bronze Age are frequently associated with sacred wells and pools.

Portishead

Half way up St Mary's Lane is the **Simmery Well** (ST461757)*, or **St Mary's Well**, a squat stone box of a structure at the bottom of a steep wooded bank. The water now barely more than seeps out of the ground due to the debris which fills the well chamber and the effect of housing development reducing its flow. Once, however, it had a reputation for miraculous healing powers for those with poor eyesight, indeed local people were so sure of its virtue that they sent the water off for laboratory analysis in the 1940s, although the results demonstrated little more than a high magnesium content. St Mary's Well is one of only four known 'pin wells' in the Bristol region—places where women who wanted children would offer up pins to the spring. This tradition was observed up to at least the 1960s. The medieval chapel of Our Lady at Capenor once stood nearby and remains including what is believed to be the head of a 'wand', have been found further down the lane.[80]

St Mary's Well, one of the region's four 'pin wells'

The Bronze 'wand' head found at Portishead. It doesn't appear to be Roman, but no medieval parallels have been found either

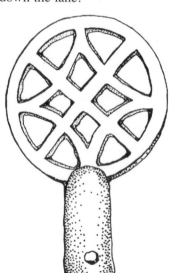

Priston

At the eastern end of the parish, on the border with Englishcombe, is a field called **Holywell** (ST700610). It is likely that the name derives from a small streamside spring, although there is no known folk-lore connected with it.[81]

St Catherine

The beautiful quiet valleys north of Batheaston shelter the hamlet of St Catherine: the church, Court and scattered farms which grew around a grange of Bath Abbey. Between the church and the Court

St Catherine's Well

there is an arched alcove containing an urn erected in the 1920s to replace a rough, square hole in the old Jacobean wall through which flowed the water of **St Catherine's Well** (ST777702)*. Before the alterations a trough caught the water, and by this there was a large stone on which pilgrims could kneel and pray as they took the waters. However, the well's true springhead (ST774698) is on the lip of Holt's Down high above the Court, where it is channelled into a stone wellhouse which draws the water of several springs together and which is then piped downhill to the alcove. There is no tradition of veneration at the source, all attention appears to have been paid to the site by the church where even into the 1920s large numbers of local people would come throughout the year to take away bottles of the healing water. In the adjacent churchyard the tragic ghostly figure of a white lady is occasionally seen.[82]

South Stoke

Five hundred metres south-west of the village lie a group of springs which are listed as part of the boundary of the Anglo-Saxon estate of South Stoke—the '**westran seofen wyllas**' (ST742609) or 'western seven wells'. The magical number seven must have made the springs ideal boundary markers, and given the site a greater strength in the local imagination.[83]

Stowey-Sutton

Two notable springs rise on private land east of Gold's Cross in the northern part of the parish. With **Drumhill Spring** (ST597612) we are reminded of the prophetic 'drumming wells' that are scattered throughout Britain. These springs were supposed to drum periodically, a phenomenon caused by air being trapped in rock cavities. Drumhill Spring emits a continuous low-pitched tattoo that can be heard ten feet away and is particularly impressive when heard at the springhead.[84]

100 metres to the north-east is the **Lining Spring** (ST600612), also called the Holwell. In this instance the name Holwell probably derives from the spring's situation in a 'hollow', rather than being a 'holy well'; nevertheless the deeply sunken springhead exerts a powerful presence, its dark wooded surroundings easily evoking the atmosphere of a sacred grove. Remains of a masonry wall across the spring imply that it was once enclosed by a well-house.[85]

The Church of St Nicholas and St Mary which may have started as a wayside well-shrine to the nearby petrifying spring

A third **spring** (ST599593) which rises above Stowey's medieval church has long drawn the interest of historians and topographers. Rising in open ash woodland at the foot of the prehistoric earthwork Mudstock Castle, it is reputedly never failing and is famous for its petrifying properties; whatever the water comes into contact with becomes encased in a hard lime crust. Contrary to its external petrifying qualities, in 1730 John Strachey described how it, 'Hath a different Effect on humane bodys for it has not been in memory of man of any one Inhabitant hath been afflicted with the Stone', (*i.e.* kidney stones). It has also been suggested that the church itself, far from any known settlement, originated as a wayside shrine associated with the spring.

Tickenham

Just north of Jacklands Bridge is Sunnyside cottage. At the bottom of the garden is a **healing well** (ST471717) which rises 'against the sun', rising as it does on the eastern side of a hill and flowing east. Popular lore held that most springs rose on the southern, western, or northern slopes and flowed 'away from' the rising sun, endowing springs such as this in the popular imagination with magical properties. In the days of coalmining at Nailsea the local doctor would send miners who came to him with eye complaints to this spring to bathe their eyes in its waters. Miss Fisher who lives at Sunnyside has drunk nothing but well water all her 92 years and survived a potentially fatal spinal tuberculosis. With the mind and skin of a woman thirty years her junior, the power of the well is hard to deny.

West of Sunnyside there is a crossroads on the B3130 with a road leading south to Tickenham Church and a track north to Folly Farm. In the north-western angle of this cross was the **Devil's Hole** (ST457718), a muddy pool surrounded by a small copse. This was reputedly the haunt of tramps but a more frightening presence must once have been felt for local children on their way to school were so frightened of this spot that they would cross to the other side of the road. Some would even run past it.[86]

Timsbury

At Northfield there was once a **field well** (ST673594) which children were instructed to avoid, for it was the abode of a mermaid!

195

Wellow

One of the most famous holy wells in north Somerset was **St Julian's Well** (ST742585)* which rises in the bank of the old canal, north-east of the parish church which shares its dedication. The well is now piped into a metal tank but once formed a large pool, its water was taken to the church for use in baptisms and the spring itself reckoned a wishing well. As a healing well its specialities were in the cure of weak eyes—'secured by bathing the lids'—and the granting of good fortune and longevity, guaranteed to those who drank its waters.[87] This gave rise to its alternative name of 'the lucky well'.[88] However the well's greatest fame rested in the form of 'the White ladye', a spectral figure who appeared at midnight on St Julian's Day, 'mourning by the crystal stream'. Her appearance was of ill omen to the house of Hungerford, who were once Lords of the Manor of Wellow, for it was said that misfortune was sure to befall the family when she appeared. The ghost was believed to have been of a tragic figure in the family's history murdered many centuries

*The old stone base of St Julian's Well rediscovered;
the spring now flows into the metal tank*

196

ago. Sometimes the white lady walked the district, though keeping the well as her base where she was seen to drink its water. The Hungerford family eventually left the parish and it is said that the white lady went with them, for she has not been seen since, and took her curse with her for this branch of the Hungerford family duly became extinct.[89]

Elsewhere in the parish an Anglo-Saxon estate charter of 766 AD lists the **Diornanwiel** or 'hidden spring' as a boundary marker.[90]

West Harptree

At Fair Ash, near the western parish boundary with Compton Martin, an intermittent pond known as **Stonystyle Pool** (ST551568)* was believed to be the place where strange, otherworldly creatures would vanish after haunting the lanes by the crossroads.[91]

Weston-Super-Mare

Weston was once famous for its 'miraculous' **ebbing and flowing wells** (ST313620), five of which issued on and above the strand line near the present Marine Lake. Two of these were on the eastern end of Manilla Crescent, one in the grounds of Glentworth Hall, one in Grove Park and one in the grounds of Cairo Lodge.[92]

The fascination of these springs lay in their curious interaction with the tides, being full at low tide and empty on a high tide. The main spring at Manilla Crescent was also thought to be a 'miracu-

The sea front at Weston-super-Mare.
The ebbing and flowing wells rose in this area

lous' wishing well with medicinal waters that were especially good in the treatment of eye disorders. The old people believed that this spring would always flow, but only so long as the fishermen threw back the first of their catch in the belief that, 'You look after they and they'll see you don't come to want', 'they' presumably being marine spirits who had to be shown respect.[93] All the springs are now built over and hidden from view.[94]

In Spring Cove, on the north side of Worlebury Hill, there was once a cave which was only accessible at low tide. In it was the **Dripping Well** (ST309625): 'a solemn place, high vaulted with water pure and cold, dripping from the roof into a crystal pool.'[95] The spring was famed for its medicinal waters which had 'great sanative virtues in diseases of the eyes.'[96] A secret tunnel was also believed to run from the well up to the Worlebury hillfort. Unfortunately a landslide destroyed the cave in 1861, however some token of the well's presence remains in the clear spring water which still drips from these cliffs.[97]

In Ashcombe Park there is a small reservoir covering what was once **Ernall's Spring** (ST335621)* next to which stood a large mound which was presumed to be ancient and was known locally as Ashcombe Batch. No folklore has been recorded at this site but just above it is the area known as Peep o'Day, believed to be the

The Celtic carved stone head found on Steep Holm in 1991

first place in Weston to be reached by the rays of the morning sun.[98]

In the old parish of Worle there was once a spring known as **St Julian's Well** although its location remains a mystery.[99]

Five miles off the coast of Weston, the small and deserted island of Steep Holm seems an unlikely site for a holy well, but just above East Beach is the **Monk's Well** (ST231607). The oily water from this spring certainly supplied the small Benedictine Priory which existed here in the Middle Ages, however it seems to have been venerated even earlier, for a carved human face found in woodland above has been declared a 'shouting head', a Celtic symbol of life. Indeed, it is even suggested that the head could have been part of a Celtic or Romano-British shrine built above the well.[100]

Whitchurch

A small field spring 300m south-west of the parish church is known as the **Snakewell** (ST610673)*. No folklore is recorded for this site.[101]

Winford

By the churchyard wall of St Mary and St Peter is a stone-lined **spring** (ST542649)*, the water of which now flows a foot lower than of old and runs below ground into the adjacent stream. The spring is thought to have provided water for baptisms, but its main virtue was its medicinal power. Gypsies were great believers in its potency and when camped in the area would drink no other water. It is said that

*The overgrown holy well in the churchyard of
St Mary and St Peter*

once a young gypsy boy had a serious leg injury which it was feared could only be addressed by amputation, but the boy was brought to the well, his leg bathed and a swift recovery ensued.[102]

Winscombe

Many springs rise in this Mendip parish but the most impressive is the **East Well** (ST414563)* lying in a spinney along Eastwell Lane which once served as the funeral path from the district of Sidcot. The well is said to derive its name from its situation east of the parish church, although an alternative name, Ice Well, exists, which is curious given its reputation of never freezing. The spring has never been known to fail but surprisingly there is no recorded folk-lore except the belief that a vapour can sometimes be seen above the water.[103]

The **Hale Well** (ST429565)* in Hale Combe is another inter-esting ancient spring, once renowned for its beauty and unfailing supply of excellent water, but now fallen on hard times. **Cox's Well** (ST408577), now capped and used as a domestic water supply, pours forth some 360,000 gallons of water a day. At one time it was believed to be the haunt of an unpleasant spectre but what form this well guardian took is not recorded.[104]

There were more supernatural happenings at Sandford where, before the depredations of quarrying, there was a cave known as **The Gulf** (ST420591). This site, at The Mangle, on the side of Sandford Hill, was visited by those who felt themselves bewitched. It was believed that a spell could be broken by descending into The Gulf on a rope and then walking over a narrow rock bridge which was raised above a pool of water. This was known as 'Crossing the waters of the Gulf.'[105]

Wraxall

At Failand there were once two famous wells. The first of these, the **Maiden's Spring** (ST519724), was an odd structure renowned for its beautiful clear water which rose in the south of Ox House Bottom. The young women of Failand and Easton-in-Gordano would walk up to two miles to collect pitchers of its water and were famed for their beautiful complexions and soft skin. The well's reputation extended to Bristol where carters would deliver the water to the wealthy suburb of Clifton. Its popularity was boosted by governesses and nursemaids who noticed that young boys under their charge would become far more tractable and cease their 'boyish behaviour' when they regularly drank the water. This gave rise to the well's alternative name: the Maid-makers Well.[106] It is said that before the well disappeared under a council rubbish tip in the 1960s, a laboratory analysis of its water showed the presence of trace elements that could lead to male sterility!

Not far from the Maiden's Spring was a **well** (ST520734) which rose on the northern side of a lane called The Tynings. Water from this well was used in the Wesleyan Good Friday Chapel Tea which was once a great social event drawing people from many miles around. At the feast urns of tea were brewed exclusively with water from the well even though far more convenient supplies were available. The well must once have had a reputation as a particularly blessed spot, perhaps it was an old holy well that still retained some prestige, its waters suitable for an Easter celebration?[107]

On the northern edge of the Land Yeo floodplain, east of Jacklands Bridge, there is an alder-fringed pool where strings of bubbles constantly weave to the surface from its clear sandy bottom. This is the **Whirleypool** (ST475717)*. Before the excavation of the Severn railway tunnel tapped its source in 1886, this was a powerful, seething spring that sent jets of water several feet into the air. People of the Mesolithic period (10,000 - 3500 BC) camped here and subsequent people left a bronze torque nearby. Several tales are told of the site, some noting its reputation for being bottomless and others that it was a Roman swimming pool![108]

Wrington

The **Lady Well** (ST466629)* is a spring which rises in sheep pasture just north of the parish church. The water was used in the cure of eye disorders and it was also once the custom for women to deposit small coins and pins into the well, a practice that was believed to bring them luck, good husbands and fertility. In the early 1980s the landowner decided to bottle the Lady Well water for commercial

The Lady Well, now in need of repair, but once a fertility well

use, but the venture did not succeed. A modern borehole thirty yards away may be connected with this, indeed it may have sucked the holy well's springhead dry. Today the Lady Well is a neglected jumble of collapsed railings and concrete posts and offers a rather sad spectacle.[109]

Just south of the runways of Lulsgate airport is a collapsed Neolithic dolmen called the **Waterstone** (ST500644). Strictly speaking it is the fallen capstone which bears this name for there is a hollow in it which is believed to never run dry even in the hottest summers. It was once the custom for the unmarried women of Wrington to walk up to the stone early on May morning and decorate it with garlands of primroses and offer libations of milk, a practice held in common with ancient stones in Scotland where the milk was offered to propitiate the resident deity. Although recumbent, the Waterstone is said to dance when the moon is full on Midsummer's Day, whilst it is believed to be visited by the Wimblestone monolith of Shipham which travels over Mendip to slake its thirst at the Waterstone. There is no proof that the Waterstone's water ever held any potency, but its importance in local folklore means it was almost certainly perceived as having such. At Penmaenmawr in north-west Wales, rainwater from a depression in the Stone of Sacrifice was taken home and sprinkled on the threshold as a protection against witches. Perhaps the Waterstone held this power too?[110]

Just over a mile north-west of the Waterstone is the mysterious **Abspit Pond** (ST485651)*, a perennial pool hidden amongst the trees on the edge of Wrington Warren. When this whole area was the limestone heath of Broadfield Down, an ancient Monolith known as the Bethel Stone, stood by the pond, although by the 19th century it had been removed.

The Anglo-Saxon estate charter for Wrington, (904 AD), lists a group of minor springs on the border with Butcombe parish as the **Merewellen** (ST510623) or 'boundary springs'. A little way to the south of the Merewellen is **Long Sutton Spring** (ST504616) which rises on a hillside within a small ash spinney. Water pours out of its stone springhead and the amount of dressed stone lying around suggests there may once have been a wellhouse here. The spring never fails and was recently analysed and found to be fit for human consumption. A former occupant of Pigeonhouse Farm would walk up to the spring each day to collect water and until her death, aged 92, she would drink no other water believing it to be 'most beneficial to health.' Local people go further, declaring how good it is mixed with a glass of Scotch![111]

Writhlington

A 17th century property deed refers to a **Holywater Elm** (*c*.ST7055) in this parish although its precise location is unknown.[112]

Yatton

In the meadows between Yatton village and Claverham rise the **Bishop's Well** (ST441656) and the **Holwell** (5T440659)*, the latter believed to be a corruption of Holywell. The Bishop's Well is on private land immediately to the north of Claverham Road, but the Holwell rises 500 metres to the north alongside a footpath on the way to Yatton village. Both wells were 'formerly accounted efficacious in consumptive maladies' but are now almost completely forgotten.[113]

Another Claverham site, Court-de-Wyck, now a factory but formerly one of the most renowned medieval houses in the district, was said to possess an **ancient well** (ST448662) which was the start of a secret underground passage leading to the road junction and gallows site of Brockley Elm, 2.3km to the east.[114]

An unplaced well

In 1912, H. Hay Wilson wrote of his experiences in north Somerset in a work entitled *A Somerset Sketch-Book*. In one chapter he mentions **Pearce's Well**, a healing well for eye complaints and describes its virtue as due to its rising on the eastern side of a hill. From his description the well can be placed in the Winford-Nempnett Thrubwell-Stowey Sutton area, with Winford a strong contender given the predominance of the surname Pearce in and around this parish. No map has recorded this well and local memory does not recall its existence.[115] How many other wells have fallen beyond the threshold of knowledge and record to be lost for good?

Wells on the Somerset Border

Compton Bishop

Within the hamlet of Cross there was said to be a **healing well** in the garden of the old forge, later known as Fairfield. The water was believed to be exceptionally pure and it is said that the doctor from neighbouring Axbridge would come here to gather water for treating his patients.[116]

Another **spring** served most of the domestic needs of local people, but its prosaic use was once possibly complemented by ritual and veneration for when the pumping station, which currently marks the site, was being constructed in 1898, workmen unearthed a golden bracelet which was dated to the Bronze Age and is now on display in the British Museum. Such a find in association with a spring suggests ritual activity, as attested elsewhere throughout Bronze Age Britain and Europe.

Stratton-on-the-Fosse

Situated some 3km south of Midsomer Norton this parish straddles the Fosse Way—the Roman road from Exeter to Lincoln. The much restored parish church is dedicated to St Vigor, one of only two such dedications in England, and west of the church is Downside Abbey, a large Benedictine foundation dating back to 1814 and once home to Somerset holy well enthusiast Dom Ethelbert Horne. It is Horne who informs us of the parish's holy well, which he suggests may once have been called **St Vigor's Well** (ST659507). Rising on the bank of Loocombe Brook, and now within a fenced poultry enclosure, the well was said to be 'good for the eyes' and is supposed to rise beneath the church itself. This core area of Stratton is also the haunt of a ghostly 'green lady'.[117]

Wells on the Wiltshire Border

Box

A great many springs rise in this parish. By the church rises the **Frog's Well** (ST822684) which was believed to have similar properties to St Anthony's Well in the parish of Bathford, being renowned for its 'efficacy in the cure of Inflammations and Rheums in the eyes.'[118] South-west of the village, and on the northern tip of Kingsdown Hill the 18th century topographer John Wood wrote of 'the marks of a **Well dedicated to Mars**', (possibly the spring rising at ST812679), with 'a couple of Ash Trees consecrated to him' standing close by. Wood was a noted Druid and in his writings frequently compares indigenous folk beliefs to the romantic notions of Celtic and Classical mythology which were prevalent amongst his class at this time. It may thus be that he was interpreting local belief rather than reporting it verbatim; even so it is fascinating to consider what it was about this site and its holy trees that caused him to equate it to the god Mars.[119]

In 1783, north of the village and on the right bank of By Brook, a baker named West sank a well to provide a domestic water source

Visitors' accommodation fronting Middle Hill Spa

for a new house he was building. The water it held was saline and slightly sulphurous, but in keeping with many another local entrepreneur he decided to turn a problem to his advantage, building a pump room over the well and opening it as a spa. The water of the **Middle Hill Spa** (ST820689)* was mildly laxative, but was most usefully employed as a powerful diuretic. A local physician, William Falconer, recorded a number of detailed case histories of local people who had been cured at the spa, and published them in *A Brief Account of the Qualities of Middle-Hill Water* (1789), a shameless piece of promotional advertising. Nevertheless, it is fascinating for the detail with which the virtues of the water and the sufferings of its visitors are expounded. He writes of John Plaisted, a butcher's clerk from Bath suffering a seasonal rash and depression; Jane Milsom of Colerne suffering severe skin problems; 18-year old George Croome of Wraxall, a farm labourer afflicted by a scab which covered his entire head; Richard Strange, a Bath butcher suffering from an ulcerous inflamed sore; and most movingly he writes of the sufferings experienced by seven-year old James Solerol, a boy who had long suffered 'an acrid moist eruption in divers parts of his body' coupled with near-blindness resultant upon an outbreak of smallpox. All drank the water and bathed the afflicted parts of their bodies; all had been given up as hopeless cases. Falconer then relates how within one or two weeks all showed signs of rapid improvement and at the time of writing were fully cured; rounding off his eulogy with an account of a leper who was then well on the road to recovery after taking the water.

Limpley Stoke

In Stoke Wood, above Chatligh House, is the **Shingle Bell Well** (ST780614)*: 'a famous spring' Its waters were once held in high regard and were especially useful in the cure of eye disorders. Moreover there was an old tradition that when sufferers came to bathe in its waters they would hang strips of cloth amongst the branches of surrounding trees as votive offerings. Nearby are the foundations of a ruined building, a chapel said to be part of a fortification known as Spy Castle. The well is difficult to find and is best reached by heading north along the footpath from the A36 and when a large grassy clearing appears head south-east amongst the jumbled rock. The sound of the spring and its brook should draw the visitor on from here.[120]

Monkton Farleigh

Just to the north of Monkton Farleigh village there stands the most impressive well-house still remaining in the Bristol region. A perfect stone building with steeply pitched roof encloses the

The Monk's Well

Monk's Well (ST803656)*, a cistern which collected the waters of several small springs which rise in the field behind. It is claimed that the well house dates from 1250, but it seems likely that it has been repaired in the past. The cistern fed a conduit which ran south-east to supply the Cluniac priory of St Mary Magdalene. No healing virtues nor folklore are known for this well but its age, beauty and the perfection of its architecture make it well worth a visit.[121]

Winsley

On the border between Bathford and the Wiltshire parish of Winsley is the small hamlet of **Conkwell**; the first part of the name believed to derive from a Celtic word for a small mound—perhaps there was once a barrow here?[122] The county boundary runs down the lane dividing the hamlet in two, and at the bottom of which is the Conkwell (ST791626)* itself built into the grassy bank, a right-angle of moss-encrusted masonry holding a basin of dark, still water where ferns and liverworts thrive. To the left of the spring-head basin are three further basins, cut from a single block of stone. The Conkwell was a renowned and much-frequented wishing well and, until the early 20th century, a popular site where visitors would, 'go through the ceremony of crawling to the well on hands and knees, then letting the water gather in the left hand, and after forming a wish in their mind, they drink.'[123] The water is beautifully cold and clear, and on all counts one of the most accessible holy wells in the region.

*Modern visitors following the old wishing ritual
at the Conkwell, Winsley (Marilyn Morris)*

The Snakewells

On the south-western fringes of Bristol are four springs unique in the area for bearing the name Snakewell. One of these springs is at Whitchurch, the other three are found in the contiguous parishes of Flax Bourton, Long Ashton and Abbots Leigh.

The geography of the Snakewells suggests that a common theme explaining the origin of their name may once have existed; unfortunately no folklore or written documentation has survived for any of the wells so now there is solely speculation. A possible guide is the Romanesque tympanum over the south door of Flax Bourton's parish church of St Michael. Here the saint, or some other religious figure, is depicted trampling a coiled serpent, his crozier thrust through the animal's jaws transfixing it to the earth, and a sword in the saint's other hand held upright in a gesture of victory. Is this simply a standard representation of the church's patron depicted in a conventional pose found in many of his images throughout the Christian world? This is indeed the most likely scenario, but the imagery of the slain serpent is particularly interesting given the presence of the Snakewell one kilometre to the north-east of the church. Could there once have been a tradition of a serpent either living in or being killed at the well in the manner of well-known serpent-slaying traditions such as The Lambton Worm in Northumberland, its presence or demise commemorated by the church's Norman masons?

Map showing the location of parishes in North Somerset mentioned in the gazetteer

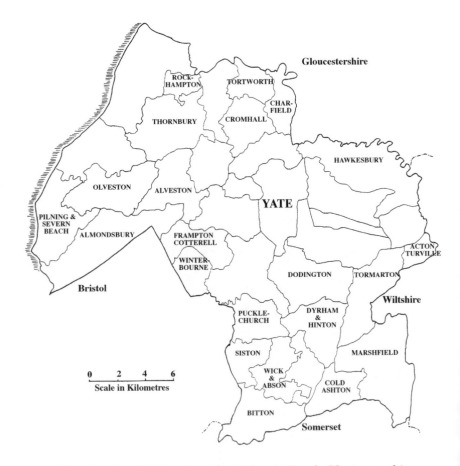

Map showing the location of parishes in South Gloucestershire mentioned in the gazetteer

South Gloucestershire

Acton Turville

Near the parish church, and at the village crossroads, is an old **draw well** (ST809808)* which R.C.S. Walters called a holy well, although he offered no explanation why this should be so.[1]

The disused draw well at Acton Turville

Alderley

South of Glentworth Farm, Tresham, the **Twizzlewell** (ST799904) rises in a steep south-facing coombe. It has been suggested that the name means 'twisted stream', but another explanation has it deriving from the local pronunciation of St Oswald, *i.e.* 'Twasole'. Oswald was a popular saint in the Middle Ages, especially in sheep-rearing areas like the Cotswolds, so it is possible we could have here a St Oswald's Well.[2]

A less problematic spring is the **Abbot's Well** (ST767887) on Lovetts Wood Farm, south of Hillesley. The abbot in question was that of Pershore, as lord of the Manor of Hawkesbury. The spring rises on a steep bank amidst a tangle of old brick reservoirs and pieces of metal; a modern pipe carries the water down to the farm. A retired farm worker recently asked the farmer who owns the well for some water from the spring, convinced it would do him good in his fight against heart trouble.

Almondsbury

A small **lake** (ST585821) in the grounds of Over Court is the haunt of a tragic female ghost. It is said that she only appears on the night of November 22, the anniversary of her death, when she was shot by her jealous husband before staggering to the lake where she drowned. She is described as being a bright white figure wearing a tall pointed headdress. In 1937 the Easter Compton prize band, on their way to perform at the Court, saw the ghost and were so frightened that they dropped their instruments and ran!

Stretching from the village of Hallen to Crook's Marsh is a ditch known as **Monk's Well Rhine**, however the position and history of the Monk's Well itself are unknown. (ST540819 - ST552803)

800 yards east of Junction 17 of the M5 is St Swithen's Farm which takes its name from a ruined medieval chapel which stands close by. Near the farm buildings there is also a **spring** (ST584815) from which flow the western headwaters of the River Trym. In the Anglo-Saxon estate charter for Henbury one of the boundary points is given as Haselwell or Hazel Well and some commentators have equated this with the St Swithen's Farm spring.[3]

Bitton

A **spring** (ST675703) of 'purging mineral water' rises in Kimber Coombe near Oldland, but Bitton's most noted well was the **Goldwell** (ST660706) which rose by the Bath Road at the top of Willsbridge Hill. Samuel Rudder (1779) reckoned it, 'very fine and pure. There is a pump erected, and a can chained to it for the use of travellers, to drink as they go along.'[4]

Charfield

There are two field names in this parish suggestive of holy wells but the springs involved are lost. A document of 1635 mentions a **Pennywells** in the parish and the 1839 Tithe Awards record the field name **Lukewell** (ST721907), which may derive from St Luke's Well.[5]

Cold Ashton

In the middle of an ancient field system of strip lynchets, between Greenway Lane and Nimlet, a strong spring gushes forth in a field called **Bridewell** (ST744721)*. However, if any lore once surrounded this well it has failed to survive. **St Anne's Well** (ST731715) is a vigorous spring just to the west of Hamswell House. It supplies the adjacent hamlet with all its water, but no lore has been recorded here either.[6]

A field well, on private land, just to the north of St John's Wood at Hamswell, has no official name but local people have taken to calling it the **Hameswelle** (ST731721) after the unlocated Anglo-Saxon spring which gave the hamlet its name. St John's Wood—the name for the adjacent copse is curious and may preserve the original dedication of the well. The Hameswelle is never failing and flows

The Hameswelle

into a large stone basin from which it runs out to form a stream. The stone structure of a three-sided enclosure, flagstone roof and revetments either side is all drystone and of a medieval date. Carved initials and date—T.W. 1788—could be those of a grateful visitor to the well who found health or good fortune here should it have once been a holy well, or could be the mark of local landowner Thomas Whittington, relative of Dick, the famous Lord Mayor of London. It is said to be Dick's ghost which rides out on November nights from Hamswell House, past the well and onto Toghill Barn.

On the boundary with Charlcombe parish, to the south of Hamswell, a small spring is believed to be the **Eanswythe Wyllas**, (ST734705) or St Eanswyth's Well, of the Anglo-Saxon estate charter (931AD).[7]

Cromhall

To the south of Tortworth Park is a hill formerly called Anchoret Hill after a hermit, or anchorite, who had his abode here. Legend tells of his counsel being sought by the monks of Bangor in Glamorganshire who were on their way to debate with St Augustine at Canterbury. A nearby spring took the name **Anckerswell** (c.ST6990) after the hermit, but its exact location is not known.[8]

The **Lake** (ST691919) in Tortworth Park is haunted by the ghost of a mounted rider galloping across its surface; it is thought that the ghost appears over the course of an old road that was flooded beneath the waters of the lake. This site is within the grounds of Ley Hill Prison but is open to the public on the first Sunday of each month.

Dodington

At the eastern edge of Dodington Park there are two streams which rise from notable springs. The northernmost spring is called **Tormery Well** (ST762791)* and has a petrifying quality 'of turning wood into stone.'[9] The name of the well is thought to derive from the adjacent parish of Tormarton, the parish boundary being 100m to the east. To its south are the **Seven Springs** (ST762790)*, the acknowledged source of the River Frome, which emerges from an unsympathetic concrete drain, and although its appearance is

The Seven Springs, now piped, the source of the River Frome

now unremarkable R.C.S. Walters found that in the 1920s it 'was much respected by those who live in the neighbourhood.'[10]

Dodington House itself, one of the great houses of the southern Cotswolds, was repositioned in the 18th century when the old medieval parish church, which stood close by, was demolished. A **spring** (ST751798) rising in the cellars of the house could have been associated with the old church. When the house was open to the public the enterprising owner placed a sign above the well declaring it to be a 'Wishing Well' and successfully persuaded the public to part with a not insignificant quantity of loose change!

Following her death, a 19th century resident of the great house, Lady Georgiana Codrington, returned to Earth as a fiery-tempered ghost to haunt the flooded **gravel pit** (ST749801) nearby, until 12 clergymen gathered within a circle of blood to successfully exorcise her.[11]

Dyrham and Hinton

Between Lower Field Farm and Barleyclose Farm a small spring called **Bridewell** (ST713770) rises in a blackthorn thicket near the parish boundary; no folklore has been recorded. Half a mile to the east, and north of Bridehill Farm, is a field called Pucklewell (ST720770), probably deriving from the Old English *pucela* or 'little goblin'.[12]

In the hamlet of Hinton an old track called Bier Path was the traditional route along which to carry the dead to Dyrham Church. Along the Chapel Lane section a ghost has been seen on several occasions by the site of an **old well** (ST732764) that stood by the now demolished medieval chapel.

Frampton Cotterell

The **old iron mine** (ST669821), now obscured in woodland behind the church, once sold waste water pumped out of the shafts. It was believed to be similar to the water of Buxton Spa, Derbyshire and was in demand for medicinal purposes.[13]

Marshfield

At West End, on the southern side of Brookhouse Lane where the track begins its descent into the valley, there rises the elusive **St Pancras Well** (ST764741)*. The spring flows even in a drought and was once associated with a chapel of the same dedication that stood in a neighbouring field. 'St Pancras' is a very rare dedication, found mostly in association with Roman sites, and there may have thus been a connection with the small Roman settlement that once existed at West End.[14]

A **spring** (ST783733) rises at Cadwell Hill on the other side of the valley to St Pancras' Well and its immediate vicinity has been the scene of a recent haunting (ST765750). South of Marshfield village is Ringswell Common, at the western end of which, in a dense hedge, rises the **Ringswell** (ST783733)—a springhead formed from drystone walling built in a 'beehive' fashion.[15]

Olveston

Amidst the wooded gullies and brooks of Stroud Common is the **Dropping Well** (ST624877)*. Its old masonry surround has decayed but lumps of worked stone can be found where the two headwaters of the brook converge. Only a small trickle runs out from the well but this always seems to have been the case. Before mains water Olveston people would often get up in the night to be the first in the queue at the well. In times of drought the well would serve a radius of several miles as it was often the only local water supply that could be depended upon. There are no traditions of any medicinal virtue associated with the site but the Dropping Well was once the venue for May Day festivities of an undisclosed nature.[16]

Alongside the driveway of Ivywell House in the hamlet of Tockington the beautifully clear **Ramswell** (ST608862)* rises in a three-sided stone courtyard. It has a metal grill to prevent children and animals falling in, but which can be lifted, for the inhabitants of Tockington still have a right to draw water from it. Some have claimed that the name is a corruption of Romans Well, but a more likely derivation is the Old English *hramsa wylle*, or 'wild garlic spring'.[17]

600 metres to the north-west, at the side of Olveston Road, there is a pile of masonry which marks the site of the **Miles Well** (ST603866). A stone wellhouse stood here until 1994 when the construction of a pavement saw it quite needlessly demolished. The name is a corruption of **St Michael's Well** although it was also known as Eye Well in honour of its reputation in curing eye disorders; indeed local doctors would recommend its water for this purpose even until the advent of the NHS. The well was enclosed by a square wellhouse with a galvanised metal roof, a gate in one side leading to steps down to the water. However the well was filled in during the 1950s after concerned parents felt it presented a danger to their children. Burials have been unearthed in the neighbouring field and it is believed that the well is the 'Ringswell' mentioned in the Saxon Estate charter for Olveston in 995. The well sits at the foot of Eastcombe Hill where village festivities were once held.[18]

Pilning and Severn Beach

An **old pond** (ST557873) at Northwick, just west of the A403, was the site of frequent hauntings believed to be the ghost of a man who was hanged nearby.

Pucklechurch

There are three holy wells in this parish; all still flow, although to varying degrees. North of Gingells Farm a field called **Bridewells** (ST685759) is the site of a well-preserved tumulus and a brick-built reservoir surrounded by vigorous hawthorn trees. The reservoir marks the site of St Bridget's Well renowned as being, 'very good for sore eyes and Diet drinks.'[19]

To the east of the village, and north of Redford Lane, is a field called Hollywells, a corruption of **Holywell** (ST707758). In 1779

Samuel Rudder noted that this spring shared the medicinal virtues of St Bridget's Well.[20] The water from the spring is now piped into a lane-side ditch.[21]

The most famous of Pucklechurch's wells was **St Aldam's Well** (ST704772) which rises at St Aldam's Ash Farm. Aldam, or Aldhelm, was an extraordinary Saxon saint who had a number of bizarre and rather un-Christian attributes including a great skill in magic. He was respected for his wisdom and was once summoned to Rome to prove the Pope's innocence on a charge of fathering a child. As Aldhelm had only two days to get there he summoned a spirit that took the shape of a black horse and they flew to Rome. He made a vestment hang on a sunbeam and gave a bell to Malmesbury Abbey which had the power to make thunder and lightning cease. He was also a noted preacher and musician and in 666 became Abbot of Malmesbury and later Bishop of Sherbourne. For much of his career he led an itinerant lifestyle and it was on one of his preaching circuits that he came to Pucklechurch. A sick child was brought to him, he took water from the spring, blessed it, and put it on the child, curing its illness. At the same time he struck his ash staff in the ground and it miraculously sprouted to provide shelter for those gathered around him. As a consequence the well became perceived as holy and henceforth bore his name. The well is reputed to never run dry and, like the other Pucklechurch holy wells, its waters were 'esteemed very good for sore eyes, and for its virtue in diet drinks.'[22] Many places associated with Aldhelm were considered health restoring and it is recorded that a girl from Pucklechurch with a spinal disease was cured at his shrine in Malmesbury. An old stone cover once protected the well but during the Second World war the Luftwaffe scored a direct hit and the old stonework was destroyed. Today the well lies beneath a modern manhole cover in the farm driveway, and is used for domestic purposes.[23]

Pucklechurch has the most holy wells of any south Gloucestershire parish, but Gloucestershire's historians cannot agree on how many there were. By using a number of documentary sources we can now identify the three described above but the frequently inaccurate Sir Robert Atkyns (*The Ancient and Present State of Gloucestershire*, 1712) only describes St Aldhelm's Well and his successor, Samuel

Rudder (*A New History of Gloucestershire*, 1779) wrote of 'Holy-well and St Bridget's Well' but nothing of St Aldhelm's. To further complicate matters, Dorothy Vintner, writing in 1966, describes St Bridget's Well as rising in 'a field called Holywell'!

Rockhampton

Halfway along Pennywell Lane a very clear spring bubbles up next to the stream running alongside the road. This is the **Pennywell** (ST653930)*, so highly regarded in the cure of eye complaints that bottles of its water were sent for by the old Union Workhouse in Thornbury. It was the custom to throw a coin into the well when visiting it for medicinal reasons and it is claimed that this practice was witnessed by Edward Jenner, pioneer of vaccination, who was visiting a relative in the parish. Very old people still come and take the water for domestic drinking purposes, a reminder of when its never-failing spring was the only supply for a considerable part of the parish.

St Anne's Well, Siston. The well is at the foot of the large tree on the bend in the road. In the foreground is 'St Anne's Bridge'

Immediately on the parish boundary with Ham and Stone is **Puckwell** field (ST663941). The road running alongside this field, from Rockhampton to Lower Stone, is haunted by a 'white lady' who disappears in a **pond** (ST673945)* south of Lowerstone Wood.

Siston

St Anne's Well (ST686749)* rises on the roadside immediately north of St Anne's Bridge, amidst the dangerous bends of Siston Lane where the visitor must be extremely careful of fast-moving traffic. It is a stone trough set into the bank at ground level and backed by a stone revetment. The trough is divided into two unequal parts and now sadly holds little more than rainwater and field drainage run-off as its springhead near the B4465 was affected by road widening some years ago.

In its heyday local people would once tell visitors of how 'Queen Anne' would visit the well, walking the ten metres to St Anne's Bridge where she would sit and drink a glass of the health-giving elixir. At the height of its power the well was one of the most famous in the Bristol area and drew 'large numbers of poor persons who have weak eyes.'[24] It was also a wishing well and had a reputation for curing other ailments, the most important of which was infertility. Women would come to the well with pins to drop in, in the hope of bearing a child. This fascinating ancient custom is recorded at only three other wells in our region—the Lady Well at Wrington, King's Castle Well in East Harptree, and St Mary's Well, Portishead.[25]

A posed photograph depicting a visitor to St Anne's Well (Reece Winstone Archive)

Thornbury

A spring called **Ludgareswell** (*c*.ST6390) was recorded in 1346 and formed a small stream which flowed west to the marshes. Its exact position is unclear though the name is thought to derive from St Lodgar, better known as St Leger.[26]

The most famous well in the parish, **St Arild's Well** (ST617903)*, is more often thought of in connection with Oldbury-on-Severn where the parish church shares the well's dedication. St Arild's Well flows from behind a stone revetment wall at the head of a stream south of Willow Farm, Kington. It takes its name from a local Christian martyr called Arilda who refused to sleep with Muncius, 'a cruel pagan tyrant.'[27] In anger, Muncius cut off her head and on the spot the spring arose with patches of Arilda's blood staining the stones. Local tradition points out that these stones are still stained red with her blood; they are indeed stained red but by an alga, *Hildebrandia rivularis*, which is found at other holy wells with beheading traditions. By another coincidence the water leaves a slight stickiness on the skin and the palate when drunk, very much like blood would do.

After Arilda's death many miracles were performed around her body and the spring of never-failing water. She was soon sanctified and Oldbury's parish church, on the site of an old temple of Jupiter,

St Arild's Well

was dedicated to her. When the Normans came to the area they removed the body to a shrine in Gloucester Cathedral, as part of a policy of centralising potentially nationalistic local cults, though it is said that miracles were still being performed at the shrine until the Dissolution. A Latin hymn composed to Arilda in the 12th century has survived; it is essentially a hymn to the saint as an intercessory with God and was sung either at the well, church or cathedral. The miraculous waters were still being sought for their curative properties within living memory and each year since the late 1980s there has been a private pilgrimage by local residents to the well.[28]

Tormarton

A **pond** (*c*.ST7778), now filled in, which stood at the eastern end of this Cotswold village, was famed amongst the country people for being the source of a continuous rain brought on by an easterly wind. On wet mornings people to the west of the village would say, 'It'll last the day thee know, it be coming from Tarmarton.'[29] This is an identical belief to that of the Kalahari San people of southern Africa who believe that the rain lives in a well; this could suggest an ancient origin for the Tormarton tale.

Tortworth

Virgin's Well (ST713934) is an inconspicuous spring that flows out from under rough stonework in a field below Little Tortworth Copse. It is never failing and in the drought of 1921 was recorded as flowing at 25 gallons per minute. Until just after the First World War, village women would go to the well on May Day morning and dress it with locally gath-

The Virgin's Well

ered wild flowers; they would then bathe their faces in its water, an action that was believed to bring them both fine complexions and good husbands. No men were allowed to see any part of this ritual, and strict precautions were taken to this end. Water from the well was believed to cure eye complaints and until the turn of the century it is said that the Bristol Eye Hospital would send for a supply. Its purity and clarity is remarkable given its location in the middle of a well-used field, the water tastes good and has a slight peaty aroma.[30]

Tytherington

At Stidcote Farm there once rose three **spring-fed pools** (ST683885). Near them was found a ceremonial macehead of the late Neolithic or early Bronze Age. Not far away a Roman tessellated pavement was discovered in the 18th century and it has been suggested that this could have been a shrine of a water deity.

Wick and Abson

There are three holy wells along a one kilometre stretch of the headwaters of Holbrook Brook, whilst in the garden of Abson Edith Farm is a **well** (ST697744) which is believed to be the source of the brook itself. The farm and its immediate area are haunted by the ghost of a woman with fair hair and who wears a long garment; many people have testified to either seeing her or

The Tunywell

feeling her presence. In the field opposite is the site of a deserted Anglo-Saxon village and its lost church of St Bartholomew.

500 metres to the south a spring rises close by the brook, its waters doubling the size of the stream. This is the **Tunywell** (ST696740) and it sits in Toneywells field, both names believed to be a corruption of St Anthony's Well.' It is said locally that an old man was dying nearby and gave as his last request 'a glass of water from the Tunywell.' It is a common belief around the world that for the dying to drink sacred water either prolongs life or aids the soul in its passage from this life to the next.[31]

Some 400 metres south of Tunywell is **Holy Well** (ST697735)*, a spring which rises amongst rough grass and rushes at the north-east of Holbrook Common. It once supplied the local drinking water but is now covered by a metal plate, whilst its stonework surround is inconspicuous. However, its waters were famed even up until the 1920s as being 'good for the eyes'; the whole parish was once an estate of Glastonbury Abbey and it is said that 'the monks used to come here and bathe their eyes' and so bestowed holiness upon the well. It is thought that this never-failing spring was originally dedicated to the Holy Virgin with the adjacent stream thus becoming called the Holy Brook.[32]

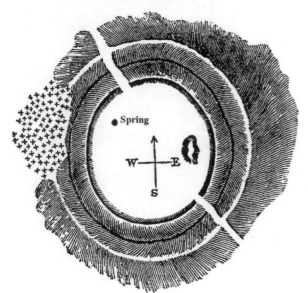

A plan of Bury Camp, Winterbourne Parish, showing the site of the 'never-failing spring'

Winterbourne

The Iron Age earthwork of Bury Hill Camp, on the southern boundary of the parish, once contained a powerful **never-failing spring** (ST651791) in its north-west corner that fed a well roughly one metre deep. The spring was lost to quarrying some time after 1926.[33]

West of Winterbourne Court Farm is the **Monk's Fishing Pool** (ST638810), once used by the Carmelite Friars of Bristol who lived at the Court before the Dissolution.[34]

Wells on the Gloucestershire Border

Boxwell with Leighterton

St Mary's Well (ST815927) rising within the wooded combe at Boxwell was used in the cure of weak and inflamed eyes and also for relieving rheumatism. As with many holy wells in this region there are accounts of people visiting the site well into the 1920s and taking bottles of the holy water away with them. In 1807 the Gloucestershire historian Thomas Fosbrooke was so impressed with the reputation of St Mary's Well that he felt fit to exclaim, with uncharacteristic enthusiasm, that 'The place is remarkably healthy'. Fosbrooke also noted a tradition that the site was part of an Anglo-Saxon nunnery, the main buildings of which may once have stood on the site of the present Boxwell Court. There is also a strong suggestion that St Mary's Well was a rag well where strips of cloth were left tied to adjacent trees and bushes by those seeking cures for their ills; if so it would be only one of three known and suspected rag wells in the Bristol region. St Mary's Well rises in what is now a cottage garden on a private estate and permission to visit it should be sought from the landowner at Boxwell Court.[35]

North Nibley

The **Crow-well** (*c*.ST7496) which rises in the north of the parish was recorded in 1712 by Sir Robert Atkyns as a mineral water spring, but little more is known about it.[36]

Ozleworth

Two kilometres due west of Boxwell's St Mary's Well there rise **The Seven Holy Springs** (ST797928)* described by John Smyth in 1618 as 'seaven excellent fountaines, springs of admirable water and Holy virtue (as speake the inhabitants)' and which 'issue forth in restless abundance'.[37] Six springs rise together on the north bank of the stream in Ozleworth Bottom; whether the seventh well really existed is not certain as it was the practise to christen several springs rising together as 'seven', or more rarely 'nine', irrespective of the actual number present. The site of the Ozleworth springs is one of great beauty and tranquillity within one of the most unspoilt of Cotswold valleys.

REFERENCES

Bath

1. Wood p.24; Holt p.165
2. Kellaway p.237
3. Cunliffe 1985, p.8 & p.4
4. Stewart p.26
5. Cunliffe 1985 p.35, Stewart p.42 & pp.47-60
6. Stewart pp.62, 67 & 70
7. Stewart p.70
8. Wade p.17
9. Stewart p.67; Strickland p.99
10. Cunliffe 1985 p.187 fig.10
11. Tunstall p.67
12. Tunstall pp70-1
13. Jorden p.42
14. Cunliffe 1993 p.2
15. Cunliffe 1993 p.18
16. Hutton p.239
17. Cunliffe 1988 p.232
18. Cunliffe 1993 pp.26-7
19. Cunliffe 1985 p.76, 1993 p.31; Nightingale p.367
20. Cunliffe 1985 pp.11-2
21. Strachey; Coxe p.833; Russell p.193; Bath Corporation p.35
22. Jorden p.88
23. McNalty 1991, Heywood 1991 and Devereux 1990
24. Russell p.195; Heywood p.71; Rolls p.57
25. Turner
26. Coxe p.731
27. Oliver p.100
28. Pierce p.244; Russell pp.197 & 201
29. Coxe p.833
30. Pierce p.195; Oliver p.100
31. Tunstall p.105
32. Tunstall p.106
33. Russell p.195
34. Warener p.34
35. Pierce pp.255 & 260; Ibbetson p.55
36. Tunstall p.52
37. Peach 1888 p.143; Warner p.34; Kellaway p.17; Coxe p.731
38. Tunstall p.65
39. O'Donnell p.14
40. Cunliffe p.38
41. Rolls p.57
42. Cunliffe 1993 pp.39 & 45
43. Thomas Venner, Via recta ad vitam longam, 1637
44. Manco p.49, Coxe
45. Peach 1888 p.46
46. Russell p.196
47. Egan p.91
48. Jorden
49. Strachey
50. Pevsner p.113; Kellaway p.53
51. Russell p.195
52. Jorden p.85
53. Venner p.312; Cunliffe 1985 p.10; Russell p.194
54. Strachey
55. Coxe p.731
56. Pevsner p.72
57. Wood pp.117 & 96
58. Phelps p.35
59. O.S. 6inch Bath 1886 XIV.1.19; Schickle pp.8-9; L. Richardson 1928 p.196
60. Schickle pp.8-9; Tunstall p.41
61. Wood p.78
62. Tunstall pp.42-3
63. Collinson Vol 1 p.29
64. Collinson Vol 1 p.31
65. L. Richardson 1928 p.196
66. Collinson Vol 1 p.53
67. Thorpe 1740
68. Wood p.21; Horne 1923 p.19; Peach 1883 p.5
69. Horne S.A.N.H.S. collection
70. Schickle p.17
71. Wood p.78
72. Holt p.165; Tunstall p.195

229

73. Weston Tithe Award 1844 TN608
& TN339—alias 25 Acre Field;
Davenport p.154; Scarth p.113
74. Wood p.21; Scott p.14; Schickle
p.6
75. Wood p.21
76. Wood p.268
77. Phelps p.36; Scott p.7
78. Nightingale p.189; Wood p.22;
Collinson Vol 1 p.169; Warner
p.14
79. Kellaway p.33; Scott p.33
80. Horne 1915 p.99
81. Tunstall p.103
82. Thorpe 1740
83. Phelps p.36
84. Edwards p.6; Walcot
Townswoman's Guild p.20

Bristol
1. Boucher pp.97 & 101; Barrett p.520
2. Leech p.23; BAFC Vol 10 1905
p.256; F.C. Jones c.1933; Rattue
p.90
3. Clinch p.68
4. F.C. Jones 1946 (i) p.107; Wells
p.52
5. Smith p.96; Worcester
6. Worcester
7. Fedden 1963 pp.45-6; Dallaway
p.136; Worcester
8. F.C. Jones 1946 (i) p.106
9. Mellor p.61; Fedden 1964 p.63;
Anon 1835 p.9; Leech p.27
10. F.C. Jones 1946 (i) p.108; Mellor
p.61
11. Mellor p.56; R. Palmer p.29
12. Mellor p.56
13. R. Palmer p.29; F.C. Jones 1946 (i)
p.108; Fedden 1964 p.62
14. Worcester
15. F.C. Jones 1946 (i) p.108; Smith
p.96; Nicholls & Taylor p.26
16. F.C. Jones 23/5/28; Noble &
Gardiner p.8; Hawkins &
Kellaway p.190

17. Noble & Gardiner pp.8-10;
Vaughan & Martelett p.7
18. Atkyns p.360
19. Noble & Gardiner pp.8-10; L.M.
Griffiths p.29
20. Walters p.148
21. Hawkins & Kellaway p.190
22. F.C. Jones 1946 (i) p.47
23. Seyer Vol 2 pp.545-6
24. Pryce p.67; Fedden 1963 p.8;
Jones & Chown p.82
25. Nicholls 1887 p.80; R.C.S. Walters
p.148; Pryce p.309; F.C. Jones
1927 p.44
26. Boycott p.7; Leech p.20
27. Boycott p.7
28. Pryce p.68; F.C. Jones 1946 (ii)
p.12; Leech pp.8-9
29. Saniger p.10
30. Leech p.21; Pryce p.67
31. Temple History Group 1984
32. Nicholls 1896 p.119; Pryce p.67
33. Mellor p.36
34. Mellor p.129
35. A Gentleman of the Faculty, p.XIII
36. Waite p.4; Evans p.129; Heath
p.208
37. Worcester
38. Russell p.185; Hawkins &
Kellaway p.197; Evans p.121
39. Johnson p.12; Worcester;
Whitehead p.6; Barrett p.93;
Macpherson p.37
40. Venner p.361
41. Underhill pp.18-20
42. Matthews p.17; Barrett p.93
43. Keir p.117
44. Coxe p.384
45. Underhill p.21
46. Underhill p.11; Matthews p.101;
Nott p.15
47. Underhill p.37
48. Russell p.181
49. Underhill p.25
50. Russell p.181

51. Major p.15; Russell p.185; Matthews p.101
52. Anderson p.34; Evans p.21; Matthews p.102
53. Owen pp.126 & 159
54. Manby p.25
55. Anderson p.34; Owen p.136; L.M. Griffiths p.47
56. Saniger p.28
57. Heath p.2066
58. Chilcott p.290; Masters pp.20 & 26; Saniger p.29
59. Dolman
60. Dolman pp.3 & 14
61 Winstone p.123
62. Salmon p.127
63. *Gloucestershire Life* 1971; Underwood 1986 p.131
64. J.F. Nicholls in Proc. of the Society of Antiquaries 17/6/1880 p.1
65. Smith p.134
66. Anon: Rambles Oct 1857
67. McEwan-Smith & Tonkin p.91
68. F.C. Jones 1946 (i) p.111
69. Salmon p.127
70. F.C. Jones 1927
71. Wright
72. Avon Fed. W.I. p.146; Ethel Thomas p.192
73. S. Watson p.47
74. Jones & Chown p.22; Winstone p.15
75. Jones & Chown p.40
76. Bristol Evening Post 19/2/65
77. Bristol Free Journal 3/1/2/94
78. Bedminsetr Tithe Award 1843 TN1181/1184 & TN1152/1153
79. F.C. Jones 1946 (i) p.113; Vear p.28
80. Horne S.A.N.H.S. collection
81. Sinnott p.11; Rev. A. Richardson p.188; Powell

82. Horne 1923 p.13; F.C. Jones 1946 (i) p.117 and in *Bristol Times and Mirror* 24/6/32
83. F.C. Jones 1946 (i) p.117; Rev. A. Richardson p.193
84. F.C. Jones 1946 (i) p.117
85. F.C. Jones in *Bristol Times and Mirror* 24/6/32; Winchester p.25; Rev. A. Richardson p.197; R.C.S. Walters p.154
86. *Western Daily Press* 20/7/1889
87. Sinnott
88. F.C. Jones 1946 (i) p.117
89. J.F. Nicholls in Proc. of the Society of Antiquaries 17/6/1880 p.1
90. Bedminster Tithe Award TN951
91. Map of Lands at Knowl 1808
92. Horne S.A.N.H.S. collection; Winstone p.61; Elliott p.104; F.C. Jones 1946 (i) p.114; Royal and Girvan p.8
93. Longwell Green W.I.
94. F.C. Jones 1927 p.42
95. Scherr 1990; O.S. 25inch Glos. 1883 LXXII.14
96. Scherr 1990; Oldland Tithe Award 1841 TN168/171
97. Braine p.213; F.C. Jones 1927 p.145
98. Matthew p.105
99. H.G. Thomas
100. F.C. Jones 1946 (i) p.110
101. Fedden 1963 p.58; Rudder p.459; F.C. Jones 1946 (i) p.110
102. F.C. Jones 1927 p.42

North Somerset
1. Hood p.3; Jones and Chown p.91
2. Gelling p.259
3. Matson p.7
4. Francis Jones p.95
5. Urban p.105
6. Costen p.153
7. Bailey 12/9/63, 30/11/51; Hunt p.28

8. Collinson Vol.3 p.568
9. Grundy 1935 (i) p.168
10. Royal and Girvan 1976 p.30
11. Barrow Gurney Tithe Awards 1838 TN176
12. Horne SANHS collection
13. Thorpe 1742
14. Mackay-Heriot p.171
15. Gandy op. p.326
16. Wood p.70
17. Bathford Tithe Awards 1839 TN51; Horne SANHS collection; Tunstall p.288.
18. Wood p.30
19. Grundy (i) p.176
20. Bailey 25/2/55; Usher 25/2/83 p.17
21. Burrington Tithe Awards 1838 TN409
22. Bailey 25/2/94; Cartwright p.33
23. Tunstall p.226
24. Wheatcroft 1899 p.21
25. Pevsner p.215
26. Vintner p.28
27. Collinson p.143; Horne 1915 p.97
28. Tongue p.20
29. Hope p.150
30. Avon Fed. W.I. p.42; Chew Magna W.I. p.35)
31. Lovatt p.23; Aston and Isles p.67; Rahtz and Harris p.15
32. Room and Rice-Jones pp.5 & 8; Avon Sites & Monuments Record; Collinson Vol.2 p.93
33. Bailey 16/4/88
34. Churchill Tithe Award 1841 TN231
35. Neale p.102
36. Usher 7/3/85, 6/9/84, 11/6/87
37. Village Pump
38. Horne SANHS collection
39. Compton Martin Tithe Award 1841 TN203/113; Wareing p.30
40. Collinson Vol.2 p.131
41. Wareing p.29
42. Poole p.75; Tongue p.220

43. Long Ashton Tithe Award 1845 TN894
44. Underwood 1985 p.96, Tongue p.96
45. Ordnance Survey 25" Somerset 1886 XIX.13; Kettlewell pp.9 & 53
46. Kettelewell p.49
47. Wood p.131
48. Scherr 1986 p.83; Wheatcroft 1899 p.50; Collinson Vol.3 p.340
49. Bridges and Jones p.27
50. Bridges and Jones p.26
51. Bridges and Jones p.27; Hudd p.5
52. Mr. R. Llewellyn, Backwell. Per com. April 1996
53. Williams and Jeffery, Rattue p.90
54. Ketchley
55. Avon Fed. W.I. p.91
56. Gray p.5; quotation from Michael Pennell via Messrs. Len Lambert and Ian Marlow of Hinton Charterhouse. Per com Aug 94
57. Beedle pp.39-40, Bailey 24/7/53
58. Phelps p.36, Kelston Tithe Award 1838 TN 170-3
59. Grundy (i) p.222
60. Bailey 22/7/83
61. Tomalin; Bailey 22/7/83; Francis Jones p.51
62. W.G. Watson p.379
63. Golledge p.26
64. W.J.R.
65. W.J.R.; Bailey 5/2/82
66. Anon 1982
67. Long Ashton Tithe Award 1845 TN289
68. Anon - Malago Local History Society Magazine 1979 (No9)
69. Long Ashton Tithe Award 1845 TN216
70. Worcester; Saniger p.38; Collinson Vol.2 p.296; Strachey; L.M. Griffiths p.15

71. Marksbury Tithe Award 1843 TN98
72. Grundy (i) p.189
73. Royal and Girvan nd p.46
74. Rutter 1829 p.123
75. Ekwall p.321
76. North Stoke Tithe Award 1838 TN138/143
77. Howell p.253
78. Horne 1923 p.22; Tongue p.218; Swift
79. Marlor p.58
80. Wigan p.46; U.B.S.S. p.39; Vintner
81. Priston Tithe Award 1839 TN164
82. Cooke p.45; Wheatcroft 1899 p.43; Horne 1923 p.22
83. Grundy (i) p.207
84. Chew Magna Tithe Map 1839
85. Chew Magna Tithe Map 1839
86. Tickenham Domesday Festival p.23
87. Fussell p.92
88. Whynne-Hammond p.21
89. Tunstall pp.161-2; Nightingale p.161
90. Grundy (i) p.198
91. Kettlewell p.52
92. Weston Mercury 1/4/55
93. Tongue p.21
94. W. Jackson p.48; unidentified newspaper cutting held in North Somerset Museum
95. Baker 1911
96. Bennett p.1097
97. Baker 1928
98. John Bailey 12/4/57; 4/1/80
99. Horne SAHNS collection
100. Rendell p. 21, pp.46-7
101. Whitchurch Tithe Award 1839 TN323
102. Hobbs p.5
103. Compton 1882 p.7
104. Knight p.92; L. Richardson 1928 p.163; Compton 1892 p.7
105. Sandford-in-Winscombe W.I. p.49

106. Mr. R.L. Woolley; Wraxall. Per com. Sept. 1994
107. Avon Fed. W.I. p.68
108. Sykes and Whittle p.206; Margaret Thomas p.2
109. Usher 1/2/84
110. Tongue p.12; Bord 1976 pp.33, 144, 159; K. palmer p.29
111. Grundy (i) p.175
112. Horne SAHNS collection
113. Collinson Vol.3 p.616
114. Neads
115. H. Hay Wilson, *A Somerset Sketch-Book* 1912 9.172
116. Compton Bishop & Cross W.I.
117. Horne 1915 p.24
118. Wood p.70
119. Wood p.78
120. Barnes
121. Horne SANHS collection
122. Grundy (i) p.216
123. Horne 1915 pp.98-99

South Gloucestershire
1. R.C.S. Walters p.115
2. Smith p.34; J.Jackson p.416
3. Kerslake p.5
4. Rudder p.294
5. Smith p.27; Charfield Tithe Awards 1839 TN327
6. Cold Ashton Tithe Award 1841 TN318
7. Smith p.64; Grundy (ii) p.92
8. James p.85; Smith p.6
9. Atkyns p.784
10. R.C.S. Walters p.108
11. Griffiths Collection
12. Dyrham and Hinton Tithe Award 1841 TN8/9 & TN48
13. West Gloucestershire water
14. Russett p.95; Fosbroke pp.112-3
15. Scherr 1986 p.81
16. O.S. 25inch Glos. 1881 LXIII.10; Alveston W.I. p.54; O.M. Griffiths p.13
17. O.S. 25inch Glos. 1881 LXIII.13

18. O.S. 25inch Glos. 1881 LXIII.13
19. Atkyns p.655; Pucklechurch Tithe
    Award 1841 TN210b
20. Rudder p.610
21. Pucklechurch Tithe Award 1841
    TN377-80
22. Atkyns p.611
23. Taylor p.118; Browne p.213
24. Braine p.188
25. Anon: Rambles Nov. 1857; R.C.S.
    Walters p.69
26. Batchelor p.138
27. Rudder p.756
28. Atkyns p.617; R. Palmer p.65,
    Wilshire p.96
29. Couzens p.104
30. L. Richardson 1930 p.163
31. Wick & Abson Tithe Award 1841
    TN252/253; Smith p.73
32. Atkyns p.201; R.C.S. Walters
    p.101
33. Winterbourne Down W.I. p.12
34. Ludwell p.12
35. R. Palmer p.28; Fosbroke
36. Atkyns p.580
37. Smythe pp.371-2

BIBLIOGRAPHY

Abbreviations:
B.A.G.A.S: Bristol and Gloucestershire Archaeological Society
S.A.N.H.S.: Somerset Archaeological and Natural History Society
Proc.: Proceedings
Trans.: Transactions

'A GENTLEMAN OF THE FACULTY' *The New Alternative Mineral Spa Guide*,
    Hotwells Road, Bristol
ALVESTON WOMENS INSTITUTE *Alveston - Our Village Within Living
    Memory*, 1953
ANDERSON, A. & M. *Vanishing Spas*, 1974
ANON 'A Magic Spring' in *South Avon Mercury* 12/2/82 p.10
ANON 1835 *Curiosities of Bristol and its Neighbourhood No 2*, October 1835
ANON 1857 (i) 'Rambles Around Bristol' in *The Bristol Magazine and West of
    England Monthly Review*, October 1857
ANON 1857 (ii) 'Rambles Around Bristol' in *The Bristol Magazine and West of
    England Monthly Review*, November 1857
ANON - MALAGO *Malago Local History Society magazine No 9*, 1978
ASTON, M. & ISLES R. (eds.) *The Archaeology of Avon*, 1987
ATKYNS, Sir Robert *The Ancient and Present State of Gloucestershire*, 1712
AVON FEDERATION OF WOMENS INSTITUTES *The Avon Village Book*, 1988
BAARG (Bristol & Avon Archaeological Research Group) *Parish Surveys of
    Flax Bourton, Bathford and Queen Charlton*, 1983
BAKER, Ernest *Weston-super-Mare Jottings*, 1911
BAKER, Ernest *The Village of Weston-super-Mare*, 1928
BARNES, P. (alias 'Quip'): Sportsman's Jaunts No 25 'Beauties of the Upper
    Avon Valley' in *The Sportsman's News* 4/5/1929
BARRETT, William *The History and Antiquities of Bristol*, 1789
BATCHELOR, K.B *The Flowing Tide: chapters in the story of two Severnside
    villages*, 1980
BATH CORPORATION *Bath as a Health Resort*, c.1925
BEEDLE, T. (ed.) *Beedle's Visitor's Handbook to Weston-super-Mare*, 1870
BENNETT, George 'Topographical Description of Weston-super-Mare' in *The
    Gentleman's Magazine*, 1805
BORD, Janet & Colin *The Secret Country*, 1976 (1986)
BORD, Janet & Colin *Sacred Waters*, 1985 (1986)
BOUCHER, Charles 'St Edith's Well and St Peter's Cross, Bristol' in *Trans.
    B.A.G.A.S. Vol 61*, 1939
BOYCOTT, Dr Tony 'Ravenswell, Still Sweet and Pure?' in *Temple Local
    History Group Newsletter No 4*, 1984-88
BRAINE, A. *History of Kingswood Forest*, 1891
BRIDGES, Patrick & JONES, Grenville *Farmborough 901 - 1977. A Jubilee
    Record*, 1977
BROWNE, Bishop G.F. *St Aldhelm: His Life and Times*, 1903
CARTWRIGHT, Rev. W.H 'A Sketch of the History of Butcombe' in *Bath
    Archaeological Field Club Vol 3 No 1*, 1877
CHEW MAGNA WOMENS INSTITUTE: *The Story of Our Village*, 1954
CHILCOTT, J. *Descriptive History of Bristol*, 1835
CLINCH, Rosemary *Curious Bristol*, 1987

COLLINSON, Rev. John: *The History and Antiquities of the County of Somerset*, 1791

COOKE, Robert *West Country Houses*, 1957

COMPTON, Rev. Theodore *Winscombe Sketches Amongst the Mendip Hills*. 1st ed., 1882

COMPTON, Rev. Theodore *Winscombe Sketches Amongst the Mendip Hills*. 2nd ed., 1892

COMPTON BISHOP AND CROSS WOMENS INSTITUTE *The Story of Our Villages: Compton Bishop and Cross*, 1967

COSTEN, Michael *The origins of Somerset*, 1992

COUZENS, P.A. *Part of the Continuing Story of the Sodburys*, 1972

COXE, Thomas: *Magna Britannia et hibernia antiqua et nova. No 60 Somerset*, 1727

CUNLIFFE, Barry *The Temple of Sulis Minerva at Bath Vol 1*, 1985

CUNLIFFE, Barry *The Temple of Sulis Minerva at Bath Vol 2*, 1988

CUNLIFFE, Barry *The Roman Baths: A View over 2000 Years*, 1993

DALLAWAY, James *Antiquities of Bristol in the Middle Centuries*, 1834

DAMES, Michael *Mythic Ireland*, 1992

DAVENPORT, Peter (ed.) *Archaeology in Bath 1976 - 1985*, 1991

DEVEREUX, Paul *Places of Power*, 1990

DOLMAN, John *Contemplations amongst St Vincent's Rocks, Near the City of Bristol*, 1755

EDWARDS, Conway T. *Observations on the Medicinal Properties of the Bladud Spa water*, 1837

EGAN, P. *Walks through Bath*, 1819

EKWALL, Eilert *The Concise Oxford Dictionary of English Place Names*, 1960

ELLIOTT, C.H.B. *Winterbourne, Gloucestershire*, 1936

EVANS, Rev. John *Picture of Bristol; or a guide to objects of curiosity and interest in Bristol, Clifton, the Hotwells and their vicinity etc.*, 1814

FEDDEN, Marguerite *Medieval Churches in Bristol*, 1963

FEDDEN, Marguerite *Bristol Vignettes*, 1964

FOSBROOKE, Thomas *The History of Gloucestershire*, 1807

FUSSELL, Rev. L.W. *Via Old England. 20th Century Pilgrimage to Wellow*, 1946

GANDY, Violet 'Haunts of Saints and Sinners', in *S.A.N.H.S. Proc. Bath & District Branch*, 1933

GELLING, Margaret *Place-Names in the Landscape*, 1984 (1993)

GOLLEDGE, Emmie *A Short History and Record of the Village of Saltford*, 1933

GRAY, Rev. Frederick *Locus Dei: The Story of Hinton Charterhouse*, 1921

GRIFFITHS, O.M. et al *The Story of Alveston*, 1938

GRIFFITHS, O.M. Collection of miscellaneous notes held in the Gloucestershire County Records Office, Gloucester

GRUNDY, G.B (i): *The Saxon Charters and Field Names of Somerset*, 1935

GRUNDY, G.B (ii): *The Saxon Charters and Field Names of Gloucestershire*, 1935

HAWKINS, A.B. & KELLAWAY G.A. (ed.) *The Hot Springs of the Avon Gorge, Bristol, England* in KELLAWAY G.A. (ed.)

HEATH, Rev. George *The History, Antiquities, Survey and Description of the City and Suburbs of Bristol*, 1797

HERIOT, Capt. Mackay 'The Mineral Spring at Batheaston' in *Bath Archaeological Field Club Vol 3 No 2*, 1874-5

HEYWOOD, Audrey *Lead, gout and bath spa therapy* in KELLAWAY, G.A. (ed.)

HOBBS, Rev. A.J. *History of the Parish of Winford*, 1954

HOLT, Rev. Alan *Old North Somerset: Romantic Routes and Mysterious Byways*, 1987

HOOD, Shirley *The Story of Our Village - Abbots Leigh*, 1965

HOPE, Robert Charles *The Legendary Lore of the Holy Wells of England*, 1893

HORNE, Dom Ethelbert 'Some of the Holy Wells of Somerset' in *S.A.N.H.S. Proc. Bath & District Branch*, 1914 -18

HORNE, Dom Ethelbert 'Holy Wells Round Downside' in *The Downside Review Vol 34*, 1915

HORNE, Dom Ethelbert *Somerset Holy Wells and Other Named Wells*, 1923

HORNE (*S.A.N.H.S.* Collection) Collection of personal papers, photographs, notes and cuttings amassed by Dom Ethelbert Horne, held in the Somerset Local Studies Library, Taunton.

HOWELL, Chris *Round Here in Them Days*, 1980

HUDD, A.E. *Romano-British Internment at Farmborough*, 1886

HUNT, J.W. 'Banwell—The Saxon Conquest and After' in *Search No 5*, 1965

HUTTON, Ronald *The Pagan Religions of the Ancient British Isles*, 1991 (1995)

IBBETSON, J.C., LAPORTE & HASSELL, J. *A Picturesque Guide to Bath, Bristol Hotwells, The River Avon, and the Adjacent Country*, 1793

JACKSON, John Edward *Wiltshire: The Topographical Collections of John Aubrey (1659-70) corrected and enlarged by J.E.J.*, 1862

JACKSON, Rev. W. *A Visitor's Handbook to Weston-super-Mare*, 1877

JAMES, John 'Short Notes on the Parish of Cromhall' in *Gloucestershire Notes and Queries Vol 3*, 1885-87

JONES, Francis *The Holy Wells of Wales*, 1954

JONES, F.C. *Old Traditions of Bristol Suburbs and Legends of Old Bristol Thoroughfares*, 1927

JONES, F.C. 'Old Bristol Wells and Pumps' in *Bristol Times and Mirror*, c.1933

JONES, F.C. 'Old Traditions of Bristol Suburbs' in *Bristol Times and Mirror* 23/5/98

JONES, F.C. 1946 (i) *The Glory that was Bristol*, 1946

JONES, F.C. 1946 (ii) *The Bristol Waterworks Company 1846 - 1946*, 1946

JONES, F.C. & CHOWN, W.G. *History of Bristol's Suburbs*, 1977

JORDEN, Dr Edward *A discourse on naturall bathes and minerall waters*, 1631

KEIR, P. *An Enquiry into the Nature and Virtues of the Medicinal Waters of Bristol and their Use in the Cure of Chronical Distempers*, 1739

KELLAWAY, G.A. (ed.) *The Hot Springs of Bath*, 1991

KELLAWAY, G.A. *The Work of William Smith at Bath (1799 - 1813)* in KELLAWAY (ed.)

KERSLAKE, Thomas *Henbury: A Gloucestershire parish a thousand years ago*, 1883

KETCHLEY, C.P. *A Short Guide to Bitton*, 1952

KETLLEWELL, Florence *Trinkum Trinkums of Fifty Years*, 1927

KNIGHT, Francis A. *The Heart of Mendip*, 1915

LEECH, Joseph *The Pipes, Pumps and Conduits of Bristol*, nd (c.1850)

LONGWELL GREEN WOMENS INSTITUTE *The Story of Our Village*, 1958

LOVATT, C.M. *10,000 BC - 700AD* in *The Natural History of the Chew Valley*, 1987

LUDWELL, H.W.N. *A History of Winterbourne*, 1967

MACKAY-HERIOT, Capt. 'The Mineral Spring at Batheaston' in *Bath Antiquarian Field Club Vol 3, No2*, 1874-5 p.171

MACPHERSON, John *Our Baths and Wells: The Mineral Waters of the British Islands*, 1871

MAJOR, S.D. *Handbook to Bristol, Clifton and neighbourhood*, 1879

MANBY, G.W. *Fugitive Sketches of the History and Natural Beauties of Cliflon, Hot-wells and Vicinity*, 1802

MANCO, Jean 'The Cross Bath' in *Bath History Vol 2*, 1988

MARLOR, Rosemary (ed.) *A Question of Paulton*, 1990

MASTERS, Rev. John *Beauties of Clifton: or, the Cliflon and Hotwells Guide*, 1820

MATSON, Rev. George 'Backwell' *(S.A.N.H.S). Northern Branch*, 1898

MATTHEWS, W. *The New History, Survey and Description of the City and Suburbs of Bristol*, 1794

MCEWEN-SMITH, R. & TONKIN, M. *Lost farms of Henbury*, 1996

MCNULTY, M. *The radium waters of Bath* in KELLLAWAY, G.A. (ed.)

MELLOR, Penelope *A Kingsdown Collection*, 1987

NEADS, R.H. 'The legends and leather of Court-de-Wyck' in *South Avon Mercury* 4/1/80, p.13

NEALE, Frances et al *Wrington Village Records. Studies of the history of a Somerset Village*, 1969

NICHOLLS, J.F. *Pleasant Trips out of Bristol*, 1887

NICHOLLS, J.F. *How to see Bristol*, 1896

NICHOLLS, J.F. & TAYLOR, John *Bristol Past and Present Vol I & 2*, 1881

NIGHTINGALE, Rev. Joseph *Topographical and Historical Description of the County of Somerset*, 1810

NOBLE, T. & GARDINER T. 'Brief History of Jacob's Well' in *The Bristol Templar*, Spring 1989

NOTT, John *Of the Hotwell Waters near Bristol*, 1793

O'DONELL, Elliot *Phantoms of the Night*, 1956

'OLD TEMPLE' letter in *Felix Farley's Bristol Journal* 14/3/1835

OLIVER, Dr William *A Practical Dissertation on Bath Waters*, 1707

OWEN, Edward *Observations on the earths, rocks, stones and minerals for some miles about Bristol, and on the nature of the Hot-Well, and the Virtues of its Water*, 1754

PALMER, Kingsley *Folklore of Somerset*, 1976

PALMER, Roy *The Folklore of Gloucestershire*, 1994

PEACH, R.E. *Historical Houses in Bath and their Associations*, 1883

PEACH, R.E. *Bath Old and New*, 1888

PEVSNER, Nikolaus *The Buildings of England. North Somerset and Bristol*, 1958 (1986)

PHELPS, William *A History of Somersetshire Vol 2*, 1836

PIERCE, Robert *Bath Memoirs: or Observations in Three and Forty Years Practice at the Bath*, 1697

POOLE, C.H. *The Customs, Superstitions and Legends of the County of the County of Somerset*, 1877 (1970)

POWELL, Martin in *Bristol Evening Post*, June 1986

PRYCE, George *Popular History of Bristol*, 1861

RAHTZ, Philip & HARRIS, Leslie: 'The Temple Well and Other Buildings at Pagans Hill Chew Stoke, North Somerset' in *Proc. S.A.N.H.S Vol 101*, 1956

RANDOLPH, George *Enquiry into the medicinal virtues of Bristol water; and the indications of cure which it answers*, 1750

RATTUE, James *The Living Stream: Holy Wells in Historical Context*, 1995

RENDELL, Stan & Joan *Steep Holm. The Story of a Small Island*, 1993

RICHARDSON, Rev. A. 'St Anne's Chapel, Brislington' in *Proc. S.A.N.H.S. Vol 44*, 1898

ROLLS, Roger *Quest for the quintessence* in KELLAWAY, G.A. (ed.)

ROOM, Miss E. & RICE-JONES, Mrs (Chew Stoke Womens Institute)*The Story of Our Village*, c.1954

ROYAL, Margaret & GIRVAN, Ian *Local Ghosts*, 1976

ROYAL, Margaret & GIRVAN, Ian *Bristol Ghosts and their neighbours*, (nd)

RUDDER, Samuel *A New History of Gloucestershire*, 1779

RUSSELL, Richard *Account of the Nature, Properties, and medicinal uses of the mineral waters in the different parts of England*, 1760

RUSSETT, Vince *Marshfield: An Archaeological Survey of a Southern Cotswold Parish*, 1985

RUTTER, John *Delineations of the Northwestem Division of the County of Somerset*, 1829

SALMON, Arthur *Bristol: City, Suburbs & Countryside*, 1922

SANDFORD-IN-WINSCOMBE WOMENS INSTITUTE *A History and Record, Past and Present of Sandford-in-Winscombe*, 1933

SANIGER, W.T. *Ancient Water Supplies of Bristol*, 1933

SCARTH, Rev. Prebendary: 'Notes on a pair of Celtic spoons found near Weston, Bath in 1866' in *Bath Archaeological Field Club Vol 2*, 1870-73

SCHERR, Jennifer 'Springs and Wells in Somerset' in *Nomina Vol 10*, 1986

SCHERR, Jennifer 'Names ofsome English Holy Wells' Paper presented at XVIIth Intemational Congress of Onomastic Sciences, Helsinki, Finland, Aug 13-18 1990

SCOTT, Maurice *Discovering Widcombe and Lyncombe*, 1984

SEYER, Rev. Samuel *Memoirs Historical and Topographical of Bristol and its Neighbourhood*, 1821

SHICKLE, Rev. C.W. *Early Water Supply of Bath*, 1917

SHIERCLIFF, E. *The Bristol and Hot Well Guide*, 1789

SINNOT and another v Tuckett *The Proceedings of the case of St Anne's Chapel, St Anne's Ferry and paths through St Anne's Wood*, 1891

SMITH A.H. *The Place-Names of Gloucestershire. English Place-Name Society, Vol XL, Part 3*, 1964

SMYTHE the Elder, John *A Description of the Hundred of Berkeley ln the County of Gloucester and of its Inhabitants*, 1634 (1885)

STEWART, R.J. *The waters of the Gap*, 1989 (2nd ed.)

STRACHEY, Rev. John *History of Somerset, 1730*. Unpublished manuscript

STRICKLAND, Edward *Roman and Fashionable Bath* in WALTERS, Cuming (ed.)

SWIFT, Myra *Midsomer Norton Memories*, 1960s

SYKES, C.M. & WHITTLE, S.L. 'The Birdcombe Mesolithic Site, Wraxall' in *S.A.N.H.S. Vol 104*, 1959-60

TAYLOR, Rev. T.F. 'St Aldhelm, Magician' in *Somerset and Dorset Notes and Queries, Vol 28*, 1961-67

TEMPLE LOCAL HISTORY GROUP *An account of St John's Conduit Medieval Water System. Report and survey of features surviving in August 1984*, 1984

THOMAS, Ethel *Shirehamplon Story*, 1983

THOMAS, H.G. letter in *Bristol Times and Mirror* 18/11/27

THOMAS, Margaret *Nailsea*, 1991

THORPE, Thomas A Plan of the Parish of Walcot in the County of Somerset. Survey'd for - Gay Esq. 1740

THORPE, Thomas An Actual Survey of the City of Bath, in the County of Somerset, and Five Miles Round, 1742

TICKENHAM DOMESDAY FESTIVAL - Village Booklet, 1986
TOMALIN, D.J. *Woodspring Priory, Somerset*, 1993
TONGUE, R.L. (ed. K. BRIGGS): *Somerset Folklore*, 1965
TUNSTALL, James *Rambles about Bath*, 1856
TURNER, Dr William, *The Book of the Natures and Properties of the Baths, of England*, 1562
UNDERHILL, John *A Short Account of the Virtues of the Bristol hot-well Water*, 1703
UNDERWOOD, Peter *The Ghosts of Somerset*, 1985
UNDERWOOD, Peter *Westcountry Hauntings*, 1986
U.B.S.S. (University of Bristol Spaeological Society Proceedings), 1965-66
URBAN, Sylvanus (ed.) *The Gentleman's Magazine, Vol LXXXI*, 1811
VEAR, Leonard *South of the Avon - Glimpses of old Bedminster Life*, 1978
VENNER, Thomas *Via recta ad Vitam longam*, 1637
W.J.R. 'Manor Houses near Bristol', articles in *Bristol Times and Mirror*, 1912(?)
WADE, G.W & J.H. *Rambles in Somerset*, 1923
WAITE, Vincent *The Bristol Hotwell*, 1960
WALCOT/LARKHALL TOWNSWOMEN'S GUILD *A History of the Parish and Manor of Walcot. Book 2*, 1989
WALTERS, Cuming (ed.) *Bygone Somerset*, 1897
WALTERS, R.C.S. *The Ancient Wells, Springs and Holy Wells of Gloucestershire: their legends, history and topography*, 1928
WAREING, Marion *The Story of Compton Martin*, 1963
WARNER, Rev. Richard *Excursions from Bath*, 1801
WATSON, Sally *Secret Underground Bristol*, 1991
WATSON, Willis G. *Calendar of Customs, Superstitions, Weatherlore, Popular Sayings and Important Events connected with the County of Somerset*, 1920
WELLS, Charles *Historic Bristol*, 1902
WEST GLOUCESTERSHIRE WATER *Brief for the Corporation of Bath, in Opposition*, 1887
WHEATCROFT, Mrs L. *Round Bath in Twenty Picturesque Rambles*, 1899
WHEATCROFT, Mrs L. *Round Bath in Twenty Picturesque Rambles*, 1901
WHYNNE-HAMMOND, Charles *Ten Somerset Mysteries*, 1995
WIGAN, Eve *Portishead Parish History*, 1932
WILLIAMS, H. & JEFFEREY, F. *A Map of the Manor of LongAshton*, 1746
WILSHIRE, Lewis *The Vale of Berkeley*, 1954
WILSON, H. Hay *A Somerset Sketch-Book*, 1912
WINCHESTER, Evelyn *St Anne's, Bristol. A History*, 1986
WINSTONE, Reece *Bristol Suburbs Long Ago*, 1985
WINTERBOURNE DOWN WOMENS INSTITUTE *A Guide to Winterbourne Down*, 1953
WOOD, John *An Essay towards a Description of Bath. 1st ed.*, 1742
WORCESTER, William *Itineraria*, 1480
WRIGHT, Mary *Make your way around Montpelier*, Montpelier Conservation Group, 1992
VAUGHAN, BOB & MARTELETT, JOHN 'Jacobs Well Rediscovered' in *Newsletter No 3/87* of the Temple Local History Group
'VILLAGE PUMP' Local History in *South Avon Mercury*, 2/10/81 p.3
VINTNER, Dorothy 'Holy Wells near Bristol' in *Gloucestershire Countryside*, June/July 1966-7

INDEX